Preface

Throughout my career in credit and finance, I have been in daily contact with the owners and officers of small and moderate-size business organizations. I am firmly convinced that this segment of our commercial and industrial population is vital to the continuing strength of our American enterprise system, and my experience has made me aware that management of the small company is in need of—and deserving of—greater financial understanding and more efficient financial tools for making profitable decisions.

Over the years, I have been privileged to become very close to thousands of manufacturers, wholesalers, and retailers and have enjoyed their confidence, shared their problems, and taken pleasure in their successes. As a result of my intimate acquaintance with their financial affairs, a great many of these businessmen have revealed their aspirations to me and have candidly discussed the handicaps they face in realizing their goals. They frequently ask me, "Do I have my company on the right track?" and, "How can I inform myself as to how my company compares with others, especially in determining profits and growth?"

This book has been written to answer such questions by furnishing fundamental financial guidance to aid and encourage thoughtful analysis by businessmen, many of whom do not realize that financial proficiency can be acquired without a specialized education. I hope, also, that the ideas presented here will be studied and implemented by the trade associations which, through their collective facilities and the confidence of their membership, can furnish meaningful information and standards of measurement for the benefit of the entire business community.

The method of analysis presented in this book is not intended to supersede other modern analytical techniques such as cash-flow projections, budgets, and forecasts, but rather to give the business manager a basic financial understanding with which he can apply them more effectively. Certainly, it is not intended as a substitute for judgment.

Unfortunately, the labeling of financial diagnostic tools as "ratio analysis," "cash-flow analysis," and so forth has led many individuals to assume that the various approaches are mutually exclusive—that one method is old-fashioned and another is very modern. The fact is that cash-flow analysis and ratio analysis are closely linked. Each adds insight and dimension.

For instance, adherents of cash flow as a total method of financial understanding concentrate upon determining the cash throwoff of the company under study. This throwoff figure (consisting of net profit and noncash charges, such as depreciation, amortization, and deferred income tax) represents funds theoretically available to service debt. This total, however, does not represent a bundle of cash sitting idle at the end of the period. A substantial portion of cash throwoff may in fact be channeled into increased fixed assets, inventory, or receivables as fast as it is taken in by the company. Because such diversions of funds obviously affect repayment of debt, the analyst should assess the likelihood of their occurrence through a more detailed study of debt service—a projection of sources and applications of funds.

In order to make a reasonable determination of the probable application of funds during the period, the analyst should turn to *ratios*. The ratio of sales to fixed assets often indicates the extent to which a company is likely to add to plant and equipment. Similarly, the probable diversion of funds into additional inventory can be projected by referring to another key ratio— sales (or cost of sales) to inventory—for prior periods. The likelihood of an increase in receivables can likewise be anticipated from the historical pattern of the indicated collection period or the ratio of sales to receivables. A company which projects substantial growth in sales volume can usually expect a corresponding expansion of receivables and inventory.

Thus this refined approach to ratio analysis injects realism into future projections and serves as a base for making sound management value judgments, particularly for the executive or owner who does not possess financial expertise.

Donald E. Miller

Contents

1 The Importance of Financial Understanding to Management / 1

2 The Nine Ratios That Measure Effect / 15

3 The Six Causal Ratios / 55

4 Application of the Causal Ratios / 107

5 Guidelines for Applying the Cause-and-Effect Technique / 152

6 Liquidity Crisis or Profit Squeeze? / 176

7 The Uses of Industrywide Statistics / 210

Index / 229

1 The Importance of Financial Understanding to Management

A company's success depends upon management awareness. Every businessman must know the full potential of his company and be thoroughly aware of the means by which this potential can be realized before he can guide his organization to ultimate success. And no manager can consider himself entirely informed about the position of his company, his competitors, or his industry unless he understands financial statements and the information they contain. He cannot rely upon general impressions of financial structure or vague notions of the competitive climate to provide him with an adequate background for making the exact decisions which successful operations demand. Precise financial knowledge is absolutely essential, and this knowledge is within the grasp of every manager who understands and applies the principles of *cause-and-effect ratio analysis.* In companies where managers do not have this kind of financial knowledge, serious difficulties are more than likely to limit the growth and profitability which determine business success.

Every day the doors of hundreds of businesses are closed forever. Tax lien notices are posted; "for sale" or "for rent" signs appear; business owners undergo examination in bankruptcy or receivership courts. These daily failures mount to a staggering annual loss—measured in dollars and cents and in the disappointment of those whose efforts and hopes were once placed in companies that have collapsed. Yet most of these business disasters can be averted. Countless other companies struggle along; they neither attain success nor succumb to failure but hover constantly at a level far short of their goals and their real potential. Still other businesses appear reasonably successful when they are compared with many firms in their line; yet they do not achieve all that is within their capabilities. These companies are not failing, but they can certainly improve their performance. In all of these cases, the application of cause-and-effect ratio analysis can markedly enhance financial understanding and be a key factor in profit improvement and business success.

Financial Management in Companies of Small and Medium Size

Large and complex business organizations, the giants of industry, are staffed with numerous specialists who supply the policy makers and the line officers with documented information regarding virtually every phase of operations—the kind of information that leads to sound decisions and detailed planning. The small business with limited funds and relatively few employees must, on the other hand, count on its management ranks to furnish both background and decision. The manager in a small concern cannot turn to the tax department, the purchasing agent, the legal staff, the production-planning manager, the personnel officer, or the credit manager for background information. The management of the concern of small or moderate size generally consists of five or fewer officers; this group must supply comprehensive management skills if the company is to prosper. Balanced management is not easily secured, because the majority of management people come either from the ranks of salesmen or from the ranks of production personnel. Far too few managers have a really comprehensive background in the financial aspects of the business that are so essential to success.

Although the relatively few corporate titans account for the greater part of national production, numerically speaking the American business scene is dominated by small companies. The Small Business Administration (SBA) has consistently reported that approximately 95 percent of all concerns in the United States meet their standards for classification as "small." The "small" category includes any manufacturer employing fewer than 500 persons and any wholesaler with sales volume under $5 million, as well as any retailer with sales below $1 million annually. The U.S. Department of Commerce statistics regularly disclose that nearly 99 percent of all business ventures—approximately 5 million concerns—have fewer than 100 individuals on the payroll.

Companies of small or moderate size clearly have qualities and problems quite dissimilar from those of the relatively few concerns employing 500 or more or possessing net worth greater than $1 million. The bulk of today's financial material, however, is written about and for large corporations and their specialists. Managers of small companies generally require more basic information, for they themselves must provide comprehensive management, either as a team of individuals with diverse experience and skills or by acquiring the necessary talents through education and self-improvement.

Management deficiencies—"unbalanced experience, lack of experience in the line, lack of managerial experience, or incompetence"—are the underlying cause of nine out of ten business failures, according to Dun & Bradstreet. These basic causes, of course, lie behind the specific factors—such as undercapitalization—that cause businesses to fail. Evidence of management groping for improved knowledge and skills can be seen in the rapid turnover of the business population. The average life of the American business is five years; in other words, one of every five companies active today will cease operations or undergo a change in ownership by this date next year. Sound management can greatly reduce this toll, and sound management is an acquired technique.

Far too many businesses, particularly those of small size, suffer from inadequate financial management. In a great number of these concerns, the treasurer's function is merely to keep the *books* in balance. But the skilled financial officer must do a great deal more than that; he must keep the *business* in balance as well. What a difference in approach this demands! The books will balance with red ink; they will even balance in bankruptcy court. But surely neither of these results represents the objectives of the owners.

To illustrate the inadequacy of financial management among small concerns, and to test the correlation between this inadequacy and lack of business success, I have periodically conducted surveys of the experience backgrounds of officers or owners of struggling manufacturing and wholesaling firms. These studies have concentrated on companies with net worth of $200,000 or less, whose condition reflects severe financial imbalance accompanied by slow payment patterns, and the picture which emerges is one of unvarying consistency.

Approximately 90 percent of the presidents or principals have been former salesmen or relatives of the founder of the company and have had no other work experience. Of their supporting cast of line officers, perhaps 15 to 20 percent have either production or product knowledge (engineers, production managers, foremen, purchasing agents). Another 20 to 25 percent come from backgrounds generally altogether unrelated to their companies' lines of endeavor or to financial expertise (clerical workers, boat captains, television repairmen, messengers, insurance agents). Nearly half of the vice presidents, secretaries, or treasurers are characteristically wives, sons, daughters, or in-laws of the president, with limited educational history and no outside employment experience. Rarely will these periodic surveys disclose as many as 5 percent of officers or partners with any identifiable connection with the vital area of financial management.

For a manufacturer, balanced management is generally thought to consist of skills in sales, production, and financial control. Although the wholesaler has no production problems to contend with, product knowledge is obviously of value in the selection of merchandise lines; sales and financial abilities are as important to merchants as they are to manufacturers. Nearly all the companies included in these studies had an inordinate share of problems, and in the overwhelming majority of cases their difficulties stemmed from inadequate financial management.

Excessive concentration on sales contributed to the plight of many of the marginal companies in the foregoing group. The primary danger to a business directed predominantly by salesmen is the strong inclination of management to assume that a business is formed to produce and sell or to buy and sell and that if these functions are performed, the success of the company is assured. Often no real thought is given to costs or to prices or to the effects a given course of action may have on the financial stability and growth potential of the enterprise. Certainly a competent salesman can become a very fine financial officer, but to attempt to develop and refine financial talent through trial and error is risky at best. Unless the sales-dominated management can hire someone with financial skill as a part of its team, a member of its own ranks must acquire fundamental knowledge in the area of finance to give the business the balance and guidance it needs.

Financial proficiency is not an inherited trait; it can be acquired—and hundreds of hours of university courses or professional lessons are not needed to master the essentials. Some companies have even built their management education in the bankruptcy courts, although this is hardly the recommended method. A renowned bankruptcy referee, who has presided over some 5,000 cases in his long career, has said that in more than half the bankruptcy cases he has handled, the concerns have succeeded in reorganizing and thriving after initial payment problems. Those that thrived after discharge from bankruptcy undoubtedly reversed their former unsuccessful practices not simply because they were freed from court domination but because the court and the creditors' committee taught them some sound financial-management techniques. If a bankrupt company can surmount its problems, how much more easily can a struggling but still independent and free concern do so? Owners' and officers' interest in learning how to diagnose their own problems is the first step and the most important step toward solving those problems.

Acquiring Financial Skill

The business officer need not be an accountant, an auditor, an industrial engineer, or a credit manager. He can master fundamental financial skill and make major policy decisions with assurance if (1) he knows the meaning of each asset and liability on his balance sheet and the meaning of each major item appearing on his profit-and-loss statement and (2) he is thoroughly familiar with the ratio analysis of his financial statement so that he can accurately assess his company's position and draw meaningful conclusions when comparing the results of his company with those of its industry.

A manager needs no formal education in accounting or bookkeeping to learn the meaning of financial-statement items. Bookkeepers and accountants are hired to make all of the various debit and credit entries which culminate in the end products—the balance sheet, the profit-and-loss statement, various expense schedules, cash-flow statements, and reconciliations of net worth. Auditors and public accounting firms are brought in to check the accuracy of the internal records, to verify certain assets and liabilities, and to certify the validity of the closing statement prepared for the owners. It is not necessary for the manager to follow a particular figure from its derivation all the way through to its entry on the books; but he must be aware of the meaning of each item that appears on his statement. The "how"—the mechanics of bookkeeping—is of secondary interest only. The "what," the "why," the "when," and the "where" should hold the owner's interest, for in the answers to these questions rests the future of his company. The term "prepaid expense and deferred charges," for instance, should be immediately understood by the business manager. He should instantly recognize the term "fixed assets" and what it represents, even though his comprehension of the computation of depreciation reserves may be somewhat cloudy. He should know what is meant by "accounts payable" without necessarily knowing the specific debit and credit entries posted to the subsidiary ledgers. While the routine entries are not within the province of management concern, the end product of those entries is very much within the scope of the manager's job. That end product consists of the financial statement which the businessman—the decision maker—must be able to read with understanding.

The assumption that all owners and managers of businesses are able to read financial statements with real understanding is false. The financial columnist of one New York newspaper has pointed out that in preparing for an examination that would-be partners in member firms of the New York Stock Exchange must take, the brokers—who belong to Wall Street's highest echelon—do the most "cramming" to prepare themselves for the part of the examination involving questions about the balance sheet. If these men have trouble mastering the intricacies of the balance sheet, it cannot be assumed that this knowledge is inherent with the managers of businesses. The business manager, however, has even greater reason to learn the fundamentals, to obtain a basic understanding of balance-sheet and operating-statement items, than has the broker. The partners in an investment house have available a staff of analysts to whom they can turn for interpretation; the small businessman normally does not. Also, the entire future of the company hinges on the manager's ability to decode relevant financial data as a means of planning profitable moves. Learning to read financial statements is the first essential element in any businessman's attempt to acquire financial-management skills.

Ratio analysis, the second element in mastering financial management, is not new. For many years, analysts have attempted to add meaning to financial-statement figures by comparing different items through the use of ratios. For instance, the ratio (or comparison) of current assets to current liabilities is somewhat familiar to many businessmen. However, earlier attempts to relate key elements of the financial statement have suffered from a definite lack of systematic application. Often, understanding of this valuable management tool has been clouded because analysts have not been aware of the fundamental principle of cause and effect. Some analysts have even gone so far as to give equal weight and equal value to all ratios. Ratios are not equal in importance any more than people are equal in ability or wealth or power; some ratios lead and others follow; some represent cause and some, effect. And even when ratios have not been given equal weight and value, they have seldom been effectively used because no guidelines have been available to indicate what comparative weight and value particular ratios deserve. Moreover, the importance of comparing the individual company's ratios with those of similar concerns in the same line of business activity and the need for broadly based, accurate industry averages have not always been understood. These aspects of ratio analysis are stressed in the cause-and-effect approach. The understanding of cause-and-effect ratio analysis makes fundamental financial-statement analysis comparatively easy for every businessman, whether his background happens to be in finance or in some other business area.

The ratio—the mathematical relationship between two quantities—is of major importance in financial analysis because it injects a qualitative measurement and demonstrates in a precise manner the adequacy of one key financial-statement item relative to another. The 15 ratios which have proved themselves to be of greatest value in actual business applications are described and applied in detail in the following chapters. But the cause-and-effect technique cannot be understood in bits and pieces; it must, instead, be viewed as a complete system of financial analysis. Knowing the XYZ Company has $350,000 in inventory—of which $120,000 is in finished goods, $60,000 in work in process, and $170,000 in raw materials—is, in and of itself, of little value to management even though the accuracy of these figures may be confirmed without qualification by the best firm of certified public accountants. What is the sales volume of the XYZ Company? How much working capital does it possess? By answering these questions and relating them to the inventory figure, the analyst can begin to judge the quality of inventory rather than its quantity. And by comparing the important ratios of the XYZ Company with industry averages derived from the financial statements of similar concerns in the same line of activity, the analyst can determine XYZ's strengths and weaknesses as well as its competitive position within the industry. This, then, is the significance of ratios: ratios relate one financial-statement item to another, and they impart meaning or reason (*ratio* means "reason" in Latin) to solely quantitative members.

Understanding Financial Statements

The soundness of management decisions depends, of course, upon the accuracy of financial data. Unfortunately, financial statements vary significantly with respect to quality and scope. In any analysis of a company's financial position, the type of statement from which the figures are derived must be considered. Financial statements may be broadly classified in the following manner.

1. *The audited statement.* The audited statement covers a specific period, generally the fiscal year. Prepared by certified public accountants, audited statements are normally quite reliable—subject, of course, to the degree of competence of the auditor. Accompanying every audited financial statement is a declaration by the auditor in which he may (a) express an unqualified opinion that the statement presents fairly the financial position and results of operations of the subject company during the accounting period, (b) limit the scope of his opinion because of incomplete examination or confirmation of accounts, (c) set forth an adverse opinion based upon the company's failure to adhere to generally accepted accounting principles, or (d) state that certain factors preclude an expression of opinion regarding the overall adequacy of the financial statement. The analyst must read the accountant's opinion with care, for only through such scrutiny can he determine the degree of reliance to be placed on the figures presented.

2. *The interim statement.* Depending upon management's needs, interim figures may be prepared monthly, quarterly, or semiannually. Because interim statements are seldom subject to audit, some inaccuracies may find their way into the figures. The interim statement is nevertheless of substantial aid to the businessman who is interested in evaluating performance periodically to determine adherence to budgets and forecasts and to detect incipient problems. The analyst must recognize that interim figures are often subject to radical year-end adjustments, and hence these statements should be accepted with some reservations.

3. *The unaudited year-end statement.* Some small companies do not have their year-end statements audited. Such unaudited statements may either be signed by a company officer or unsigned. Although an unaudited interim statement is generally acceptable, failure to have fiscal-closing figures audited is a very

unwise procedure. While many companies have never engaged a public accountant to verify their internal records, these concerns are, in general, marginal financial risks. Audits performed on insolvent concerns all too often disclose that the statements upon which management had been relying were totally unrepresentative of the actual condition of the companies—a fact learned too late to permit corrective action.

4. *The "estimated" statement.* Only the most naïve businessman would base management decisions upon estimated figures. Successful competitive moves cannot be approximate; they must be clearly defined and precisely executed. One cannot buy an "estimated" piece of machinery or hire an "estimated" salesman or sell on an "estimated" final price. Approximations can lead business managers into dangerously erroneous beliefs regarding their financial position.

Although an independent verification of the financial statement is indeed important, the auditor is not a valuer or appraiser. He may establish, for instance, that the accounts receivable of the XYZ Company are $111,512.26 through 100 percent verification; but confirmation of book value in no manner indicates the collectibility of these receivables. While a good auditor will age and reserve accounts, the final interpretation of the auditor's figures, and the decisions based upon them, are the responsibility of the business owner or manager. Nor does the auditor attempt to determine whether a company's working capital can support its receivables or whether they are justified by the company's volume of sales. Qualitative measurement of quantitative figures is performed by the financial analyst—a business manager, a credit grantor, or an independent industry counselor.

Items on the Financial Statement

Before discussing the details of ratios and ratio analysis, we should note briefly the broad categories of financial-statement items with which we will be dealing in cause-and-effect analysis. A definition and description of each asset and liability that might appear on a company's balance sheet is purposely omitted because this important and complex area of classification has been covered in excellent fashion in numerous accounting texts. Moreover, managers should already know the meaning of such items as "accounts receivable," "mortgages payable," and so on. If they do not, they should certainly consult with their own accountants or their auditors to gain an understanding of each item appearing on their financial statement. Primarily as a review, then, the major categories of financial-statement items are outlined in the following paragraphs.

Assets can be divided into four distinct categories: (1) current assets, (2) fixed assets, (3) intangible assets, and (4) miscellaneous assets.

Current assets consist of cash plus those items which the company plans to convert to cash in the course of its normal manufacturing or marketing process in the regular conduct of its business. They are available for conversion to cash as needed.

Fixed assets, briefly, are the tangible, physical facilities utilized by the company in performing its avowed business function. These assets generally represent a permanent investment in such items as land, buildings, machinery, autos and trucks, furniture and fixtures, and leasehold improvements. The important distinction between fixed assets and current assets is that fixed assets are not sold in the normal day-to-day operation of business, although they obviously can be sold. Plant and equipment tend to lose value through age, use, or obsolescence and hence are subject to periodic downward adjustment in value through either depreciation or amortization charges (in some fields, through depletion as well). Fixed assets include only facilities owned directly by the company and do not extend to any investments in subsidiaries or affiliated concerns. Investment in a subsidiary or affiliate constitutes a miscellaneous asset.

Intangible assets are difficult to define because in some cases they represent definite money value, while in most others they do not have any measurable cash value. Within this category are found organizational expense, patents, franchises, and goodwill. As a rule, intangible assets are not available for payment of debts of a going concern. Sometimes, however, they can be converted to cash; for instance, some companies have sold certain of their franchises or patents as a means of extricating themselves from temporary problems. Intangible assets seldom have value if the company itself is liquidated, but this is not universally true. A large independent soft drink bottler, for example, may possess exclusive franchises which retain their market value despite the company's insolvency. The difficulty of assigning an accurate money value is, however, the characteristic which distinguishes intangible assets. This characteristic, in turn, suggests that analysts should remove intangible assets entirely and reduce net worth in direct proportion when analyzing financial statements.

Miscellaneous assets are identified through the process of elimination. If the asset is tangible, if it is not intended for conversion into cash in the normal operation of the business, and if it is not a part of the physical facilities by means of which the business function is performed, it falls automatically into the miscellaneous category. Included among miscellaneous assets are such items as the cash-surrender value of life insurance; investments in subsidiaries; money due from officers, directors, and employees; deferred charges; and prepaid expenses.

Turning now to *liabilities*, we find three basic categories: (1) current liabilities, (2) long-term liabilities, and (3) net worth.

Current liabilities are those obligations which mature within one year from the closing date of the financial statement; this category includes demand notes which have no fixed maturity date. Current liabilities include, among other items, accounts payable, notes payable to banks and trade suppliers, trade acceptances payable, loans payable, tax liabilities or reserves, accrued items (such as rent and wages), customers' deposits and advance payments, dividends declared but unpaid, and reserves for contingencies (which are in reality established as claims to be paid but which may be subject to court appeal or some other deferment or possible nullification).

The sole distinction between current and *long-term liabilities* is the time element. Any obligation due within one year from statement date is current; any claim falling due beyond one year is long term. Certain company obligations, of course, include both long-term and current elements—for example, serial notes, mortgages, debentures, and other types of bonds of which certain portions come due within one year and the balance mature at clearly defined dates in subsequent years. Some companies list among their long-term liabilities "Notes payable, officers" for some stated amount, but they fail to list the maturity dates of the notes. Investigation may disclose that these notes are payable on demand, and despite the avowed intention of the note holders not to press their claims "until the company can afford to repay," such notes should be reclassified as current liabilities. If, however, the maturities are clearly indicated and the due dates extend beyond one year, these notes may properly be treated as long-term indebtedness despite their being owed to the owners. The analyst should acquaint himself with some of the more common forms of long-term debt and should know the nature and extent of the assets which serve as collateral for secured borrowing in specific instances.

The final category on the liability side of the balance sheet is *net worth*, the excess of total tangible assets over total debt (current and long term). In effect, net worth is what the business owes to the owners as their equitable share. A proprietorship or partnership statement normally shows the difference between assets and liabilities as simply "net worth," while the corporate statement is generally more complicated and may subdivide net worth among any or all of the following: preferred stock, common stock, class A and B stock, capital surplus, earned surplus, and undivided profit.

One final balance-sheet term with which the analyst should be familiar is *working capital*. The amount of this item is found very simply by deducting current liabilities from current assets. The significance of working capital will be explored in later pages as the actual use of ratios by the analyst is explained.

The income, or profit-and-loss, statement has received less attention from financial analysts than has the balance sheet. Consequently, profit-and-loss items are far less standardized; and in this area, great effort is required to provide management with clearly defined, accurate, meaningful facts about industry performance. Detailed analysis of the income statement—the study of each individual expense item—will demonstrate why Company A made money while Company B recorded a loss. The member firms of an industry have, through their trade association, the opportunity to avail themselves of the guidance of industrywide expense figures. Of course, each industry will necessarily develop its own presentation of expense items according to the particular characteristics and needs of that industry.

Only through standardized reporting of financial-statement items can individual ratios and industry averages be sufficiently comparable to serve as meaningful analytical tools. Trade associations should take the lead in setting forth for their members uniform standards governing the classification of assets, liabilities, net worth, and expense entries. Companies need not, of course, keep their books in complete agreement with the industry method, but in reporting annual figures to the association for the compilation of industry averages, each company must reclassify any items at variance with common practice. If, for instance, the industry should exclude deferred charges and prepaid expenses from current assets and if the individual company in computing its ratios should include such items in the current-asset category, not only would the disparity distort the industry average but the resulting ratios would lose much of their significance for purposes of comparison. In other words, like items must be related to likes if ratios are to provide understanding of the company's position in relation to industry norms. In order to maximize the usefulness of ratio analysis, industries must adopt clearcut systems of classification which are known to all firms within particular industries and to which all firms conform when reporting financial data. This important aspect of cause-and-effect ratio analysis will be examined in greater detail later in this book.

2 The Nine Ratios That Measure Effect

Cause-and-effect ratio analysis is based upon 15 key financial relationships expressed as mathematical proportions between major balance-sheet and income-statement items. Each of the 15 ratios demonstrates a significant connection between two important elements of the company's financial structure. An almost infinite number of other ratios can, of course, be calculated by pairing financial-statement entries at random; and certain of these are useful in specialized operations. But the 15 ratios of cause-and-effect analysis have been applied and tested as a unified system in thousands of business situations and have demonstrated that, taken together, they provide the fundamental financial understanding needed by business managers, credit grantors, and independent analysts.

In this and the following chapters, each of the 15 ratios is considered in detail. The present chapter is devoted to a study of the nine secondary ratios, those which yield important information about the financial structure and the competitive position of the company but which do not individually indicate causes of strength or weakness. The six primary, or causal, ratios—those which reflect the relationships which directly influence the firm in its entirety—are presented in Chapter 3. In order to achieve a true working knowledge of cause-and-effect analysis, one must not only read about ratios but also apply them to business problems. Hypothetical cases have been used in the text to help the reader gain familiarity with the cause-and-effect technique.

As we shall point out frequently throughout the book, it is highly important that the ratios derived from any company's financial statement be related to averages or norms for the industry in which that concern is engaged. Only in this way can deviations—either good or bad—be detected.

In the discussion of individual ratios in this and the next chapter, reference will be made to certain specific sources of statistical data on the business community. While each will be explored in greater depth in Chapter 7, it is appropriate here to make brief mention of the two most readily accessible sources.

For nearly 50 years Robert Morris Associates of Philadelphia has published its "Annual Statement Studies," which include composite balance sheets, operating ratios, and profit-and-loss studies on a broad spectrum of American business establishments. In the 1971 edition 262 separate lines of activity are covered, including 123 identifiable lines of manufacture, 55 wholesaling operations, 44 types of retail establishments, 32 services (such as hospitals, insurance agents, laundries, and dry cleaners) and 8 diverse groups difficult to classify (horticultural services, seed companies, and so on).

Robert Morris Associates is the national association of bank loan and credit officers and is actively engaged in promoting improvement in the principles and practices of commercial lending, loan administration, and asset management in commercial banks. Its figures are compiled by the voluntary contribution of statement data for approximately 30,000 different companies on an anonymous basis by its membership of some 1,200 commercial banks. Its figures thus serve as valuable guidelines in the evaluation of industry standards and of the comparative performance of each individual company.

A disclaimer statement by Robert Morris reads:

"RMA cannot emphasize too strongly that their composite figures for each industry may *not* be representative of that entire industry (except by coincidence), for the following reasons:

"1. The only companies with a chance of being included in

their study in the first place are those for whom their submitting banks have recent figures.

"2. Even from this restricted group of potentially includable companies, those which are chosen, and the total number chosen, are not determined in any random or otherwise statistically reliable manner.

"3. Many companies in their study have *varied* product lines; they are "mini-conglomerates," if you will. All they can do in these cases is categorize them by their *primary* product line, and be willing to tolerate any "impurity" thereby introduced.

"In a word, don't automatically consider their figures as representative norms and don't attach any more or less significance to them than is indicated by the unique aspects of the data collection."

Despite this qualification, I have found RMA figures to be the most complete and representative of all industry statistics available to the general public today. While they lack the refinements and added features which will be suggested in Chapter 7, they are indicative enough of industry characteristics to serve our purposes in illustrating the use of ratios as a means of detection of individual company strengths and weaknesses.

Dun & Bradstreet, Inc. has for many years published and distributed free to subscribers its 14 ratios for a substantial segment of industry, including 125 manufacturers, wholesalers, and retailers.

Each of these sources is readily available to the small firm as well as to the very largest organization. Their individual applicability for the analyst's use will be explored further in the concluding chapter.

Let us now become acquainted with the 15 ratios; we begin here with the 9 secondary ratios.

Current ratio (current-assets-to-current-liabilities).
Current-liabilities-to-net-worth.
Total-liabilities-to-net-worth.
Inventory-to-working-capital.
Trade-receivables-to-working-capital.

Long-term-liabilities-to-working-capital.
Net-profit-to-net-worth.
Net-sales-to-fixed-assets.
Net-sales-to-working-capital.

In the remainder of this chapter, the method of computation and the significance of each of these ratios will be explained.

Current Ratio (Current-Assets-to-Current-Liabilities)

The *current ratio* gives the analyst a general picture of the adequacy of a company's working capital and of the company's ability to meet its day-to-day payment obligations. It likewise measures the margin of safety provided for paying current debts in the event of a reduction in the value of current assets. This is not a ratio which can stand alone; the story it tells is conditioned by the *quality* of the major component parts of current assets—receivables and inventory. To the extent that receivables and inventory can be established as valid and liquid, the current ratio assumes importance as a specific measure of a company's capacity to meet its daily financial operating requirements.

The current ratio is computed by dividing total current assets by total current liabilities. For instance, the XYZ Company, with $750,000 in current assets and $200,000 in current liabilities, would have a 3.75 current ratio; the ABC Company, with only $180,000 in current assets and $200,000 in current liabilities, would have a current ratio of .90. (This ratio figure is expressed in "times" rather than the percentage value given to many of the other ratios.)

The current ratio is generally recognized as the patriarch among ratios. At one time it commanded such widespread respect that many businessmen regarded it as being endowed with the infallibility of nature's laws—a law of gravity applied to the balance sheet. And a 2-to-1 value became the inflexible standard—the minimum value that analysts thought this ratio should have in a properly operating concern. Financial analysis surely owes something to the creator of the current ratio, for at least he recognized the importance of relative values in preference to isolated figures. Using the current ratio, the credit manager or lending officer could put away his "flipping coin" and could instead make decisions based on some degree of logic and accuracy. Prompting inquiry into other areas, the current ratio has played a significant part in the evolution and general acceptance of a reasonably objective approach to financial analysis.

In the long run, however, the originator of the 2-to-1 current-ratio theory has done more disservice than can be imagined. An alarming number of credit grantors and business owners look for easy solutions to problems, and what could be easier than to resolve all doubt by one simple test? A credit manager appears—on the surface—to be quite professional when he says, "Yes, we can accept the order from XYZ Company, for I have analyzed its statement, and the company is liquid; it has a 2.78-to-1 current ratio." Or, "I don't see my way clear to go along with XYZ on its present $5,000 order, for its current ratio has slipped to 1.89-to-1 and is now in the danger zone." Similarly, some business owners have pointed with pride to their better than 2-to-1 current ratio as evidence of prosperity, even though they may be in constant conflict with their suppliers over their inability to pay within terms of sale. Blind reliance on a 2-to-1 standard for the current ratio is an indication of the constant groping for panaceas and easy solutions by businessmen who do not possess financial understanding. This sort of oversimplification is very dangerous and often leads directly to financial disaster.

At the very outset, the 2-to-1 theory fell far short of original expectations. This arbitrary standard implied that any company with a 2-to-1, or better, current ratio was a sheep and could be admitted to the credit fold. Companies which fell below that all-important dividing line were goats; the door was barred against them, or very stringent conditions of sale were imposed upon them. Strangely enough, it was discovered that many 2-to-1's—or even 3-to-1's or better—floundered; and a surprisingly large number wound up in the bankruptcy courts or in some form of insolvency. On the other hand, an impressive number of "goats"—less than 2-to-1 and frequently even less than 1-to-1—found the path to success and often were able to discount their bills while the sheep were dodging creditors.

How could this happen? In theory, $2 in current assets should be adequate to cover $1 in current liabilities. The answer is, quite simply, that the current ratio tests quantity, not quality. The current ratio measures only total dollars' worth of assets and total dollars' worth of liabilities. But how good are those assets and liabilities? There is no need for fear about the quality of liabilities, for they are very real and worth every dollar of debt shown on the balance sheets. Liabilities, assuredly, are not subject to shrinkage. But current assets—which generally consist in large measure of cash, accounts receivable, notes receivable, and inventory—may indeed decline in value. If a company's books are loaded with doubtful receivables or with slow-moving and unsalable inventory, then not only is its ability to pay greatly impaired, but its solvency may be threatened. Experience has taught that the current ratio is subject to further questioning, for the margin of error involved in blind reliance on a 2-to-1 figure has proved to be too great.

Logically, in their various endeavors to improve the current ratio, the analysts focused on the component parts of current assets; they concentrated initially on the influence of inventory on the current ratio. Twenty or thirty years ago, inventory represented a much larger dollars-and-cents figure than did accounts receivable, and hence its impact on liquidity or debt-paying ability was much greater than it is today. Then too, methods of valuation of inventory were not well defined, nor were there perpetual inventory systems or any of the modern refinements in inventory and purchasing control. The early analysts had seen inventory values rise and fall in rhythm with economic cycles and thus had considerable reason to view inventory as the element which caused their 2-to-1 current ratio yardstick to prove so unreliable.

The first major refinement of the current ratio was the "acid test" ratio. The name implied that absolute certainty would now reign and that the analyst's life would become serene through the elimination of all doubt surrounding future decisions. If inventory was the stumbling block that had thwarted the infallibility of the 2-to-1 current ratio, then it was thought that doubts about inventory should be eliminated from the analysts' thinking and calculations. The analysts reasoned that if there was one dollar in cash and receivables for every dollar in current liabilities, the credit grantor was taking no chances. So the 1-to-1 acid-test ratio became the vogue and is still regarded by some adherents as a definitive test. Again, however, the basic weakness which caused the current ratio to falter plagued the acid-test ratio. It, likewise, is a quantitative rather than a qualitative standard.

The acid-test ratio measures the total amount of cash and receivables against the total amount of current liabilities, with no allowance for the collectibility of receivables. It does not take into account that a company's terms of sale may be considerably longer than those of its suppliers, a situation which might impair the concern's ability to meet obligations within terms. In any case, a margin of error exists. To the extent that receivables were not as important an item on the balance sheet several years ago as they are today, the 1-to-1 acid-test ratio proved more reliable than the 2-to-1 current ratio. But today receivables have passed inventory in total value on the balance sheets of many American businesses. Moreover, receivables are stretching out in age and declining in quality of collectibility, whereas with regard to inventory, business has taken great strides toward assuring overall stability, salability, and control.

The acid-test ratio failed to pass its own acid test, for there were far too many companies with 1-to-1, or better, current ratios which ended in failure and too many "substandard" companies (less than 1-to-1) which performed beautifully and became outstandingly successful organizations. The trouble lay in oversimplification—in a failure to recognize that working capital does not just exist but is influenced by other forces within the financial structure of a company. Working capital ebbs and flows to the extent that these forces, which are measurable from the financial statement, are kept in balance.

The current ratio has not lost significance, nor has it lost its place in the analysis of today's financial statement. However, the analyst must bear three points in mind.

1. The current ratio must be subjected to qualitative tests. The major components of current assets—receivables and inventory—must be carefully assessed to determine their quality; otherwise the ratio may be grossly misleading.

Table 1

	COMPANY A	COMPANY B	COMPANY C
Cash	$ 10,000	$120,000	$ 15,000
Accounts receivable	125,000	300,000	85,000
Inventory	165,000	480,000	100,000
Total current assets	$300,000	$900,000	$200,000
Notes payable	$ 30,000	$150,000	$ 10,000
Accounts payable	110,000	430,000	60,000
Taxes and accruals	10,000	20,000	10,000
Total current liabilities	$150,000	$600,000	$ 80,000
Working capital	$150,000	$300,000	$120,000
Current ratio	2.00	1.50	2.50

2. The current ratio is subject to the influence of other financial forces which can depress or revive it dramatically overnight. Not only does the movement of receivables and inventory cause it to fluctuate, but it responds to fixed-asset investment, to sales, and to profit or loss as well.

3. The 2-to-1 current ratio must be abandoned as a convenient and flexible standard. Each industry has its own peculiar problems reflected in its own specific averages. A current ratio of 1.5-to-1 might be perfectly acceptable in one line of business activity, whereas a 3.5-to-1 ratio would be typical of another.

Keeping these qualifications in mind, let us examine the current assets, the current liabilities, and the working-capital position of three separate companies and note the significance of the current ratio. Table 1 shows the applicable financial-statement figures for the three companies in this case. All other factors being equal, the higher a company's current ratio, the more liquid is that company. Thus, as the current ratio increases, the company has a greater likelihood of meeting day-to-day operating expenses and of either discounting suppliers' invoices or paying within net selling terms. A firm with a higher ratio is better able to take in stride unforeseen or nonrecurring emergencies while not only surviving but remaining fluid and relatively free from creditor pressure.

The ratio of current assets to current liabilities is far more important than the actual amount of working capital. While Com-

Table 2

	PRESENT WORKING CAPITAL	LOSS THROUGH WRITEOFF	REMAINING WORKING CAPITAL (OR DEFICIT)
Company A	$150,000	$145,000	$ 5,000
Company B	300,000	390,000	(90,000)
Company C	120,000	92,500	27,500

pany B, in our example, has twice the working capital of Company A and 2.5 times as much as Company C, B is the least liquid of the three (provided that current assets are of equal quality in each case). Company C, with the least working capital, is the most liquid and feels the least creditor pressure. If for some reason each company suffered a 50 percent decline in the value of both receivables and inventory, what would happen to its working capital is illustrated in Table 2. While such an occurrence may seem farfetched, writeoffs or markdowns of this magnitude have in fact occurred, and this exercise demonstrates that the relative position of current assets to current liabilities (the current ratio) is more important than the actual dollar amount of working capital.

The current ratio presents a *general* picture of the adequacy of the working-capital position of a company. If, through later tests of receivables and inventory, the analyst should find that these two assets are normal with regard to collectibility and turnover, then the current ratio assumes importance as a *specific* measure of the working-capital position of the company under analysis. Liquidity and flexibility are clearly essential to the achievement of many company objectives.

Current-Liabilities-to-Net-Worth; Total-Liabilities-to-Net-Worth

The operating freedom of every company is conditioned by the relative stake creditors have in the business in contrast with that of the owners. The company with a lower-than-average ratio of debt to net worth—which denotes a strong ownership interest or position—enjoys relative freedom from creditors demanding repayment of debts or attempting to impose their wills on the company's management decisions. Conversely, if the debt ratios are higher than industry norm, management must be more apprehensive and may be compelled by creditors to courses of action that rob the company of valuable initiative and innovation.

Although both debt ratios are considered in this one section, there are some important differences between the two. A preponderance of debt which is current in status carries with it more immediate danger to the company's operating freedom because of its early maturity. From the point of view of time, the current-liabilities-to-net-worth ratio is the more pressing of the two. On the other hand, long-term debt has its own peculiar peril in that it is generally more exactly fixed as to maturity and repayment requirements. Moreover, repayment of long-term obligations is usually more enforceable because almost all long-term debt is backed by pledge of specific collateral.

The first of the debt ratios—*current-liabilities-to-net-worth*—is computed by dividing all current liabilities (those due within one year of the statement date) by the tangible net worth of the company. If the XYZ Company has $120,000 in current liabilities and $300,000 in net worth, its ratio is 40 percent. The ABC Company with $60,000 in current liabilities and net worth of $40,000 has a ratio of 150 percent. The second of the debt ratios—*total-liabilities-to-net-worth*—simply adds long-term liabilities to the current-liabilities figures to arrive at the total debt of the company, which is then divided by net worth. Using the XYZ and ABC Companies' figures from the preceding example, let us assume that the XYZ Company has $30,000 in debt of a long-term nature and that the ABC Company has none. This brings XYZ's liabilities to a total of $150,000, and thus its total-liabilities-to-net-worth ratio is 50 percent. ABC's ratio of total liabilities to net worth remains the same as its ratio of current liabilities to net worth—150 percent.

For illustration, let us turn to Table 3 and examine the debt ratios drawn from the financial statements of three more hypothetical companies—D, E, and F. As will be shown in detail in the next chapter, a company's financial position derives from particular causal factors—decisions or other actions traceable

Table 3

	COMPANY D	COMPANY E	COMPANY F
Current-liabilities-to-net-worth	40.0%	75.0%	150.0%
Industry average	75.0	75.0	75.0
Total-liabilities-to-net-worth	50.0	125.0	250.0
Industry average	90.0	90.0	90.0

through the six primary ratios. But for our present exercise we are not concerned with cause, but with effect (and its measurement); we are now interested in assessing the relative debt positions of Companies D, E, and F. (All of these companies, incidentally, are in the same line of business activity, which accounts for the uniformity of industry average.)

Certainly Company D is in an enviable position, with its total debt being only half as great as its equity capital. Owners have twice the stake in this business as do all types of creditors. While we do not know from the cited figures what Company D's current assets might be, we can, with reasonable assurance, assume that ample coverage is afforded to permit prompt payment; the possibility of creditor restrictions or limitations on D's operations is quite remote. Although the bulk of its debt is of a current nature, here too Company D is considerably less burdened than is the typical firm in its industry, and great latitude in management action and decisions is possible for this firm. Company E is strictly average with respect to the ratio of current liabilities to net worth but is a bit top-heavy in terms of total debt. Restrictive clauses or covenants might possibly be imposed on E's long-term borrowing; such an eventuality would depend on the nature of E's collateral, if any, and the length of time permitted for repayment of the loan or loans. But in general, Company E's current debt position is normal and its total debt structure, while above average, does not appear dangerously excessive.

The current debt of Company F, on the other hand, is twice the industry average when related to net worth, and F's ratio of total debt to net worth is nearly three times that of other concerns in this line of business. In addition to heavy short-term borrowing from banks, the company's long-term obligations, while not defined as to their nature, are exceedingly large and no doubt collateralized in major part, with restrictive agreements covering any unsecured portion. Such agreements may require that a certain level of working capital be maintained ($200,000, for example) or that the current ratio may not drop below 1.5-to-1. Or perhaps officers' salaries are limited in amount during the life of the loan, or dividends are suspended until the balance is repaid. The notes payable to trade suppliers are hardly evidence of financial health, since they probably represent conversion of overdue open-account balances, acknowledged in note form at the suppliers' request. In Company F's case, then, because of the disproportionately high ratio of debt to worth, it is likely that considerable limitation on the independent actions of management is being imposed by trade creditors and by lending institutions.

Pressure or the fear of pressure may, as Dun & Bradstreet has stated, "cloud business judgment, and . . . sap management energies." A business under creditor pressure is much like a poker player going into a sky's-the-limit game with only about $10 or $20 in his pocket. For fear of losing his limited capital and for fear of his wife's recriminations if he returns home with empty pockets, he folds his cards on many a winning hand. His wealthier competitors can easily run bluffs on him because they do not have his fears. Timing is all-important in the development and implementation of major business decisions, and a certain amount of imagination and daring is also helpful. If management knows that certain actions are beyond its reach or is fearful that those to whom the firm is indebted may veto management's plans, owners and officers can easily lose both their drive and their vision. In our present example, Company D has initiative in its grasp, for it is under little or no obligation to anyone other than the owners. Conversely, Company F's freedom of action is undoubtedly limited, subject to the concurrence of a variety of creditors whose views of any planned management gambit might necessarily be influenced by the element of risk rather than by potential profit. A negative vote—or even the thought of being turned down—might well deflate the ambitions of the officers of Company F. Management can ill afford a negative or frightened frame of mind.

The company skating on thin financial ice—slow in paying suppliers, heavily extended, and indebted in several quarters—lacks the resilience to sustain severe or sudden reverses. Its ability to exist and function is often limited by the extent of grace given it by understanding and lenient creditors whose satisfaction is highly contingent upon uninterrupted production, sales, and collections. Heavy indebtedness is often a characteristic of overtrading (attempting to do too much with one's invested capital), and overtrading is geared to prolonged optimum operating conditions. If, however, an unexpected difficulty should arise, few resources would be available to support the company. A strike may occur, shutting off production. Inventory will lie idle, but suppliers' bills will continue to come due, and the heavily extended company with no cushion and with already restless creditors to satisfy may collapse under the strain.

These ratios—current-liabilities-to-net-worth and total-liabilities-to-net-worth—measure the freedom of action of management by contrasting the equity owners have in the business with the interest of those on the outside.

Inventory-to-Working-Capital

Working capital represents the excess of current assets, which consist of cash and other liquid assets expected to be converted to cash, over current liabilities, those obligations which must be repaid within the current fiscal year. (When current debts exceed current assets, a working-capital deficit occurs.) Working capital thus represents the margin of protection a company provides for the payment of current debts in the event of possible reductions in the value of current assets or the need for diversion of current funds into fixed or miscellaneous assets. Because inventory is usually a very large and important element in the composition of working capital and because it is sometimes subject to major downward value revisions, management has need to measure the dependence of working capital on the stated value of inventory. The *inventory-to-working-capital ratio* provides this measurement.

To compute the ratio of inventory to working capital, the first step is to determine the company's working capital by subtracting

Exhibit 1. Rate of growth in net working capital, trade receivables, and dollar inventories.

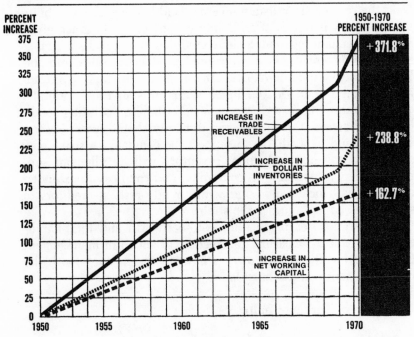

Reprinted by permission of Dun & Bradstreet

its current liabilities from its current assets. Let us assume that current assets of the XYZ Company total $150,000 (including $50,000 inventory) and that current liabilities are $70,000. Then XYZ's working capital is $80,000. Next, by dividing the book value of inventory—or $50,000—by the $80,000 working-capital figure, we determine that XYZ's ratio is 62.5 percent. If the ABC Company had $120,000 inventory and $40,000 working capital, its ratio would be 300 percent.

Historically, inventory has been the asset item most often responsible for business losses or failure—having been replaced by receivables only during the most recent five to ten years. During the past 20 years, a combination of computerized inventory controls and major changes in marketing and purchasing methods has seen the danger of inventory loss diminish, particularly in comparison with the rise in importance of receivables on the bal-

Table 4a. Percent of Total Assets, 1970.

	MANUFACTURERS	WHOLESALERS
Inventory	31	40
Fixed assets	29	13
Receivables	23	31

These figures were derived from data copyrighted by Robert Morris Associates, 1971.

Table 4b. Rank of Importance on Company Balance Sheet, 1970.

	MANUFACTURERS			WHOLESALERS		
	FIRST	SECOND	THIRD	FIRST	SECOND	THIRD
Inventory	64	38	21	35	13	7
Fixed assets	50	29	44	4	6	45
Receivables	9	56	58	16.	36	3

These figures were derived from data copyrighted by Robert Morris Associates, 1971.

ance sheets of American corporations. (See Exhibit 1.) Even so, it will be noted from Exhibit 1 that inventories increased at a 47 percent more rapid rate than working capital. Thus inventory remains a problem for American business—particularly for smaller companies.

Much of the improved relative position of inventory is due to the dynamic changes just referred to, but these refinements are far from universal. True, major companies have made great strides in this area, and their combined contribution has had great impact in improving the lot of inventory on the total American corporate balance sheet. Smaller companies, too, continue to benefit from the techniques of the leaders, but to a lesser degree.

It is generally conceded that the capital-goods investment is the largest single asset item on the books of the giant corporations of American industry, particularly the leaders engaged in our basic industries (cars, steel, oil, chemicals, paper, and so forth). However, as shown in Tables 4a and 4b, the merchandise inventory of smaller and moderate-size companies outranks even fixed assets in dollar amount and rank. Thus, even though inventory overall is under better control (rising over the past 20 years at a rate slightly lower than sales), management of our smaller organizations must remain vigilant and strive for improved methods of inventory evaluation and control.

Book figures for inventory are subject to major reduction in value from many influences. Style change, obsolescence, physical deterioration, and customer preference for other types of material are among those conditions which account for a drastic slash in the dollar figure assigned to inventory on a company's ledgers. Undetected pilferage and theft—often of inadequately insured or even totally uninsured goods—has caused many a shock to management, when the losses were ultimately discovered through physical inventory counts. In the past, too, there were so many uncertainties as to the method of inventory valuation that neither owners nor credit grantors could place substantial reliance on the figure which appeared on the financial statement. Even today, a surprising number of auditors' reports on companies of medium or small size qualify the inventory figure as simply taken from clients' books, without physical count and without verification of materials prices.

If inventory is large, if it is to any appreciable extent of unproven or unknown value, or if it is slow moving, what is the effect on the business? Naturally, profit would be affected by any markdown. But, in addition, heavy or slow-moving inventory can affect the company's ability to meet its daily commitments— its obligations to its workers and its creditors. If working capital is important to the functioning of any business, and if inventory, as one significant element of working capital, is subject to possible decline in value, then some measure must be used to test the degree of dependency of working capital on inventory. Such a measure is the ratio of *inventory to working capital*.

Let us examine Companies G, H, and I—all engaged in the same line of business—and relate their respective inventory-to-working-capital ratios to industry averages. The applicable figures are shown in Table 5. Company G's inventory-to-working-capital position is just industry average. Company H is somewhat beyond normal for its line of business, but still within acceptable limits. Company I, on the other hand, has strayed far from the path of industry normality. If, by reason of some calamity, inventory values of these three companies were cut today by 50 percent,

Table 5

	COMPANY G	COMPANY H	COMPANY I
Cash	$ 20,000	$ 40,000	$ 100,000
Accounts receivable	160,000	160,000	400,000
Inventory	120,000	200,000	600,000
Total current assets	$300,000	$400,000	$1,100,000
Total current liabilities	100,000	150,000	800,000
Working capital	$200,000	$250,000	$ 300,000
Inventory-to-working-capital	60.0%	80.0%	200.0%
Industry average	60.0	60.0	60.0

how would this reduction affect the working-capital position of each? Company G would sustain a $60,000 reversal, which would cut into its $200,000 working capital but would still leave the company with a cushion of $140,000, an amount greater than its total current liabilities. Its current ratio would remain a respectable 2.40-to-1. Company H's loss through this 50 percent slash in inventory value would amount to $100,000, or 40 percent of its working capital. While H would clearly feel a considerable shock, the $150,000 remaining as working capital would provide total coverage for current liabilities. The company's current ratio would drop from 2.67 to 2.0. Company I's dollar loss through a 50 percent reduction would be $300,000; I's working capital would be eliminated. The company's current ratio would become 1-to-1 overnight. Unless I's receivables were in excellent shape and unless its remaining inventory were turned at a better-than-average pace, the company would face considerable difficulty in meeting its daily obligations. Company I's situation may be considered extreme, but indeed it is fairly common. Many companies have an inventory-to-working-capital ratio of hundreds or even thousands of percent because of very heavy inventory, exceedingly limited working capital, or a combination of these two factors. A number of companies, moreover, operate with a working-capital deficit, which automatically throws their inventory-to-working-capital ratios into infinite numbers. This latter group is, of course, highly vulnerable to any reduction in the quality of its current assets, particularly inventory and trade receivables. We shall consider a test of inventory quality (net-sales-to-inventory) in the next chapter.

Trade-Receivables-to-Working-Capital

This ratio measures the dependence of working capital on trade receivables; it is based upon the same principle as is the inventory-to-working-capital ratio. As receivables have gained on and frequently surpassed inventory in dollar value and as their rate of growth has attained exceedingly great velocity—and remains unchecked today—the importance of this asset item in the working-capital structure of most companies has increased dramatically.

To compute the *trade-receivables-to-working-capital ratio*, add together all accounts receivable, notes receivable, and trade acceptances receivable arising from the normal trading activity of the business, and divide this total by the company's working capital. Special or unusual receivables—such as an amount due from a purchaser of a piece of surplus machinery or receivables due from officers, directors, or employees—are excluded from the calculation because the receivables of interest to the analyst are those created by selling the company's products or services to its regular trade. A firm possessing current assets of $100,000 (including $45,000 in trade receivables) and showing current liabilities of $40,000 has working capital of $60,000 and a trade-receivables-to-working-capital ratio of 75.0 percent.

When we examine the collection-period ratio in the following chapter, we shall consider in detail the many dangers involved in carrying massive receivables which have reached advanced age. Such situations are, understandably, much more common among small companies than among major corporations that have staffs of credit specialists. Many smaller companies do not subscribe to credit-reporting services, such as Dun & Bradstreet, or to such specialized industry publications as the Blue Book or the Red Book (publications reporting on packers and shippers of perishable fruits and vegetables), United Beverage Bureau (publishers of studies covering bottlers of carbonated beverages, beer, and soft drinks), or the Lyon Furniture Mercantile Agency reports. Nor do most small firms belong to the National Association of Credit Management, from which their officers could derive the benefit of mingling with others who extend credit, attending group meetings with persons in their own industries whose problems may closely parallel theirs, or going to classes presenting the rudiments and advanced techniques of good credit and financial management. Nor do the majority of small firms subscribe to credit-interchange services through which they would gain at least some knowledge of their customers' payment practices. In the majority of cases, the small company hires no employee with training in credit management or collection techniques, specialties which require considerable professional education and experience. Because of the large number of firms that operate with inadequate informational tools and without trained credit experts on their staffs, it is not surprising that even in periods of unprecedented prosperity, receivables of many small and medium-size businesses rise to highly dangerous proportions relative to sales, relative to working capital, relative to invested capital, and relative to profit.

On what basis are credit decisions made by smaller companies? Many credit grantors reason in this fashion: "He drives a Cadillac, so he must have some money," or "They've got a beautiful plant, the best-looking one in town," or "They always seem to be busy." These visual observations of apparent affluence hardly fall within the definition of scientific financial appraisal. Many credit decisions, reached without fundamental financial facts, follow entirely from the credit grantor's personal evaluation of his customer's character, based upon a personal meeting with the principal. Far too many officers and owners of small businesses feel that no loss can come from dealings with a man who appears honest, and more often than not, the credit decision of the small company is made on a trial-and-error basis. If Company A paid its last bill in reasonably prompt fashion, Company A is to be trusted again. The credit decision, like all management decisions, must be future-oriented, and yesterday's performance is only one factor among many that must be considered.

Realizing that unprofessional credit judgments are a major factor contributing to today's record receivables (which now

Table 6

	COMPANY J	COMPANY K	COMPANY L
Cash	$ 10,000	$ 20,000	$ 50,000
Trade receivables	60,000	200,000	500,000
Inventory	70,000	250,000	300,000
Total current assets	$140,000	$470,000	$850,000
Total current liabilities	40,000	270,000	550,000
Working capital	$100,000	$200,000	$300,000
Trade-receivables-to-working-capital	60.0%	100.0%	166.7%
Industry average	75.0	75.0	75.0

stand at their highest historical levels in terms of dollar amount, age, and percentage of total assets), the analyst simply cannot ignore the impact of receivables in the study of any company. Evaluation of the collectibility of receivables (which will be fully explored in the next chapter) is not entirely sufficient. The analyst must also determine the extent of working capital's dependence upon the continued validity of the reported receivables and upon the conversion of these receivables into cash at a satisfactory rate.

Let us observe selected figures for the hypothetical Companies J, K, and L in order to note the significance of the trade-receivables-to-working-capital ratio. The relevant data is presented in Table 6. Several subsidiary considerations must enter into our final appraisal of this ratio. Among these considerations are four points.

1. How many days' sales are outstanding at statement date and what is the industry average for collection period?

2. What are the respective terms of sale for each company, what are standard terms of sale for the industry, and what are the terms of purchase received from suppliers?

3. How many accounts are sold? Is any major percentage of receivables owed by a few accounts, or is the exposure widespread among many accounts?

4. Is a seasonal element involved?

In any of these cases, the potential harm to working capital stemming from possible slowness or writeoffs of receivables increases from Company J to Company L. If Company J should encounter payment slowness on the part of its customers, it could still pay its own debts. If it should sustain a severe bad-debt loss, it could survive. If Company J lost every dime now on the books—which is obviously pure fantasy—it would still have a positive working-capital position. The company might not have any customers left, but it would nonetheless have working capital. Company K is more vulnerable because its working capital is at the mercy of receivables. From the figures at hand, we do not know the exact nature of K's indebtedness, to whom money is owed, or the terms of sale under which K buys; but should severe slowness develop among K's accounts, very likely this slowness would have to be passed on to Company K's suppliers. Further, any major bad-debt writeoffs would be severely felt in a proportional shrinkage of working capital and a corresponding decline in the current ratio. Company L is comparatively, if not actually, in rather serious straits. Receivables are $200,000 greater than working capital. The firm's current liabilities are roughly equal to its receivables, which considerably outweigh inventory in dollar total. Unless L's receivables show evidence of exceptionally high quality (as determined through study of the collection-period ratio), L has a very narrow margin for error. With its limited working capital and low current ratio, payment slowness by L is probable. Faltering payment by L's customers would only serve to heighten the company's own delinquency—which could easily result in L's suppliers, for their own safety, either shortening terms of sale, intensifying collection pressure, establishing maximum credit limits, or even totally withdrawing credit arrangements. Company L's resilience in absorbing major bad-debt losses is minimal; should major writeoffs occur, working capital would be dangerously weakened and conceivably might disappear.

An increasing number of concerns find themselves in the bankruptcy courts, either voluntarily or involuntarily, because of inability to collect their receivables. (Exhibit 2 shows that reported bad-debt losses have risen at a rate almost double that of sales.) Often a sizable bankruptcy will set off a chain reaction of insolvencies among the bankrupt's suppliers, with occasional failure repercussions at the third and fourth levels in the progression. This domino possibility was one of the principal reasons

Exhibit 2. Rate of growth of sales and bad-debt losses.

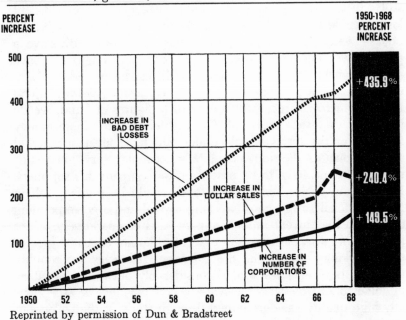

Reprinted by permission of Dun & Bradstreet

advanced by proponents of government guarantees for Lockheed borrowings during 1971.

The number of business mortalities attributable to "receivables difficulties" as the underlying cause for failure has risen, according to Dun & Bradstreet, until it is second only to "inadequate sales." Today receivables are the asset item most responsible for a firm's inability to survive ("inadequate sales" being an operating-statement item).

While current statistical sources do not publish industry figures for the trade-receivables-to-working-capital ratios, such averages can be constructed from existing ratios, if a certain allowance for error is made. Using Robert Morris Associates data, the analyst simply divides the composite figure for receivables by the composite figure for working capital. For example, Robert Morris reports 1970 figures for 186 wholesalers of meats and meat products as shown in Table 7. Working capital equals 67.4 percent in current assets minus 43.9 percent in current liabilities,

Table 7

Assets	Percent
Cash	5.1
Marketable securities	1.8
Receivables net	38.9
Inventory net	19.2
All other current assets	2.5
Total current assets	67.4
Fixed-assets net	25.8
All other noncurrent assets	6.8
	100.00*
Liabilities	
Due to banks, short term	13.9
Due to trade	17.5
Income taxes	2.2
Current maturities long-term debt	1.6
All other current liabilities	8.7
Total current liabilities	43.9
Noncurrent debt, unsubordinated	11.0
Total unsubordinated debt	54.9
Subordinated debt	1.7
Tangible net worth	43.4
	100.00

* Figures do not sum to precisely 100 percent because of rounding.

or 23.5 percent. Receivables clearly appear as 38.9 percent. Dividing 38.9 percent by 23.5 percent, we determine the ratio of trade receivables to working capital to be 165.5 percent.

Computation of the trade-receivables-to-working-capital ratio from Dun & Bradstreet figures is more complex and is based upon additional assumptions, but the resulting figures are sufficiently meaningful to serve as at least a rough indication of the significance of receivables within a particular company's working-capital structure. Take, for example, the 1970 Dun & Bradstreet averages for wholesalers of toys:

Net-sales-to-net-worth	3.74 times
Current-debt-to-net-worth	75.1%
Current-assets-to-current-liabilities	1.89 times
Collection period	60 days

Allowing certain liberties, we can develop the following.

1. Let us assume that net worth is $100,000.
2. Sales then are $374,000, since net worth turns 3.74 times per year.
3. Dividing $374,000 annual sales by 365, we find average daily sales to be $1,025.
4. Multiplying $1,025 by the 60-day collection period, we arrive at a receivables figure of $61,500.
5. Current debt is 75.1 percent of net worth ($100,000) or $75,100.
6. Current assets are 1.89 times current debt (as shown by the current ratio) or $141,939.
7. Subtracting $75,100 current debt from $141,939 current assets, we can establish that working capital is $66,839.
8. Dividing $61,500 receivables by $66,839 working capital, we find that the ratio of trade receivables to working capital is 92.0 percent.

With receivables assuming such a prominent place on the typical balance sheet, the analyst must measure his company's working-capital dependency on this highly volatile asset. The accounts-receivable-to-working-capital ratio is a secondary measurement, but one vital to total understanding of a financial statement.

Long-Term-Liabilities-to-Working-Capital

Companies generally resort to borrowing of a long-term nature for the purpose of adding new funds to deficient working capital to give the business time to generate profit and restore overall financial balance. The *long-term-liabilities-to-working-capital ratio* measures three specific aspects of the debt structure of a business concern.

1. It indicates whether long-term borrowing has been used to fulfill its principal purpose, that of replenishing working capital. If this ratio exceeds 100 percent, it is possible that funds from long-term borrowing may have been diverted into fixed-as-

set expansion, payment of unwarranted dividends, or the camouflaging of continuing operating losses.

2. It points out the possibility of future long-term financing by the company. A top-heavy percentage generally indicates that a concern has exhausted or is approaching the limit of this form of debt. Conversely, the absence of long-term borrowing or a very low percentage for this ratio points to the probable availability of long-term financing, if the analyst assumes that the company has assets of the type normally required to support loans of this nature.

3. It redirects the analyst's attention to the existence of long-term borrowing as such and—along with the debt ratios already discussed—keeps the analyst aware of the proportions between long-term and short-term credit.

To compute the long-term-liabilities-to-working-capital ratio, simply divide long-term liabilities (those maturing more than one year from statement date) by the company's working capital. If the XYZ Company has $40,000 in long-term borrowing and working capital of $120,000 its ratio is expressed as 33.3 percent. The ABC Company, with no long-term indebtedness, has a ratio of 0 percent regardless of the amount of its working capital.

Long-term debt, as we determined earlier, consists of any indebtedness payable more than one year from the date of the statement and includes intermediate financing, such as two- or three-year term loans or chattel mortgages, as well as real estate mortgages. We must remember, however, that any portion of such long-term obligations which falls due within the year following the statement date must be considered among the current liabilities of the company.

Business concerns of small and medium size generally resort to long-term borrowing to reinforce their working-capital positions. A company's liquidity, its bill-paying ability, may become impaired through operating losses, the diversion of funds into fixed or miscellaneous assets, or the accumulation of sluggish receivables or inventory. If management has properly analyzed the company's problems and has taken steps to prevent recurrence and, eventually, to restore proper balance, the company may find long-term financing of immeasurable aid during its period of return to liquidity. But money alone is not the answer. Borrowing commitments should not be made unless and until the underlying cause of the working-capital deficiency has been identified and a corrective program instituted or unless the purpose for borrowing is such that funds for repayment will be generated through improved profit expectancy, for both the principal and the interest of any such loan will have to be repaid.

Companies frequently require long-term financing to supplement invested capital in acquiring fixed assets while maintaining an adequate working-capital position. Such borrowing, of course, obligates the company to operate at a profit in order to meet interest and principal installments. The typical small company can seldom raise much new capital and likewise experiences considerable difficulty in refinancing obligations through new borrowing. Generally, a concern's repayment must be derived from earnings if it is to avoid drain on its working capital, which the loan was intended to bolster. Thus, if the borrowed funds are utilized to camouflage fundamental operating weaknesses which remain uncorrected, the same ghosts will return to haunt the company with even greater vengeance and chain-rattling.

Let us now examine hypothetical Companies M, N, and O to illustrate the significance of the long-term-debt-to-working-capital ratio. The applicable figures are shown in Table 8. Company M appears, on the basis of these rough summaries, to have made wise use of long-term borrowing. It has achieved a good volume of sales at an attractive rate of profit and, through the medium of long-term borrowing, has been able to maintain complete operating freedom as evidenced by a solid 3-to-1 current ratio. Had M not resorted to long-term financing, this ratio would have been only 1.24-to-1, and the company would probably have experienced difficulty in meeting suppliers' terms of sale, let alone earning the premium that goes with discounting. Such working-capital stringency would have carried with it the possibility of diminished sales volume stemming from curtailed lines of credit offered by suppliers. Many companies refuse to ship orders to a customer from whom an invoice is past due, and the achievement of maximum sales is—in large measure—contingent upon the ability of a business to obtain materials in the quantities needed

Table 8

	COMPANY M	COMPANY N	COMPANY O
Current assets	$ 300,000	$ 250,000	$ 275,000
Fixed assets	200,000	150,000	225,000
Other assets	50,000	15,000	20,000
Total assets	$ 550,000	$ 415,000	$ 520,000
Current liabilities	$ 100,000	$ 225,000	$ 200,000
Long-term liabilities	140,000*	100,000*	—
Total liabilities	$ 240,000	$ 325,000	$ 200,000
Net worth	$ 310,000	$ 90,000	$ 320,000
Working capital	200,000	25,000	75,000
Long-term-liabilities- to-working-capital	70.0%	400.0%	00.0%
Industry average	62.0	62.0	62.0
Net sales	$1,500,000	$1,000,000	$2,000,000
Net profit (or loss)	75,000	(20,000)	30,000

* Due in ten equal principal payments over the next ten years.

and on the dates required. Further, M's $75,000 profit, if maintained, will permit the company to reinforce its working capital while meeting its $14,000 annual principal payment with ease. Dividend payments might be justified as well. While M's percentage of long-term liabilities to working capital is slightly in excess of the industry norm, another year like the last should see the company reduce its ratio below the average for its industry.

Company N has evidently found the going a good bit thornier than has Company M. Despite long-term borrowing, Company N has virtually no working capital and its operations are being conducted at a loss. Moreover, N's opportunities for further borrowing are probably quite limited because the company is heavily debt-ridden already. While the figures at hand do not indicate the exact composition of N's liabilities, we can reasonably surmise that management has made maximum use of short-term borrowing from lending institutions (banks, factors, or finance companies), and that it has extended its lines of credit with suppliers to maximum levels and age. As the long-term debt in all likelihood represents real estate mortgages and chattel mortgages on equipment, Company N clearly has little room for added long-term borrowing. Unless the owners are able to contribute or attract additional risk capital, N faces imminent financial embarrassment. Another loss of present proportions during the coming year, coupled with the annual principal payment, will put N's working capital in deficit. But under such circumstances, owners, too, are reluctant to throw in additional money unless they are certain that they have devised a plan to reverse the company's drift toward insolvency.

Company O's condition, as evidenced by the brief data available, is neither quite good nor very bad. Management has not resorted to long-term financing as yet, but may well be obliged to do so in the near future. The company's sales have risen substantially beyond those of M—to the point where O is apparently overtrading on its capital (a common problem which we shall examine in Chapter 3)—but without the same beneficial rate of profit return. Yet O is in a far superior position to N. As it has not tapped the long-term borrowing market, some extended financing should be available to it. Despite the company's working-capital handicap, it is still making a profit which should aid it in meeting the fixed obligations resulting from long-term borrowing. Conceivably, greater freedom, promoted by relief from current-debt pressures and working-capital stringency, might enhance Company O's chances of improving its profit ratio. If, for instance, O borrowed $100,000 and used the money to pay off current bills, its current ratio would move up from 1.38 to 2.75, while its ratio of long-term debt to working capital would reach only 57.1 percent—or roughly the industry average. So, in summary, while O has not borrowed, it is in a position to do so.

In considering the significance of the long-term-liabilities-to-working-capital ratio, the analyst must bear in mind that unless existing term financing can be re-funded indefinitely, working capital eventually must be depleted by the amount of long-term borrowing.

Net-Profit-to-Net-Worth

The *net-profit-to-net-worth ratio* measures the profit return on investment, the reward for assumption of ownership risk. The businessman will seldom assume the perils that go with the operation of his own business unless he has reason to believe that his daring and his efforts will provide him with an adequate, and continuing, reward in the form of profit. And no business can provide for future growth without supplementing net worth through income from operations. Nor can the company attract more or new investment funds without a substantial return to show for present and past investments or at least the prospect of future profit attainment. However, these considerations must be conditioned by the recognition that the ratio of net profit to net worth is a secondary measurement of both profit and net worth. The analyst must be alert to the fact that when a company's capital account is abnormally low, even a substandard profit (as measured by the net-profit-to-net-sales ratio, which will be presented in Chapter 3) will appear as a sensational return on capital and create a very misleading impression of success.

The ratio of net profit to net worth is computed by dividing a company's profit after taxes by its tangible net worth (the excess of assets over liabilities after deducting intangibles). A profit of $20,000 on net worth of $120,000 gives a ratio of 16.67 percent. The same $20,000 profit on net worth of $250,000 yields an 8 percent return on invested capital.

Profit measured against net worth, the return on investment, is important as an incentive to the owners—whether stockholders, partners, or an individual proprietor—and as a means of providing for the future growth of the company. Losses, on the other hand, may threaten the concern's very existence. When an individual joins in launching a business, one of his main objectives is to reap monetary return from this action. Some individuals may be prompted by more visionary and humanitarian motives such as improving the lot of man through introduction of a product or service designed to lessen his workload or render it more pleasant or through contribution to his cultural or educational wealth. But generally the business entrepreneur expects to derive direct benefit from his contribution—not solely an esthetic pride or contentment but a reward in the form of monetary profit.

In the opening paragraph of most annual reports to stockholders, the corporation presidents express pride or modest satisfaction (or regret and apologies) for the profits (or losses) experienced by their companies. As every company president knows, not only are he and his fellow officers dedicated to making progress, expressed in terms of profit, but the owners—the stockholders—regard this objective as being of prime importance. The remainder of the annual report explains that tomorrow will be brighter because of new products, new plants, and new personnel; but many stockholders do not read beyond the line concerning present profit—the company's profit is their primary interest. In addition to immediate return, provision for future growth through retained earnings is a significant aspect of profit.

When corporate profits have been realized and when cash and liquidity positions are adequate, cash dividends are normally paid to stockholders as a return on their share of ownership. Management, however, must exercise prudence in distributing earnings, for money must be retained for financing other projects which may produce even greater profit in the future. The company with a high profit return can theoretically pay dividends while holding sufficient funds to permit expansion. Companies often require additional capital as they increase the scope of their operations through the introduction of new products, the opening of new markets, the acquisition of new plants, or the expansion of existing facilities. Some businesses, however, need new capital to cover heavy operating losses which have drained their resources to a point where their functions are threatened with drastic curtailment. Naturally, capital is more easily attracted by a proven record of profit return on net worth and an established pattern of dividend payments than by a series of losses and passed dividends.

The preceding discussion points up the importance of measuring profit by means of the net-profit-to-net-worth ratio. But this ratio serves to test net worth as well as profit. An abnormally high ratio may very well indicate an inadequate profit and even more inadequate net worth. This aspect of the net-profit-to-net-worth ratio is often ignored by those who think in terms of the blue-chip organization without considering the positions of smaller companies.

Let us examine, for example, the figures for the hypothetical Companies P, Q, and R shown in Table 9. Certainly Companies

Table 9

	COMPANY P	COMPANY Q	COMPANY R
Net worth	$40,000	$200,000	$500,000
Net profit	10,000	30,000	50,000
Net-profit-to-net-worth	25.00%	15.00%	10.00%
Industry average	8.88	8.88	8.88

Table 10

	COMPANY P	COMPANY Q	COMPANY R
Net sales	$500,000	$2,000,000	$1,000,000
Net profit	10,000	30,000	50,000
Net-profit-to-net-sales	2.00%	1.50%	5.00%
Industry average	4.38	4.38	4.38

P and Q appear substantially superior to Company R by the single standard of measurement, net-profit-to-net-worth. Company P has a ratio 2.5 times that of Company R and shows a return three times greater than the average for the industry, while Company R is only fractionally above normal profit expectancy for its line of business. So the two smaller firms appear to be making infinitely greater strides than Company R. We cannot assume, however, that as the net-profit-to-net-worth ratio increases in size, commensurate stability and progress are necessarily reflected.

Let us add another dimension to this analysis of profit before we venture a final judgment on the relative positions of the three companies. From the figures in Table 10, we can see that both P and Q recorded substandard profit return on sales, substantially less than half the normal industry expectancy. Company R, on the other hand, attained a higher-than-average percentage of profit per dollar of sales. The smaller companies are obviously placing considerable strain on their invested capital by transacting a volume of sales per dollar of net worth several times greater than that of Company R. Only by such overtrading have Companies P and Q succeeded in logging impressive profit-to-worth percentages. When we study the trading ratio (net-sales-to-net-worth) in the next chapter, we shall note the many dangers involved in attempting to support excessive sales volume on limited invested capital.

An abnormally high rate of profit may very well, then, tell

a story of inadequate net worth and demonstrate the need for additional invested capital. Thus, particularly in regard to the legion of smaller companies which numerically dominate the American business scene, this ratio must serve a dual purpose: (1) to measure the adequacy of profit return on investment and (2) to provide a secondary test of both profit and net worth.

Net-Sales-to-Fixed-Assets

The ratio of *net sales to fixed assets* measures the efficiency with which the company is utilizing its investment in land, plant, equipment, furniture, fixtures, and so forth. In addition, this ratio serves as a secondary test of the adequacy of sales volume. The analyst must keep in mind that an abnormally high ratio usually indicates the rental of property and equipment.

Computed by dividing a company's net sales by the book or depreciated value of fixed assets, this ratio is expressed in "times" rather than "percent." The XYZ Company with annual sales of $1 million on fixed assets of $200,000 has a net-sales-to-fixed-assets ratio of 5. The ABC Company recording yearly sales of $2 million on a $40,000 fixed-asset investment has a ratio of 50.

The ratio of net sales to fixed assets is indispensable in securing a total understanding of a company's financial statement; without this secondary measurement, conclusions concerning the adequacy of fixed assets would be based on a single test (the fixed-assets-to-net-worth ratio, which will be covered thoroughly in Chapter 3). While fixed-assets-to-net-worth is assuredly among the most vital of the 15 ratios used in cause-and-effect ratio analysis, it cannot be relied upon as a conclusive test of fixed assets, and an additional gauge of this important balance-sheet item is clearly necessary. Every ratio serves as a measure of both halves of the fraction, and distortion in this ratio does not necessarily point to fixed assets as the causal element, any more than it establishes beyond doubt that net worth is responsible for the resulting lack of balance. Only through further testing can the analyst determine the status of each component and its influence upon the company's financial balance.

Since fixed assets are acquired to further the sales progress of

Table 11

	COMPANY S	COMPANY T	COMPANY U
Net sales	$600,000	$1,000,000	$800,000
Fixed assets	50,000	200,000	20,000
Net-sales-to-fixed-assets	12.0 times	5.0 times	40.0 times
Industry average	8.0	8.0	8.0

a company by increasing production and service or reducing costs, or both, the utilization of these assets must be measured by reference to sales activity. An assessment of the efficiency of plant and equipment, expressed in dollars of sales to dollars of fixed assets, must be added to the analyst's findings regarding the relative size of fixed investment in order to determine present conditions and future needs in this area. In general, a high sales-to-fixed-assets ratio reflects efficient use of money invested in plant and in other productive or capital assets. If this ratio is well above industry average, the analyst must consider that plant, machinery, trucks, and other fixed assets have not only a theoretical but an actual capacity and that as this capacity is reached, profitable sales may be lost through inability to increase production. Also, an abnormally high net-sales-to-fixed-assets ratio may well be a sign that the company under study is leasing part or all of its property and equipment.

Let us refer to Companies S, T, and U to see how the net-sales-to-fixed-assets ratio is applied. The relevant figures are shown in Table 11. In the case of Company S, we find a picture of efficient use of plant investment; the firm has been able to achieve 50 percent more sales per dollar in fixed assets than has its average competitor. Through its success in limiting fixed assets, S has a larger proportion of its total assets available for working-capital purposes. Also, the company's per unit charges against sales income to cover depreciation and other fixed costs incident to plant and equipment are in all probability less than average; this fact gives management still further flexibility. In a period of intense competition, such advantages would enhance management's ability to meet possible price-cutting tactics of competitors, as long as the company's financial reserves remained roughly average for its industry. The ability of Company S to boost its net-sales-to-fixed-assets ratio is, of course, subject to an upper limit; for even though the firm might resort to 24-hour-a-day production, the total physical capacity of existing plant and equipment must ultimately be reached. As this point nears, Company S will be obliged to consider additional capital-goods investment or rental which, unless sales keep pace, will bring the ratio of net sales to fixed assets closer to the industry average.

Company T's ratio is less attractive than that of Company S. Company T's $200,000 plant investment has not yet been justified by the level of sales attained. To achieve average performance, T must increase its volume to $1.6 million—$600,000 more than present activity. The company might well find that its excessive fixed assets have caused

1. A drain on working capital.
2. Greater-than-average debt pressure, either short term or long term.
3. Reduced profit stemming from high fixed costs on each unit of sales.

In order to evaluate T's present fixed-asset commitment, the analyst must know the dates of acquisition of the major components of plant and equipment and the company's sales volume for the preceding two or three years. If the investment in fixed assets should prove to be relatively recent, quite possibly T expanded for the future somewhat beyond its immediate needs. While the company might feel temporary financial strain, such advance planning might indeed become a future advantage. The analyst must take care not to judge the significance of a financial-statement item entirely by figures recorded on a single date. If sales are moving upward at an appreciable rate, this trend tends to minimize the dangers of the concern's present deficiency. Assume, for example, that as an analyst you have found Company T's sales pattern to be:

1969	$ 350,000
1970	500,000
1971	750,000
1972	1,000,000

These figures indicate that, while the investment is now a noticeable burden to Company T, continuation of the present trend in sales will soon justify the outlay for fixed assets. Conversely, should a declining sales pattern be discovered, T's added commitment in fixed assets could not be easily justified. If the excessive investment was made several years ago, then the low ratio of 5 times assumes more serious proportions. Continued substandard performance points to an error in judgment on the part of management, in that sales to justify the expansion have not materialized. The analyst must note, too, that under these circumstances management's original expansion decision was even more faulty than is now apparent, since fixed assets are annually reduced in value through depreciation charges. In the case of Company U, a quick glance might prompt a conclusion that the firm is a tremendously efficient operator—that it has achieved peak performance from its plant investment dollar. With U's ratio currently 5 times industry average, however, further investigation would undoubtedly disclose that the company is leasing a substantial part of its fixed assets.

While industry averages for the net-sales-to-fixed-assets ratio are not generally available, useful figures can be computed from other ratios as follows:

1. Assume net worth to be $100,000.
2. If net-sales-to-net-worth for the industry under study should, for instance, be 7.2 times, then annual sales would be $720,000.
3. If the fixed-assets-to-net-worth ratio should be 90 percent, it follows that fixed assets amount to $90,000.
4. Dividing $720,000 sales by $90,000 fixed assets, the net-sales-to-fixed-assets ratio is found to be 8 times per year.

It is simpler to determine this ratio through use of Robert Morris Associates' composites. To illustrate, Exhibit 3 covers 1970 figures for manufacturers of fabricated plate work. Concentrating on those companies with asset size under $250,000, we find 24 firms' statements representing combined net sales of $9,842,000, or an average of $410,083. The average asset size, $169,375, is

Exhibit 3. Composite statement, manufacturers of fabricated plate work.

	39 STATEMENTS ENDED ON OR ABOUT JUNE 30, 1970 64 STATEMENTS ENDED ON OR ABOUT DECEMBER 31, 1970				
ASSET SIZE	UNDER $250M	$250M AND LESS THAN $1MM	$1MM AND LESS THAN $10MM	$10MM AND LESS THAN $25MM	ALL SIZES
NUMBER OF STATEMENTS	24	40	36		103
ASSETS	%	%	%	%	%
Cash	8.3	9.2	6.8		6.3
Marketable Securities	.7	1.0	.1		.7
Receivables Net	24.6	26.6	30.3		29.0
Inventory Net	26.5	26.2	27.6		28.4
All Other Current	1.3	2.1	3.1		2.3
Total Current	61.4	65.1	68.0		66.8
Fixed Assets Net	36.4	30.2	25.2		26.9
All Other Noncurrent	2.2	4.7	6.8		6.3
Total	100.0	100.0	100.0		100.0
LIABILITIES					
Due to Banks – Short Term	10.0	7.7	10.4		7.6
Due to Trade	17.9	17.8	16.4		16.0
Income Taxes	1.6	2.3	2.6		2.5
Current Maturities LT Debt	1.5	2.4	1.4		2.6
All Other Current	8.4	10.7	11.7		13.0
Total Current Debt	39.4	40.9	42.6		41.6
Noncurrent Debt Unsubordinated	11.6	12.9	9.6		10.6
Total Unsubordinated Debt	51.0	53.9	52.2		52.1
Subordinated Debt	1.4	.9	1.3		2.2
Tangible Net Worth	47.7	45.2	46.5		45.6
Total	100.0	100.0	100.0		100.0
INCOME DATA					
Net Sales	100.0	100.0	100.0		100.0
Cost of Sales	79.9	79.6	83.8		81.3
Gross Profit	20.1	20.4	16.2		18.7
All Other Expense Net	19.7	16.5	12.0		14.6
Profit Before Taxes	.4	3.9	4.1		4.1
RATIOS	1.6	1.6	1.2		1.5
Quick	1.0	.9	.9		.9
	.6	.7	.6		.6

obtained by dividing total assets of $4,065,000 by 24. Fixed assets in this particular size grouping constitute 36.4 percent of average assets (or $169,375) resulting in an average capital-goods investment of $61,653. Dividing this figure into annual sales, already determined to be $410,083, we find the turnover rate to be 6.7 times per year.

Although the analyst may have to make certain allowances in computing the net-sales-to-fixed-assets ratio from currently

ASSET SIZE	39 STATEMENTS ENDED ON OR ABOUT JUNE 30, 1970 / 64 STATEMENTS ENDED ON OR ABOUT DECEMBER 31, 1970				
	UNDER $250M	$250M AND LESS THAN $1MM	$1MM AND LESS THAN $10MM	$10MM AND LESS THAN $25MM	ALL SIZES
NUMBER OF STATEMENTS	24	40	36		103
RATIOS	%	%	%	%	%
Current	2.6 / 1.6 / 1.2	2.9 / 1.7 / 1.2	2.4 / 1.7 / 1.2		2.6 / 1.7 / 1.2
Fixed/Worth	.5 / .7 / 1.1	.4 / .7 / 1.0	.3 / .5 / 1.0		.4 / .6 / 1.0
Debt/Worth	.6 / 1.1 / 1.5	.5 / 1.3 / 2.5	.6 / 1.1 / 2.0		.5 / 1.1 / 2.4
Unsubordinated Debt/Capital Funds	.4 / 1.1 / 1.5	.5 / 1.2 / 2.5	.6 / 1.0 / 2.0		.5 / 1.1 / 2.4
Sales/Receivables	23 15.5 / 38 9.6 / 53 6.8	29 12.3 / 43 8.3 / 51 7.1	40 8.9 / 53 6.8 / 67 5.4		31 11.8 / 46 7.9 / 60 6.0
Cost Sales/Inventory	27 13.6 / 49 7.3 / 77 4.7	29 12.3 / 52 6.9 / 84 4.3	29 12.6 / 68 5.3 / 106 3.4		29 12.5 / 55 6.5 / 88 4.1
Sales/Working Capital	19.3 / 7.0 / 4.1	13.3 / 6.7 / 4.5	9.3 / 6.6 / 3.8		13.3 / 6.7 / 3.9
Sales/Worth	7.5 / 4.8 / 3.1	8.8 / 4.7 / 3.0	5.9 / 4.3 / 3.0		7.4 / 4.6 / 2.9
% Profit Before Taxes/Worth	18.7 / 4.5 / -10.1	43.5 / 14.6 / 3.9	34.8 / 16.2 / 7.1		34.8 / 13.8 / 2.2
% Profit Before Taxes/Total Assets	8.7 / 2.9 / -7.0	14.1 / 5.5 / .5	14.9 / 8.7 / 1.7		13.9 / 5.6 / .6
Net Sales	$9842M	$55193M	$225886M		$380277M
Total Assets	4065M	23542M	113865M		195273M

available information, this measure serves as a good indicator of the company's utilization of its investment in plant, equipment, and other fixed assets.

Net-Sales-to-Working-Capital

The ratio of *net sales to working capital* indicates the demands made upon working capital in supporting the sales volume of a business concern. The principle that a company's sales volume requires a certain amount of working capital is sound. The higher the level of sales in relation to available working capital, the greater the strain a company encounters in satisfying trade and bank creditors while meeting payroll, taxes, and other regular obligations. In cases where this ratio appears disproportionately high, it serves to point out working-capital deficiencies in dramatic fashion.

Net sales are simply divided by working capital to derive this ratio, which is expressed in "times." The XYZ Company with annual sales of $300,000 on $40,000 working capital has a ratio of 7.5 times, while the ABC Company with working capital of $20,000 and sales of $800,000 has a ratio of 40.

The net-sales-to-working-capital ratio is included in this study more as a bonus than as a monumental contribution to financial-statement understanding, for despite its value in emphasizing any working-capital deficiency, it usually confirms facts the analyst has already discovered through other, more fundamental indicators. In total analysis, sales are measured against (1) net worth, (2) profit, (3) fixed assets, (4) receivables, and (5) inventory. Thus the net-sales-to-working-capital ratio yields little new information about the adequacy of sales. Working capital, likewise, is thoroughly tested by comparison with (1) long-term debt, (2) inventory, and (3) accounts receivable as well as through (4) the current ratio. But notwithstanding the tendency of this ratio to confirm rather than disclose, its sensitivity to changes in working capital makes it particularly valuable under certain conditions. And, as one more measurement of both sales and working capital, it does serve to emphasize the need for operating funds to support the sales objectives of the company.

For illustration of the application of the net-sales-to-working-capital ratio, see Table 12, which shows selected figures from the financial statements of Companies V, W, and X—all engaged in the same industry. In the case of Company V, the figures indicate an extremely tight, but not unusual, working-capital situation. Although V is transacting a volume of business that appears reasonably consistent with the size of its current assets, its net-sales-to-working-capital ratio is 18 times greater than the industry

Table 12

	COMPANY V	COMPANY W	COMPANY X
Current assets	$ 250,000	$ 250,000	$ 250,000
Current liabilities	240,000	100,000	110,000
Working capital	$ 10,000	$ 150,000	$ 140,000
Sales	$1,800,000	$2,700,000	$1,500,000
Sales-to-working-capital	180.0 times	18.0 times	10.7 times
Industry average	10.0	10.0	10.0

average; thus the cause of this disparity might seem, at first glance, to lie with working capital. The firm's 1.04-to-1 current ratio tends to confirm this surface observation, but without complete financial-statement figures we cannot be absolutely certain. In any event, V clearly must do some fancy juggling to maintain cordial trade relationships. Company W has the same dollar amount of current assets as V and displays an apparently sound 2.5-to-1 current ratio. The company's net-sales-to-working-capital ratio is, nevertheless, substantially above the industry norm. We can speculate that the pressure on W's working capital results from high sales volume relative to the concern's overall financial structure, but any definitive answer must depend upon total analysis. Company X, again with the same dollar value of current assets, is roughly average with respect to the ratio of net sales to working capital and thus encounters no unusual strain in meeting current obligations.

Now let us suppose that each of these companies has just been notified that one of its major accounts is unable to meet a payment covering nearly one week's average sales. Instead of remitting within the usual 15 days of billing, this customer cannot be expected to pay for at least one month, possibly two, or perhaps even longer. Company V may well encounter considerable difficulty as a result of this unexpected development which will cause accounts receivable to mount by $35,000. Because of V's tight working-capital position, the increase in trade credit (current liabilities) needed to support additional receivables may not be readily available to the concern. Thus Company V may be required to reduce sales or to secure outside capital. Neither Company W nor Company X will likely find the added receivables burdensome. It should be noted, however, that because of W's higher net-sales-to-working-capital ratio, the increase in receivables by one week's sales ($46,000 for W and $29,000 in X's case) will reduce W's current ratio to a considerably greater extent than it will affect that of Company X.

We have seen, then, that as a measure of the amount of sales supported by each dollar of working capital, the net-sales-to-working-capital ratio is useful in total analysis of the company's financial structure.

The nine ratios that we have examined in the preceding pages are used by the financial analyst to measure and study the effects of financial forces on the operation of the business. The six primary ratios—those that set forth the six causal relationships which determine financial balance and thus point to the underlying causes of financial problems—will be defined and thoroughly examined in the following chapter.

3 The Six Causal Ratios

We have now examined nine of the fifteen ratios upon which total cause-and-effect analysis is based. Purposely, the six most important ratios appear in this chapter, for the inexperienced analyst can best learn the ratio technique if he commences with the study of the nine secondary ratios. Having developed a familiarity with these secondary measures and having acquired some facility in computing and applying them, the analyst should be ready to explore the six basic, or causal, ratios. Of course, no skill can be mastered on the first performance, but thoughtful handling of practice cases—real or hypothetical—will refine techniques and make clear the meanings of all the ratios. Another reason the study of the six fundamental ratios has been deferred until this chapter is that by beginning with the study of the secondary ratios, the reader develops a fuller understanding of *cause and effect,* the most important concept in the mastery of ratio analysis. The analyst who understands the cause-and-effect element can examine any financial statement and, within minutes, pinpoint the precise nature of any lack of balance reflected in that statement. Ignorance of cause and effect will leave the analyst jousting with windmills, concentrating on entirely incidental factors.

All of life is, of course, subject to cause and effect. If a rock is thrown at a plate glass window with sufficient force, the window breaks. The throwing of the stone is the cause; the shattering of the glass is the effect. One could hardly believe the reverse—

that the breaking glass caused the rock to be thrown. Applying the basic principle of cause and effect, we recognize that a business organization finds itself in a particular financial position because of some cause or perhaps a multiplicity of causes. The immediate situation is the effect; the cause or causes must be sought. Financial balance, measured through ratios, is clearly subject to the fundamental forces of cause and effect. Some ratios are basic, fundamental, primary. Others are resultant, secondary, derivative. The six ratios discussed in this chapter are causal; they are the keys to financial balance.

Knowledge of the meaning of each ratio is, by itself, not sufficient to provide anyone with the ability to use the ratio-analysis technique effectively. Nor can the application of individual industry averages yield complete understanding; no company can be expected to adhere strictly to industry averages in all respects. The analyst will likely find the XYZ Company deficient in several areas, but above average in others. What then can he conclude about XYZ? Is the company good or bad or somewhere between these extremes? Is the degree of deviation from normal the factor which separates the sheep from the goats? An understanding of the cause-and-effect factors in ratio analysis provides the answers to these questions. Developed some 25 years ago, the cause-and-effect system of analysis has been tested in thousands of business situations since that time. It has served numerous business principals and officers as the key to quick and accurate detection of basic financial problems and has thus guided many companies to financial success.

Let us now examine the six primary or causal ratios in order to see how variations in these ratios are reflected in the other nine and how the primary ratios interact among themselves. These six causal ratios are:

Fixed-assets-to-net-worth.
Collection period.
Net-sales-to-inventory.
Net-sales-to-net-worth.
Net-profit-to-net-sales.
Miscellaneous-assets-to-net-worth.

In the following pages, each of these ratios is examined, and the method of computation and significance of each one is explained.

Fixed-Assets-to-Net-Worth

Every solvent company has a certain amount of capital or net worth, the owners' equity in the business. This capital must be put to effective use in order for the concern to perform its business purpose and to assure its survival and prosperity. To accomplish these ends, management must make decisions regarding the apportionment of the owners' equity among current assets, fixed assets, and miscellaneous assets. The *ratio of fixed assets to net worth* measures the extent to which a company's invested capital or net worth is tied up in nonliquid, permanent, depreciable assets; and, indirectly, it measures the amount of capital that remains for investment in other, more fluid assets. A disproportionately high investment in fixed assets places a burden on the company because it limits current assets and productive miscellaneous assets, increases the debt position, and may depress profits through heavy fixed costs. The analyst must, however, be aware that a high percentage for this ratio does not automatically prove that fixed assets are excessive. The ratio of fixed assets to net worth can be distorted by inadequate net worth or may be inflated through a combination of above-average fixed assets and below-average net worth.

The ratio of fixed assets to net worth is computed by dividing the depreciated value of fixed assets by net worth. The XYZ Company, with fixed assets of $20,000 and net worth of $80,000, has a ratio of 25 percent. The ABC Company, which has fixed assets valued at $120,000 and shows net worth of only $60,000, has a ratio of 200 percent.

Every company has a limited amount of capital with which to work. This capital is supplemented by income received through profit, or is decreased by the extent of any losses sustained. In a general sense, a company is not unlike John Jones, private citizen, who over the years has accumulated a certain amount of personal net worth in the form of a savings account, some investments in the stock market, an equity in a home, and a car. Jones hopes to add to his nest egg through his annual income, although he may possibly encounter reverses through serious illness in the family or some other unforeseen personal difficulty. If Jones, with a $10,000 annual income and with accumulated personal resources of $7,000 or $8,000, decided to buy a $75,000 home in an exclusive suburb, he might well find that he had overreached himself financially. His liquid resources would be completely exhausted and the monthly mortgage payments would consume most of his salary. Real estate taxes would absorb the rest of his pay, and all his normal activities—among them the luxury of eating—would be necessarily discontinued.

The foregoing example may be regarded as an extreme and unlikely case, but there are many parallel situations in the business world. Suppose that the owners of the XYZ Company are of the same frame of mind as Jones and decide that the company name and its product require the very best public image. A new plant—complete with the latest machinery and office trappings, new automobiles, trucks, and perhaps private airplanes for the officers—seems to them to be a reasonable investment. They do expect their company to grow, and they see this investment as "planning for the future." If they have the capital resources and the income to support such an investment, if proper thought is given to the expenses involved, and if the profit to cover these costs can be realistically projected, then their commitment may be wise. But if, on the other hand, their investment is impulsive with neither the resources nor the income to support the outlay, and if the resulting expenses will actually erode or wipe out profits, then the program is obviously ill-advised and will affect the company in the same way that Jones's suburban purchase altered his way of life. Physical facilities clearly require funds, and if too much of invested capital is placed in "bricks and mortar," the little luxuries, and more, may have to be forgone. Both Jones and the XYZ Company have daily obligations to cover basic necessities, let alone luxuries, and these are difficult to meet without cash or credit arrangements. Jones must clothe his family, provide for food on the table, pay his gas and telephone bills, and satisfy the Internal Revenue Service. The XYZ Company must likewise meet its payroll, buy materials, pay its utility bills, and have enough liquid capital left to cover taxes. Any company has a fixed amount of capital with which to operate, and, necessarily, choices must be made as to where and how that capital is to be allocated, what part is to be spent currently, and what portion is to be set aside for future growth.

Before considering in detail the application of the fixed-assets-to-net-worth ratio to individual cases, let us consider how this ratio qualifies as causal or primary, and how the factors measured by this ratio influence other ratios. If a company has an excessively high percentage of net worth committed to fixed assets, its working-capital position will be greatly influenced. For example, if the XYZ Company, with a net worth of $100,000, has invested $200,000 in fixed assets, it has created a definite problem for itself; it owns outright only 50 percent of its fixed assets. In the absence of other forms of borrowing, the working capital of the XYZ Company will be penalized $100,000, and, of course, any such penalty will automatically reduce the current ratio. Hence, it follows that any ratio involving working capital will also suffer. Excessive fixed assets, then, adversely affect and distort five ratios relating to working capital:

Current ratio.
Net-sales-to-working-capital.
Inventory-to-working-capital.
Trade-receivables-to-working-capital.
Long-term-debt-to-working-capital.

To the extent that the ratio of fixed assets to net worth is excessively high, the current ratio is reduced and the other four ratios are increased, simply through the reduction of working capital. For example, if the ABC Company has current assets of $300,000 against current liabilities of $150,000, its ratio is 2 times, or 2-to-1. If the XYZ Company has the same $300,000 in current assets and the same $150,000 in current liabilities, but it attempts to expand its plant and equipment by a $100,000 investment, it must be prepared to face one of three alternatives:

1. The company's current assets will be decreased $100,000 to $200,000.

Table 13a

	COMPANIES ABC AND XYZ
Net sales	$1,500,000
Inventory	100,000
Receivables	120,000
Long-term debt	75,000

Table 13b

	ABC COMPANY	XYZ COMPANY
Net-sales-to-working-capital	10.0 times	30.0 times
Inventory-to-working-capital	66.7%	200.0%
Receivables-to-working-capital	80.0	240.0
Long-term-debt-to-working-capital	50.0	150.0

2. The company's current liabilities will become $100,000 greater, rising to $250,000.
3. The company's current assets will be decreased and its current liabilities increased to an aggregate difference of $100,000.

Assume the second alternative. The XYZ Company now has $300,000 in current assets and $250,000 (not $150,000) in current liabilities—a current ratio of 1.2 in contrast to ABC's current ratio of 2. The ABC Company's working capital remains $150,000 ($300,000 current assets minus $150,000 current liabilities), whereas XYZ has only $50,000 in working capital ($300,000 current assets minus $250,000 current liabilities). Assuming that both companies are identical with respect to sales, inventory, receivables, and long-term debt, we observe the difference in their ratios shown in Tables 13a and 13b.

Just as the throwing of the rock was the cause of the smashing of the plate glass window, and the broken glass was the result, we have identified a similar cause-and-effect relationship: excessive fixed assets caused working capital to be deficient. Deficient working capital obviously did not cause the excessive investment in fixed assets. One is the cause, the other the effect.

Someone may say that the XYZ Company's working capital need not necessarily suffer from excessive fixed assets related to net worth—that XYZ possibly may borrow on a long-term basis, thus restoring its working-capital position to normal. Agreed, but in the process the firm will simply transfer portions of its current debt to long-term status. The XYZ Company will still have its debt, $100,000 more than ABC's. So fixed assets measured against net worth, in this case, exercises a causal influence on the debt ratios, as follows:

1. The total-debt-to-net-worth ratio, which increased substantially as a result of XYZ's fixed-assets investment, will remain at the same high level.

2. The ratio of long-term liabilities to working capital will obviously rise above the previous level.

Excessive fixed assets might also influence profit adversely. If the analyst should determine that a $100,000 investment is normal for XYZ's capital strength, he will readily see that the firm's $200,000 investment in plant and equipment might very well depress the profit margin per dollar of sales. All other factors being equal, the company's annual depreciation charges are now twice as high as those of its competitors—possibly a quite substantial figure. Also, XYZ's property taxes and insurance are in all likelihood higher than average and exercise a further downward pressure on profit.

Repairs and maintenance and a variety of other charges might also enter into the picture at a higher than normal rate per sales dollar. Conceivably, this excess investment might depress the company's working capital to the point where the XYZ Company would be obliged to lose cash discounts on purchases, which its competitor, the ABC Company, would still be able to enjoy. Once again, XYZ's excessive fixed-assets commitment would have a negative influence on profits. And if, as a result of its working-capital pinch, the company should find certain key suppliers holding back vitally needed shipments of materials because of credit uncertainty, the resultant loss of productive time might substantially reduce profits. Any such negative influence, or combination of influences, would therefore affect two ratios: net-profit-to-net sales and net-profit-to-net-worth. And if the impact were sufficiently great to throw the company into red ink, such an operating loss would necessarily reduce net worth, thus affecting two

Table 14

	COMPANY A	COMPANY B	COMPANY C
Fixed assets	$ 10,000	$ 80,000	$400,000
Net worth	100,000	200,000	200,000
Fixed-assets-to-net-worth	10.0%	40.0%	200.0%
Industry average	40.0	40.0	40.0

additional ratios: net-sales-to-net-worth and miscellaneous-assets-to-net-worth.

Certainly, added investment in fixed assets without a corresponding increase in sales would affect still another ratio: net-sales-to-fixed-assets. The ratio of fixed assets to net worth qualifies without question as a causal ratio, a primary influence, for, as we have noted in the foregoing example, its effect is felt throughout the entire list of other ratios.

Let us turn to Table 14 and examine hypothetical Companies A, B, and C, noting only figures for net worth and for fixed assets in order to keep our attention concentrated on the ratio under consideration. In a later chapter we will explore total cause-and-effect analysis, but for the present it is desirable to learn fully the meaning of this primary ratio and to see how it relates to other ratios, either primary or secondary. Company A, with a fixed-assets-to-net-worth ratio of only 10 percent compared to a 40 percent industry average, appears exceedingly healthy. When an abnormally low ratio appears, however, it usually indicates that the bulk of the company's fixed assets are leased rather than owned. Whether leasing is a favorable or unfavorable condition depends largely upon the rental charges and the flexibility afforded by the rental arrangement. Company B's position is exactly normal for the industry. Other factors being equal, B has neither more nor fewer problems in this area than does its average competitor. Company C is in an extremely difficult financial position. Its excessive fixed assets, five times greater than the industry norm in comparison with net worth, have subjected C to far greater pressure than that felt by the average company in its line. As a result, many, if not all, of the other cause-and-effect ratios are probably subject to distortion.

We have seen, then, that the ratio of fixed assets to net worth clearly deserves recognition as one of the six primary financial ratios.

Collection Period

A company's credit-and-collections outlook and program, the competence of its credit manager, and the nature of its terms structure together exert direct influence on (1) sales attainment, (2) profits, and (3) need for borrowing.

The collection-period ratio is a tool to aid in the analysis of a company's trade receivables. Analysis of this particular asset item is commanding ever greater attention today because of the increasingly prominent position of trade receivables on the balance sheets of most businesses.

The collection-period ratio is computed in the following manner:

1. The total *credit* sales for the company must initially be determined. If the company in question transacts all of its business on credit terms, then the net-sales figure for the year as taken from the company's operating or profit-and-loss statement is identical with the total credit-sales figure. If, however, any significant portion of sales are on a cash basis, these sales must be subtracted, because they do not involve any credit risk, and their inclusion would thus be misleading in determining the true condition of the company's receivables. Suppose, for example, that total sales for the year were $1 million, of which 20 percent represented cash sales. The company's annual credit sales then would be only $800,000.

2. To determine credit sales per day, divide the credit sales for the year by 365. If total sales for the year are $1 million, all on credit, then credit sales per day amount to $2,740. Or, if 20 percent of these sales were for cash, credit sales per day would be $2,192 ($800,000 divided by 365).

3. Add together all trade receivables—accounts receivable, notes receivable, trade acceptances receivable—arising from regular merchandise transactions. Let us assume that these amount to $103,500.

4. Divide the total receivables ($103,500) by the credit sales

Table 15

December	$ 57,500
November	25,400
October	10,300
September	5,100
Prior	15,700
	$114,000

per day (either $2,740 or $2,192). The resulting figure is the collection period reckoned in days. If the company's sales are on a straight credit basis, it has roughly 38 days outstanding. If 20 percent of the company's sales are for cash, its collection period is approximately 47 days.

The collection-period ratio is designed to accomplish several specific objectives. First, it measures the internal credit-and-collection efficiency of the company. Second, it determines the probability of bad-debt writeoffs lurking among the concern's receivables. Finally, it measures the company's receivables position relative to the accomplishments of its own industry, provided that the analyst remembers to take into consideration the extent to which the company's selling terms differ from those which characterize its competitors.

We shall initially consider the collection-period ratio from the standpoint of internal credit-and-collection efficiency. Assuming that the XYZ Company's terms of sale are 1-10-30, let us evaluate two possible alternatives for this organization. In the first case, the company's collection period is found to be 62 days. Is this good or bad? How good or how bad? By any standard, 62 days is quite a high collection-period ratio. The company has more than two months' sales on its books; this undoubtedly hampers the company's bill-paying ability and may very well forecast some credit losses that will, some time in the future, adversely affect the concern's profit picture. The analyst would be wise to study an aging schedule of XYZ's receivables to see for himself just how seriously overdue some of the balances might be.

Suppose that in this instance the statement date is December 31 and that the aging schedule shows the exposures, by month of billing, indicated in Table 15. Viewing the foregoing results, the analyst would have every reason to be alarmed. The XYZ Company is indeed building up a heavy percentage of deadwood on its books. This deadwood represents an abnormally high bad-debt loss and charge-off potential. Such charge-offs are, of course, business expenses, which must be deducted from the company's gross profit. Even if the company is able eventually to collect most of these receivables, it will probably have to resort to drastic action to do so. Such an effort may necessitate expenditures for attorney's fees, litigation costs, and collection-agency charges, all of which would have to be absorbed before any profit could be realized.

Referring again to the 62-day collection period, but assuming for the moment that no aging schedule has been compiled, we must consider one factor which might justify such an extremely high figure—the seasonal element. If the bulk of annual sales are concentrated in November and December, due to the nature of the XYZ Company's product and its regular selling pattern, then 62 days is a far from calamitous collection-period ratio. But the analyst should bear in mind that any such significant deviation must be thoroughly studied.

Now let us suppose that the XYZ Company's collection period is 14 days on 1-10-30 terms. This record is not necessarily favorable. On the contrary, such a performance in all likelihood reflects an uncommonly severe and restrictive credit-and-collection approach on the part of the XYZ Company. In its fear of bad-debt losses, the company has evidently limited its salesmen to soliciting orders from prime credit risks only. Management has insisted upon discounting performance, and such a negative sales outlook is anything but profit-minded, for not only is volume lost, but so is the higher profit attainment that is possible from undiscounted sales to small and perhaps even marginal customers. The presence of a seasonal factor, accounting for an ebb in receivables at the XYZ Company's closing date, would, of course, tend to mitigate this harsh judgment.

In addition to measuring the company's credit-and-collections performance against its own selling terms, the analyst must compare the concern's attainment with that of its industry. If we find, for example, that the XYZ Company has a 25- or 26-day collection period on 1-10-30 terms, then its receivables appear to be quite efficiently administrated. Naturally, many customers will discount, many others will pay according to terms, and a smaller percentage will be slow payers. A 25-day collection period, then, seems to be a good overall accomplishment for the company—an accomplishment reflecting the influence of each of the three broad types of accounts to which the XYZ Company sells. If, however, the industry average should prove to be 48 days in contrast to XYZ's 25 days, the analyst must investigate the possibility that the industry sells on substantially longer terms than does the XYZ Company. Do XYZ's competitors extend perhaps 60-day-net terms, with discount privilege for 30-day payment? Or could they be granting 1 percent 10th prox, net 30th prox terms? Or, on the other hand, is the XYZ Company more efficient than the industry generally is in its approach to credit management? And having resolved these points, the analyst must probe further and determine the answers to the following questions.

1. Has XYZ lost valuable accounts and sales volume due to its restrictive credit policy?

2. Can XYZ afford the increased receivables exposure that would result from terms liberalization to match those offered by other companies in the same line? Would this limit XYZ's ability to pay its own bills or add a financing burden to support receivables?

3. Is a change desirable or necessary, or is XYZ doing well on its present basis? (While there may be "general" terms for an industry, successful operation of the individual firm does not always require strict adherence to "general" policy.)

The collection-period ratio thus provides the analyst with two significant measurements of receivables. He can initially test a company's collection period against its own selling terms to determine the collectibility of receivables and to measure credit-and-collection efficiency. Then he can gauge the company's ratio against the industry average to ascertain the concern's competitive strengths and weaknesses relative to credit terms and overall financial accomplishment.

Table 16 shows summarized figures—identical with the excep-

Table 16

	XYZ COMPANY	ABC COMPANY
Cash	$ 15,000	$ 15,000
Accounts receivable	200,000	100,000
Inventory	115,000	115,000
Total current assets	$330,000	$230,000
Total current liabilities	175,000	75,000
Long-term liabilities	125,000	125,000
Total liabilities	$300,000	$200,000
Net worth	$300,000	$300,000
Sales	$912,000	$912,000

Table 17

	XYZ COMPANY	ABC COMPANY
Current-assets-to-current-liabilities	1.89 times	3.07 times
Current-liabilities-to-net-worth	58.3%	25.0%
Total-liabilities-to-net-worth	100.0	66.7
Trade-receivables-to-working-capital	129.0	64.5

tion of accounts receivable and current liabilities—for hypothetical companies XYZ and ABC for one fiscal year. With $912,000 annual sales volume, all on account, both companies show daily credit sales of $2,500. The ABC Company has a 40-day collection period, whereas the XYZ Company has an 80-day period. While the working capital of the two companies is identical—$155,000 ($330,000 minus $175,000 for XYZ; $230,000 minus $75,000 for ABC)—consider the effect of their respective collection periods on the four ratios shown in Table 17. All other elements of the financial statement were purposely made equal; clearly, the collection period alone causes distortion in these ratios. As a consequence of XYZ's 80-day period, either of two situations is likely to occur.

1. The XYZ Company will be obligated to pass cash discounts on purchases which, in contrast, will be earned by ABC as a result of its 40-day collection period. Unless XYZ began as one of those rare phenomena, a company with superabundant net worth and more than adequate working capital, slowness of its accounts receivable will cause XYZ to be correspondingly tardy in paying

Table 18

	COMPANY D	COMPANY E	COMPANY F
Collection period	14 days	28 days	63 days
Industry average	31	31	31

its own suppliers. To the extent that one company loses discounts and the other achieves them, the working capital of ABC will, in time, accumulate to the competitive disadvantage of XYZ.

2. The XYZ Company will be obligated to write off, say, $15,000 in bad debts, while ABC will be able to avoid such charge-offs through its greater credit selectivity and collection efficiency. Such losses automatically cause a shrinkage in both working capital and actual net worth, and they necessarily depress profit.

Hence, as the XYZ Company's working capital, profit, and net worth decline vis-à-vis those elements of the ABC Company, eight additional ratios are affected:

Net-profit-to-net-sales.
Net-profit-to-net-worth.
Net-sales-to-net-worth.
Net-sales-to-working-capital.
Fixed-assets-to-net-worth.
Inventory-to-working-capital.
Long-term-debt-to-working-capital.
Miscellaneous-assets-to-net-worth.

Let us consider hypothetical Companies D, E, and F, all in the same industry and all selling on 1-10-30 terms. The collection-period ratios for these three companies are shown in Table 18. Without knowing additional facts about these three organizations, an analyst might logically conclude that Company D has a far too rigid and unimaginative approach to credit sales. One can assume that profitable sales are being lost and that the company's negativism may be holding overall sales volume to levels inadequate to cover expenses so that the resultant undertrading is leading the company toward red-ink operations. Company D is apparently not in great jeopardy from bad-debt losses, but it may very well be in danger of losing its entire business through such extreme credit wariness. By contrast, the performance of Company E—other factors being equal—indicates that management is neither too cautious nor too blindly trusting. Its credit-and-collection program is, evidently, due for plaudits. Company F has built-in trouble facing it, and the analyst can assume—without knowledge of any other segment of the financial statement—that its current ratio will be tight, its debt heavy and pressing, and its potential collection fees and bad-debt losses abnormally high. If Company F should become a failure statistic, the epitaph on its financial gravestone might appropriately read "underlying cause of failure—receivables difficulties."

As trade receivables continue to grow at a rapid rate, the significance of the collection-period ratio increases accordingly. Certainly, this measure belongs among the six causal ratios.

Net-Sales-to-Inventory

The *ratio of net sales to inventory* serves as an indicator of the inventory turnover and merchandising efficiency of a company. Generally speaking, the higher the rate of movement of inventory, the better the job a business manager has performed in the fields of scheduled and balanced buying and of inventory control. A low net-sales-to-inventory ratio points out the likelihood that some unsalable material is included in the book figure for inventory and the possibility that a writeoff will result.

The ratio of net sales to inventory is computed by dividing annual net sales by the book value of inventory; the ratio is expressed in "times." The XYZ Company, with $800,000 in sales and an inventory of $200,000, has a "turnover" of 4 times per year. The ABC Company with $20,000 inventory and $300,000 in sales has a net-sales-to-inventory ratio of 15.

While this ratio clearly does not yield an actual physical-turn-over-of-inventory figure, it is the best general measure now available to indicate the manner in which a company's inventory is "turning." The net-sales-to-inventory ratio establishes, at the least, a rough guide to the merchandising efficiency of the company under analysis. Nevertheless, most analysts deplore the present necessity for using this ratio as a "turnover" measurement for inventory. They would prefer to substitute one of *cost of sales to average inventory*, which would truly represent a great forward step in ratio analysis. One may ask why, if the cost-of-sales-to-average-inventory ratio is superior to the more general measure (net-sales-to-inventory), it is not substituted in this study. The reason is one of practicality, since most analysts do not have at hand industry figures against which to compare a company's cost-of-sales-to-inventory ratio. Because companies are reluctant to permit publication of intimate figures which would be available for study by their competitors, reporting agencies are not always able to get complete and detailed operating statements from all or even a significant percentage of firms contributing to industry surveys. Hence, the general availability of the net-sales-to-inventory ratio dictates its use. Hopefully, great changes in the compilation of industry statistics will occur in the not too distant future—changes that are discussed in detail in Chapter 7. Should these hoped-for changes occur, they will permit owners and credit grantors access to industry average figures for the cost-of-sales-to-average-inventory ratio which could then be used as a yardstick for measuring inventory turnover. When such industry averages are available, the net-sales-to-inventory ratio can go onto the discard heap—but not until then.

It should be added that Robert Morris Associates has already adopted the ratio of cost of sales to inventory, which has contributed much to the improved understanding of expected industry inventory turnover rates. Further, RMA expresses this rate two ways: both in terms of times of inventory turns, and in the number of days' sales of inventory on the typical industry member's books. (The latter is determined with the same formula as is used in calculating the collection-period ratio.)

In utilizing available industry averages to study the net-sales-to-inventory ratio, the analyst may encounter a warning that a high ratio is indicative of a perilous condition which can lead to loss of sales "through lack of adequate inventories in stock and failure to offer proper depth of selection to customers." The factual basis for this admonition is doubtful. While there is the possibility that inventory may be held to dangerously low levels relative to sales, the probability of this occurrence is exceedingly small. Obviously, the company's merchandising objectives are met with increasing effectiveness as the firm boosts sales while limiting the growth of inventory. If sales volume is substandard because of inadequate stock of goods, then the ratio of sales to inventory will still be moderately low—unless the shelves are bare and the warehouse empty. But it is not likely that even one case in many hundreds can be found in which inadequate inventory was the sole or primary cause of sales losses. Clearly, however, inventory does influence sales. Many companies have lost business because of the following inventory problems:

1. Lack of foresight in purchasing key materials or components for their products; such failure to plan ahead can cause interruption of manufacture or assembly until missing elements are delivered.

2. Curtailment of credit lines by certain prime suppliers; such restriction can result in disruption of production until new sources of supply are established or until existing suppliers are satisfied.

3. Insolvency of principal suppliers or their inability to meet scheduled delivery.

But generally such developments result in low—rather than high—turnover rates, for in such cases great quantities of improperly balanced and stagnant inventory are often on hand. Possible exceptions are the cases of converters with only one supplier or distributors of one supplier's product. If credit lines are closed to them, these companies must pay cash in advance for one order at a time, sell it, collect their money so that they can prepay another shipment, and repeat their inflexible marketing cycle. On any dates when they have sold their products but have not collected for them or replenished their supplies, their ratios of net sales to inventory will be high and will reflect inadequate inventories—but only at such times, for once their new shipments arrive, their turnover rates will fall to relatively low levels. The decline of inventory to a level inadequate to support sales almost invariably results from other, more basic causes—insufficient invested capital, perhaps, or suspended credit lines due to working-capital stringency—which in turn may be traced to factors indicated by some one of the other causal ratios presented in this chapter.

The function of the inventory-turnover ratio is quite similar to that of the collection-period ratio; both ratios measure the quality of working capital. Just as receivables become subject to shrinkage through bad debts and, indirectly, through heavy attorney and collection-agency fees as accounts reach advanced age, so inventory is susceptible to possible markdown in value for a variety of reasons. Some of these reasons follow.

1. *Physical deterioration through age and natural forces.* Many products affected by changes in temperature or humidity, among other factors, cannot withstand the passage of time without a decline in the quality of the material. Constant moving and shifting about of goods involves hazards which may likewise reduce salability or usability. The accumulation of dirt may cause quantities of inventory to be discarded with corresponding writeoff of book value, and chemical change—which would not have occurred with proper and regular movement of the material—may affect the quality or consistency of certain basic ingredients.

2. *Softening of prices of the materials comprising inventory.* No company can escape the impact of fluctuations in the price levels of goods which it buys and sells, or of the components of articles which it assembles or manufactures. The company may gain from an overinventoried position while materials prices rise, but such unforeseen profit is hardly a natural byproduct of manufacture. If the XYZ Company prefers to gamble on price rises rather than concentrate on its normal manufacturing profit, then it would be well advised to become a commodity trader and forgo the other risks that go with being a manufacturer. Flour millers and soybean processors, among others, recognize the risk of price fluctuations to the extent that they hedge their commodity position as a means of protecting their converting or manufacturing profit. For the XYZ Company, a profit through rising prices may prove an unexpected and welcome windfall, but if prices decline sharply   either as a result of general downward economic movement or as a result of an oversupplied condition of XYZ's industry or of the industry supplying XYZ's basic materials require-

ments—a very real problem develops because the decline (if management is the least bit realistic) must be reflected as a reduction in the book value of inventory. A steep decline in the value of an excessive inventory can completely wipe out a light working-capital position. And if the company is operating on a very slim margin of profit, the writeoff of inventory could easily throw its year's total into red ink.

3. *Obsolescence, change in customer preference, or the introduction of new materials or improved products.* A "new," or unused, 1970 automobile on a dealer's lot in 1972 can hardly command its 1970 price. Similarly, a machine designed to produce 1,000 razor blades an hour will scarcely find a ready market if someone else offers for sale a device of comparable price capable of turning out 8,000 blades per hour. Changing taste has greatly diminished the salability of hula hoops and Slim Jim ties.

4. *The seasonal influence.* The impact of the seasonal factor on inventory values is clearly evidenced by the drastic markdowns of Christmas cards, ornaments, and gift wrappings on December 26.

5. *Overvaluation—intentional or unintentional.* Despite the many refinements in valuation techniques developed by the accounting profession, the validity of inventory figures still depends in large measure upon the honesty, integrity, and good sense of the manager who submits them.

6. *Purchase or retention of unusable materials.* Any materials which are unadaptable to the company's regular manufacturing process or to that of any competitive producer clearly have less value than that indicated by their original cost.

7. *Failure to verify book figures through periodic physical count.* After unfortunate instances of employee pilferage—not always covered by insurance—some companies have been belatedly awakened to the disappearance of great quantities of stock which the records showed to be on hand. Recordkeeping errors, likewise, are common and may, upon detection, lead to either increase or decrease in the true inventory figure.

Slowdown of inventory turnover can, of course, hinder a company's ability to meet its current obligations and can affect its costs, particularly through the incurrence of charges to support

Table 19

	XYZ COMPANY	ABC COMPANY
Cash	$ 10,000	$ 10,000
Accounts receivable	120,000	120,000
Inventory	125,000	250,000
Total current assets	$ 255,000	$ 380,000
Total current liabilities	$ 130,000	$ 255,000
Long-term liabilities	30,000	30,000
Total liabilities	$ 160,000	$ 285,000
Net worth	$ 350,000	$ 350,000
Sales	$1,000,000	$1,000,000

Table 20

	XYZ COMPANY	ABC COMPANY
Current-assets-to-current-liabilities	1.96 times	1.49 times
Current-liabilities-to-net-worth	37.1%	72.9%
Total-liabilities-to-net-worth	45.7	81.4
Inventory-to-working-capital	100.0	200.0

the luxury of excessive inventory or through the loss of purchase discounts which may result from the slowdown of cash flow.

To focus our attention on the net-sales-to-inventory ratio, let us consider the skeletal financial statements for the hypothetical companies XYZ and ABC shown in Table 19. All figures for the two companies are identical with the exception of inventory and current liabilities. Industry average for the ratio of net sale to inventory is, in this case, 8 times per year. Note that the XYZ Company is strictly average with respect to inventory turnover, its ratio being exactly 8 times ($1 million divided by $125,000). In contrast, the ABC Company has a ratio of 4 times ($1 million divided by $250,000); this figure points to a very sluggish inventory condition with a strong possibility of imminent loss of value. The ABC Company has $125,000 more tied up in inventory than does the average concern in the industry, despite the fact that it and the XYZ Company have identical working capital, sales, and net worth. Allowing the assumption that the full $125,000 is reflected in an equivalent increase in current payables, we can see the influence of ABC's slow-moving inventory on the ratios shown in Table 20. Obviously, ABC's inventory turnover alone created the unfavorable distortion of all four of these ratios. If, as a result of its unhealthy commitment in slow-moving or obsolete merchandise, the ABC Company should be forced into either of the following courses of action, an entirely different set of ratios would be involved in a chain reaction of adverse change.

1. If the disproportionate share of funds frozen in inventory should cause ABC to borrow to support inventory—and if the XYZ Company were not compelled to such financing by virtue of its lesser exposure—then ABC would incur costs from which XYZ is exempt. Both profit and working capital would be immediately affected.

2. If ABC should be obligated to write off any portion of its inventory as unsalable or overvalued, then to that extent both its working capital and its profit would automatically be reduced. Should the drop in value throw operations into loss, then net worth would likewise decline.

In either of these situations—which are likely to develop from XYZ's overinventoried condition—an additional eight ratios would be adversely influenced. These eight ratios are:

Net-profit-to-net-sales.
Net-profit-to-net-worth.
Net-sales-to-net-worth.
Net-sales-to-working-capital.
Fixed-assets-to-net-worth.
Trade-receivables-to-working-capital.
Long-term-debt-to-working-capital.
Miscellaneous-assets-to-net-worth.

Any reduction in profit, working capital, or net worth will necessarily change any ratio involving those three major elements.

Let us now consider fictitious Companies G, H, and I with regard to inventory control, as measured by the ratio of net sales to inventory. The individual companies' ratios and the industry averages are shown in Table 21. Although Company G's ratio is roughly double the industry average, the concern's performance is, in this instance, favorable. This contention cannot

Table 21

	COMPANY G	COMPANY H	COMPANY I
Net-sales-to-inventory	15.4 times	8.3 times	3.6 times
Industry average	8.0	8.0	8.0

be indisputably demonstrated through one isolated ratio, but G's rapid turnover of inventory does indicate an efficient merchandising program. (In Chapter 6 we shall study the interplay of all ratios, but at this point we are concerned solely with the net-sales-to-inventory ratio.) Keeping inventory at the lowest levels consistent with providing the material necessary to meet production schedules offers many advantages to Company G—the most obvious of which are reduced costs, minimized risk of reduction in book value, and a freer working-capital position. Company H is an average operator with regard to inventory turnover, and, other factors being equal, its problems are no greater but no less than those of the typical firm in its line. Judging from this ratio alone, the analyst must conclude that Company I is beset with problems. All the major difficulties associated with sluggish inventory—tie-up of funds, impairment of profit, increased costs—confront Company I at the moment. The manner in which these challenges are met may well determine not only the company's future progress, but its very existence; for a great many companies have become insolvent as a result of inventory problems.

We have seen that, as the best generally available measure of inventory turnover, net-sales-to-inventory is definitely a primary ratio.

Net-Sales-to-Net-Worth

The *ratio of net sales to net worth* is rather commonly known as the trading ratio; it is a measure of the extent to which a company's sales volume is supported by invested capital. A substantially higher-than-average ratio depicts the overtrader, a company which is attempting to stretch the invested dollar to its maximum capacity. The overtrader's statement, as we shall see, is generally burdened by oppressively heavy debt, and the company's survival often hinges on the long-term continuation of optimum internal and external conditions. The undertrader, on the other hand, has either capital resources in excess of the company's needs or inadequate sales to support the business. Although the undertrading concern is less likely to be debt-ridden than is the overtrader, its most pressing need is to bring sales to profitable levels; no business can permanently survive with chronic and persistent losses. A reasonable balance must be maintained between these two extremes; the ratio of net sales to net worth measures the degree to which a company has attained this balance.

The net-sales-to-net-worth ratio is computed by dividing a company's annual sales by its net worth. The XYZ Company, with annual sales of $900,000 and net worth of $150,000, has a net-sales-to-net-worth ratio, or turnover, of 6 times. The ABC Company, which sells $250,000 yearly on a net worth of $20,000, has a ratio of 12.5 times.

Clearly, the objective of commercial ventures is to realize a profit, something which can be accomplished only by selling goods or services in adequate quantities at proper price levels. Since the majority of businesses are started by salesmen, the uppermost thought of the management of most concerns is, naturally enough, to sell as much as possible, subject only to the limit of the hours comprising the business day. The greater the number and the dollar amount of orders, the greater the profit; that seems to be the predominant philosophy. The playwright Arthur Miller has, in his various literary efforts, expressed the view that the salesman, more than any other professional group, epitomizes modern American society. In many ways, the push to "sell, sell, sell" has much to commend it. Every company must reckon with daily costs of both fixed and variable nature. And fixed costs, of course, accrue without interruption—whether the plant operates or is idle and whether a single item moves off the shelf. Only by achieving a level of sales adequate to offset fixed costs, as well as their variable counterparts, can any company hope to break even, let alone realize profit. As sales exceed the break-even level, the company's profit percentage rises sharply (if we assume that a fairly consistent level of prices is maintained). So management may logically expend strenuous effort to achieve ever higher sales in the hope of obtaining ever greater profit.

But every company possesses a limited amount of invested capital upon which attainment of its sales goals must be based. The two factors—sales and capital—are forced into correlation, whether the company likes it or not, for sales must look to capital, or net worth, for support. Only so much sales activity or turnover can be derived from each dollar of equity capital, and in order to expand business beyond this maximum point, the company must take special action; it might choose one or a combination of the following courses.

1. It could borrow money or depend upon creditor confidence or lenience. Banks, finance companies, or factors will often provide temporary support, but even at best borrowed funds cannot serve as a permanent substitute for ownership money. Nor is the answer to be found in unsubordinated loans from officers or borrowing from friends, relatives, or affiliated companies. Some trade suppliers may be willing to grant temporary special terms or carry overdue balances, but clearly this relief is more in the nature of an expedient than a solution.

2. It could develop compensating advantages to ease the strain on its working-capital and debt position. The company, for example, might shorten its terms of sale or initiate more rigid enforcement of existing terms, whereby its collection period would become substantially shorter than industry average. It might reduce its inventory exposure and speed its turnover, thus increasing its cash flow. Or it might attempt to secure a sale-and-lease-back agreement covering its plant and equipment, thus freeing cash for working-capital purposes. Many companies have successfully built into their structures—on a permanent basis—such competitive advantages that they are able to offset capital deficiencies through superior performance in other key areas. Other concerns, panicked by debt pressure into ill-considered moves, have found that precipitate actions simply alter the nature of their problems without solving them.

3. It could attract additional equity capital from outside investors. The injection of new capital may solve immediate prob-

Table 22

| | XYZ COMPANY | | | |
	1969	1970	1971	1972
Cash	$ 10,000	$ 10,000	$ 10,000	$ 10,000
Receivables	30,000	60,000	120,000	240,000
Inventory	60,000	120,000	240,000	480,000
Total current assets	$100,000	$190,000	$ 370,000	$ 730,000
Fixed assets	45,000	45,000	145,000	245,000
Miscellaneous assets	5,000	5,000	5,000	5,000
Total assets	$150,000	$240,000	$ 520,000	$ 980,000
Due banks	—0—	—0—	$ 90,000	$ 90,000
Due trade	$ 30,000	$100,000	150,000	455,000
Total current liabilities	$ 30,000	$100,000	$ 240,000	$ 545,000
Long-term liabilities	—0—	—0—	100,000	175,000
Total	$ 30,000	$100,000	$ 340,000	$ 720,000
Net worth	120,000	140,000	180,000	260,000
Total liabilities	$150,000	$240,000	$ 520,000	$ 980,000
Net sales	$360,000	$720,000	$1,440,000	$2,880,000
Net profit	10,000	20,000	40,000	80,000
Working capital	70,000	90,000	130,000	185,000

lems, but for many small businesses this may mean the weakening
or even the loss of management control.

4. It could either reduce sales or, while holding the sales line,
add to net worth through retention of all earnings in the business.
Selective selling, the elimination of less profitable or even unprofitable customers, may actually improve profit percentage
while reducing sales volume. Retaining all earnings in the business and forgoing dividends or excessive withdrawals will, in
time, bring the relationship between sales and net worth into
balance, provided, of course, that profit is earned.

Either overtrading (conducting excessive sales on limited invested capital) or undertrading (failing to utilize invested capital
to the fullest extent) is, in itself, an unfavorable condition and
requires thorough scrutiny. Let us look first at an overtrading
situation to see how excessive sales relative to net worth can
affect other key financial elements. The pertinent figures for the
XYZ Company are shown in Table 22. Reduced to ratios, XYZ's

Table 23

	1969	1970	1971	1972
Current-assets-to- current-liabilities	3.33 times	1.90 times	1.54 times	1.34 times
Fixed-assets-to-net- worth	37.5%	32.1%	80.6%	94.2%
Current-liabilities-to- net-worth	25.0	71.4	133.3	209.6
Total-liabilities-to- net-worth	25.0	71.4	188.9	276.9
Inventory-to- working-capital	85.7	133.3	184.6	259.5
Trade-receivables- to-working-capital	42.9	66.7	92.3	129.7
Long-term-liabilities- to-working-capital	—0—	—0—	76.9	94.6
Miscellaneous-assets- to-net-worth	4.2	3.6	2.8	1.9
Net-profit-to-net-sales	2.78	2.78	2.78	2.78
Net-profit-to-net- worth	8.33	14.29	22.22	30.77
Net-sales-to-fixed- assets	8.00 times	16.00 times	9.93 times	11.76 times
Net-sales-to-net- worth	3.00	5.14	8.00	11.08
Net-sales-to- inventory	6.00	6.00	6.00	6.00
Net-sales-to-working- capital	5.14	8.00	11.08	15.57
Collection period	30 days	30 days	30 days	30 days

position for each of the four years under review is shown in Table 23. In the present illustration, the XYZ Company doubled its sales volume each year from 1969 through 1972. (This may seem an extreme example, but even more exaggerated cases of overtrading do, in fact, occur.) The company's profit percentage on sales remained constant at an attractive 2.78 percent per year, so that as sales doubled, profit after taxes also doubled. One might expect the profit percentage per sales dollar to increase as volume grows substantially beyond theoretical and actual breakeven levels. In actual practice, however, many overtraders find their profit returns on sales declining as they achieve their ever increasing sales quotas. Price concessions are made to bolster sales, while marginal and unprofitable accounts are added to the roster of customers; both of these factors tend to depress rather than bolster the net-profit-to-net-sales ratio. To demonstrate the natural upward debt pressure exerted—even under optimum conditions—by overtrading, a number of factors have been arbitrarily kept at constant levels in this particular illustration. All profits were retained in the business and were applied against current liabilities. In 1970, for example, XYZ's profit was $20,000. Hence, although growth of the company's receivables and inventory totaled $90,000, the net increase in current liabilities was only $70,000. The turnover of inventory was intentionally held at a constant rate of 6 times per year. Likewise, the collection period was, by design, maintained at a constant 30-day level. To keep the statement in basic form so that our attention will not be diverted, let us assume that all taxes have been paid and that there are no accruals or other miscellaneous payables.

Despite the retention of all earnings to build up net worth, XYZ's invested capital was subject to increased activity and pressure, as reflected by the rise of the net-sales-to-net-worth ratio from 3 times per year in 1969 to 11.1 times in 1972. Even granting the XYZ Company a steady profit and giving it an identical inventory turnover rate for each of the three years, as well as an unchanged collection period, we see that serious overtrading brings with it a sharp increase in debt, particularly in current liabilities; for although the XYZ Company more than doubled its net worth in three years, its debt rose in almost geometric, rather than arithmetic, progression, as illustrated by the ratio of total debt to net worth. Of the company's debt, more than 75 percent consists of current liabilities, which have become twice as great as net worth. In 1971 and again in 1972, the company found it necessary to expand its fixed assets, for at a certain level sales begin to outrun production capacity. Determination of the activity of plant and equipment caused by sales is, of course, the primary purpose of the net-sales-to-fixed-assets ratio, which was examined in Chapter 2. The XYZ Company's 1972 figures show that, despite a recent increase in fixed assets, this ratio has climbed to 11.76 times, an even higher level than in the previous year. Unless the growth rate of sales is checked, 1973 will see the company compelled to divert additional funds into more buildings, more machinery, and more handling and delivery equipment—if financing can be found.

We have been generous to the XYZ Company in permitting it to borrow so heavily on a long-term basis. If lending institutions had refused XYZ's request for long-term borrowing, its current-debt pressure would be almost unbearable because working capital would be near the zero point. Even though the XYZ Company has applied every penny of its profit toward payment of suppliers' bills, the current ratio has been in steady decline, dropping from an attractive 3.33 level to 1.34 in just three years. It would have been 1.01 without the relief afforded by long-term loans. Working capital, in actual dollars and cents, increased sharply—from $70,000 in 1969 to $185,000 in 1972, a gain of nearly 165 percent. But the strain placed upon working capital by XYZ's skyrocketing sales volume is indicated in several ways:

1. The net-sales-to-working-capital ratio rose from a 5.14 annual rate to 15.57 times in three years.

2. The inventory-to-working-capital ratio moved upward from 85.7 percent to 259.5 percent in the same span of time, despite the fact that inventory turnover was purposely held at a constant rate.

3. The receivables-to-working-capital ratio shows the same sensational growth trend, mounting from 42.9 percent to 129.7 percent although the collection-period ratio remained perfectly constant.

4. Long-term liabilities also outgained working capital, as retained earnings were insufficient to meet the needs of an exceedingly rapid sales expansion.

Net profit to net worth, likewise, increased very substantially during the three years under study—even though every dime of profit was kept in the business as equity capital. Earlier in our discussion of this particular ratio, we found that an abnormally high net-profit-to-net-worth picture does not necessarily point to an unusually attractive profit return, but instead may depict an undercapitalized situation. This is true of the XYZ Company in 1972; its 30.77 percent return reflects adversely on net worth rather than favorably on profit. Because profit return on sales is purposely pegged at an identical 2.78 percent for each of the four years, this ratio obviously is no more attractive today than it was in 1969. Moreover, our previous review of other ratios corroborated the story told by the net-sales-to-net-worth ratio—that XYZ is overtrading or, in other words, is undercapitalized. The total profit realization, however, might look rather attractive to prospective investors in this business.

So, in establishing net sales to net worth as a causal, or primary, ratio, we see that 12 ratios have already been affected in the case of the XYZ Company, an overtrader:

Current-assets-to-current-liabilities.
Fixed-assets-to-net-worth.
Current-liabilities-to-net-worth.
Total-liabilities-to-net-worth.
Inventory-to-working-capital.
Trade-receivables-to-working-capital.
Long-term-liabilities-to-working-capital.
Net-profit-to-net-worth.
Net-sales-to-fixed-assets.
Net-sales-to-net-worth.
Net-sales-to-working-capital.
Miscellaneous-assets-to-net-worth.

Only three ratios, then, have remained unchanged in this hypothetical case, and they were purposely left constant in order to permit concentration on the causal influence of the net-sales-to-net-worth ratio. The three unchanged ratios are (1) net-profit-to-net-sales, (2) net-sales-to-inventory, and (3) collection-period. An experienced analyst will, however, note that these three seldom ride out the overtrading storm without some radical change. Let us consider them in reverse order, starting with the collection-period ratio.

The overtrader usually finds his collection period moving upward, on occasion gradually, but often quite rapidly. Total devotion to the selling objective tends to blind a company to the actuality of the risk it is accepting; this blindness leads not only to the infiltration of the receivables ledgers by slow or "dead" accounts, but also to very easygoing and erratic collection follow-up procedures. The blindly sales-minded organization is often reluctant to ask for payment of overdue balances for fear of jeopardizing its future sales relationships. The net result of this philosophy is a higher collection-period ratio; and the higher it goes, the graver becomes the working-capital strain and the debt pressure on the company. Some overtraders have found profits on sales declining, and some have gone into red ink despite burgeoning sales.

Occasionally a company will reach out too far in its search for new business by moving into the natural trading area of one of its more distant competitors. To offset the local convenience and service of rival organizations, overtraders have been known to make extreme price concessions to garner orders. Distant accounts are often relatively expensive to service; if this disadvantage is compounded by low gross profit per sale, the combination will naturally depress profit per sales dollar. Overtraders, as we noted earlier, may encounter inventory problems or receivables difficulties in effecting their aggressive sales programs, and these factors may also hinder profit attainment. Or a rapid expansion in fixed assets needed to meet mounting sales commitments can add to costs, again influencing profit adversely. On the other hand, certain overtraders record a very attractive profit return, so no generalization as to the effect of overtrading on the vital area of profit can be made. But one can note with assurance that a company's level of trading does have a direct influence on profit levels.

A common characteristic of overtrading situations is the apparent reluctance of owners to assume the full share of risk normally associated with ownership. That is, they are unwilling in many cases to put their personal resources into the corporation as capital-stock investment but, instead, capitalize at a nominal amount and advance other money to the company in the form of officers' loans, generally of a demand nature. Commonly, one finds $10,000 in capital stock and $40,000 in officers' loans, with the officers thus in a dual capacity as both owners and creditors but with the emphasis on the credit side. Capitalization of these loans would contribute materially toward reduction of overtrading and toward bolstering suppliers' credit confidence, but some overtraders are undoubtedly fearful of assuming the risk of ownership, preferring instead to share in any possible liquidation of their companies on an equal footing with their trade suppliers. Even a subordination to specific or general creditors would render the loans, in many respects, almost the same as equity capital. The typical owner-creditor claims that "tax advantages" prompt him to lend rather than invest, yet more often than not he will refuse to subordinate, an act which would in no way jeopardize any of the alleged tax benefits. This reluctance to assume outright financial responsibility, of course, tends to foster in the minds of creditors the belief that the owners of many undercapitalized firms have little confidence in their companies' ability to meet the demands of competitive existence.

The thinner the overtrading concern stretches its invested dollar, the more vulnerable it becomes to some sudden and unexpected calamity. The overtrading company is much like an army that has penetrated deeply into enemy territory at a pace too rapid for its line of supply. A breakdown in the flow of materiel at the height of battle can place the army at the mercy of its foe. The overtrader involved in a prolonged strike finds his income cut off; but bills must be paid, and generally these bills are staggeringly high and are of a short-term nature. Or he may lose several of his major accounts, either to competitors or through the insolvency of those customers. With already heavy inventory on hand and advance orders placed, such a loss of sales could create a situation that might not be solvable outside the bankruptcy courts. Acts of God—flood, tornado, fire—will strike the overtrader a heavier blow than the undertrader. A price war can be devastating to the overtrader's income and to his financial balance, which is generally so cumbersome that ability to meet changing conditions is almost nonexistent.

Statistics indicating the percentage of business failures directly attributable to overtrading are, understandably enough, not available. The death blow is not dealt directly by the fact of overtrading, but instead is the result of one of the weaknesses caused by overtrading; it comes about through a breakdown in the perfect meshing of all financial gears that is required for successful overtrading. In the postmortem, the failure of the over-extended XYZ Company might be blamed on "receivables difficulties" or "inventory difficulties," but in the final analysis the true cause was overtrading, which in time placed the company in such an inflexible position that it was not able to respond to unexpected developments.

Unsecured creditors generally lose more in an overtrading failure than in any other type of business suspension, while the undertrading failure normally proves to involve the least loss to creditors. By definition, the overtrader requires more and more materials and ever greater lines of credit. When some development upsets the delicate balance of the overtrading company and drives it to the bankruptcy court, the concern's liabilities are generally exceedingly high. Usually it has resorted to every conceivable type of financing, and the more severe the level of overtrading, the more inclined financing institutions are to request security for their advances. While the assets shown on the overtrader's books may be large, assets have a tendency to shrink a great deal in the courts or under the auctioneer's hammer, whereas liabilities and expenses flourish there and are augmented by administrative costs and attorney fees. Frequently, bankruptcy cases involving overtraders terminate as total losses to unsecured creditors as well as to owners.

The number of overtraders appears to have grown—hand in hand with increased competition and, in many industries, with a continually lessening rate of profit return per dollar of sales—with very few exceptions over the past 15 or 20 years. Given a narrower profit margin, the average company must sell more to achieve even its former rate of return on invested capital; this fact provides the impulse to overtrade, but it can be a dangerous impulse and it must be watched carefully.

A company may turn its capital too infrequently as well as too rapidly, but the undertrading situation becomes perilous only if sales are inadequate to cover operating costs; if this is the case, the company's operations are thrown into deficit. There are, of course, cases where sales are normal with respect to receivables, inventory, and fixed assets, and operations are nevertheless in the red. In many such situations sales related to net worth are somewhat low, but often not far below normal. Under these circumstances, further examination of expenses is clearly dictated. Owners and officers commonly feel that they are entitled to top executive pay despite the poor accomplishments of their companies, and often such high salary costs give an impression of undertrading which does not in fact exist. Undertrading is a low rate of sales related to net worth—not an inadequate income related to expenses.

The undertrader in difficulty displays many signs which the alert analyst will detect. A slow-pay record, declining bank balances, and diminishing activity point to the need for further investigation. The financial statement, of course, provides the analyst with direct information from which a reasoned plan of action may be developed. Undertrading, on occasion, results from excessively large capital investment or net worth. If a company has substantial equity capital with only modest sales to match, danger of loss either to creditors or to owners is minimal. The owners, however, are not receiving full value on their investment and might profitably divert the excess portion into an area which will bring them a greater return. Among companies of small or medium size, overcapitalization is a relatively rare phenomenon.

Undertrading, particularly when coupled with excessive expenses, contributes significantly to the annual toll of business failures. Although losses to creditors in the case of an undertrader are generally much more limited than those resulting from the insolvency of an overtrader, the owner or investor gains small comfort. Among manufacturers, the smaller companies almost universally have a considerably higher degree of sales activity relative to net worth than do their larger rivals. In wholesaling and retailing, however, this pattern of "overtrading" according to size does not exist. Larger units within these two areas turn net worth at higher levels than their smaller competitors in certain lines, but at lower levels in others.

One of the major weaknesses of the various industry average ratios generally available to analysts is the inclusion of all sizes of companies in one broad average. The characteristics and problems of the smaller companies are often so dissimilar from those of the giants of a particular industry that to meld them all together in one average is to distort the significance of the ratio

Table 24

INDUSTRY	SMALLER FIRMS*	LARGER FIRMS†
Manufacturers of men's and boys' sport clothing	6.8 times	4.8 times
Manufacturers of women's dresses	10.6	6.5
Manufacturers of women's suits, skirts, sportswear, and coats	7.6	5.6
Manufacturers of women's undergarments and sleepwear	8.0	5.5
Manufacturers of plastic materials and synthetic resins	5.5	3.4
Manufacturers of bread and bakery products	6.4	4.9
Manufacturers of dairy products	4.8	9.2
Manufacturers of flour and other grain mill products	9.8	7.2
Manufacturers of frozen fruits, fruit juices, vegetables, and specialties	7.2	4.8
Manufacturers of sausages and other prepared meat products	10.6	7.5

© 1971 Robert Morris Associates.
* $250 M and less than $1 MM asset size.
† $1 MM to $10 MM asset size.

in the analysis of either. And to compute averages solely from the statements of the larger companies, and then to measure the smaller concerns against them, is to create grossly false impressions. By the first method, most major concerns will appear to be undertrading, and through neither of the foregoing methods of compiling industry averages will the true undertrading of certain smaller concerns be detected.

Robert Morris Associates currently compiles four distinct groups of ratios for each major industry by segregating firms according to asset size: $250,000 or less; $250,000 to $1 million; $1 million to $10 million; $10 million to $25 million. Let us examine a few of the Robert Morris 1970 median averages for the net-sales-to-net-worth ratio, as shown in Table 24. If an analyst were relying solely on the figures for larger manufacturers of frozen fruit juices in attempting to interpret the trading activity of a canner of smaller size, he could be greatly misled, and actions

Table 25

	COMPANY J	COMPANY K	COMPANY L
Net-sales-to-net-worth	1.75 times	4.71 times	12.45 times
Industry average	4.38	4.38	4.38

based upon his erroneous conclusions could prove disastrous to the company under analysis. Let us assume, for instance, that the XYZ Company, with assets of $300,000, shows a net-sales-to-net-worth ratio of 3.9 times for the year. Referring to the 4.8 turnover rate that is typical for the larger canners, the analyst would conclude that the XYZ Company is trading very nearly at a normal pace. Yet the concern is actually guilty of severe undertrading when compared with the norm of 7.2 times for canners of its own asset size. Since most present sources make no distinction as to asset size in their published averages, and since those averages are more often than not compiled from the reports of larger companies, mistakes resulting from reliance on available averages are understandable but are nevertheless dangerous.

Very briefly, let us view hypothetical Companies J, K, and L with respect to the ratio of net sales to net worth. The value of the ratio for the three companies and the industry norms are shown in Table 25. Company J is definitely undertrading, and clearly the greatest danger to it and to its creditors is that its level of income may be inadequate to meet even the most closely supervised and controlled expenses. Red-ink operations drain working capital and depress net worth. One of the ironies of ratio analysis occurs as net worth and working capital tend to reach the vanishing point: the most flagrant undertrader then becomes an overtrader through a technicality. Suppose, for example, that during 1971 Company J transacted a $70,000 volume of sales on net worth of $40,000 in establishing its sales-to-worth ratio of 1.75 times and that the company incurred a $20,000 operating loss which reduced net worth to the present $40,000 figure. If during the next year it should suffer a $30,000 loss on volume of $60,000, its net worth would shrink to $10,000 and its turnover would rise to 6 times per year. This would make Company J technically an overtrader. So that the analyst will not be misled by such isolated figures, he must employ all 15 ratios, which together provide a complete picture of the company's financial balance. Company K is trading normally and, other factors being equal, is competing on even terms with the average concern in its line of activity. Company L's overtrading is readily apparent. Unless Company L has developed significant compensating advantages—such as extremely efficient utilization of fixed assets, fast-moving inventory, and rapidly collected receivables—it is probably subject to all the evils associated with inordinate trading on invested capital. These potential or actual problems, in brief, are rapidly mounting and excessive debt, increasing difficulty in meeting suppliers' terms, and restricted lines of borrowing from financial institutions. Company L's problems are evidenced by distortion of virtually all its ratios. The success of Company L in maintaining solvency will depend upon the continuity of optimum operating conditions.

Certainly net sales to net worth ranks among the causal or primary ratios, for we have demonstrated the manner in which its effect is felt throughout the entire range of ratios, whether the influence be from overtrading or from undertrading.

Net-Profit-to-Net-Sales

Every company has as its goal the realization of profit from each dollar's worth of merchandise it sells. The *ratio of net profit to net sales* measures the success any given company has achieved in meeting this objective.

The net-profit-to-net-sales ratio is computed very simply by dividing annual net profit after taxes by annual net sales. If the XYZ Company's sales for the year were $1 million and its profit amounted to $5,000, its ratio is .5 percent. By achieving a profit of $15,000 on sales of $250,000, the ABC Company shows a profit-to-sales ratio of 6 percent.

Robert Morris Associates relies upon a somewhat different version of this ratio, using instead pretax profit rather than net—or after-tax—income. There is much to be said in favor of this approach, for it eliminates any bias caused by unequal comparative current tax liabilities. In some illustrative cases in Chapter 6 occasional reference will be made to this adaptation of the profit ratio.

Unless a company profits from selling its goods or services, it has little reason to exist. For every dollar of sales, the successful company finds a number of pennies in profit flowing back into its coffers. The more pennies per dollar, the greater the opportunity for growth, and through growth those pennies may become quarters or dollars in the aggregate. A company losing pennies per sales dollar must reverse that trend, or it will obviously meet with extinction at some date in the future.

Profits retained in the business bolster working capital, add to net worth, and aid in restoring balance to any ratios that may be deficient. Conversely, losses on sales aggravate any financial imbalance, for they strike directly at both working capital and net worth and automatically distort any ratios that relate to those two vital areas. Subject to the qualifications that were considered in the study of the net-sales-to-net-worth ratio, the greater a company's sales volume, the greater is the likelihood of increasing profit return on sales.

Let us consider the significance of the net-profit-to-net-sales ratio of the XYZ Company for the period 1969–1972, imposing certain arbitrary conditions so that we may focus our attention solely on the changes wrought on the ratio under study. The applicable financial-statement figures are shown in Table 26. These figures, reduced to ratio form, and the comparable 1972 industry averages are shown in Table 27.

Receivables turnover and collection period have been held constant during the four years under consideration. The dollar investment in miscellaneous assets and the dollar volume of sales similarly remained unchanged during the period 1969–1972, while fixed assets were reduced $10,000 each year through depreciation charges. Although well below the industry return on sales, XYZ's 1970 profit of $15,000 (1.25 percent on sales of $1 million) exercised a salutary influence on all other ratios, except the secondary profit measure, net profit to net worth, and the two ratios held constant by design. Had the $5,000 used to bolster the bank account been applied to current obligations, the current ratio and the debt-to-worth ratios would have shown still further improvement. Thus retained profit, though substandard, significantly

Table 26

	1969	1970	1971	1972
Cash	$ 15,000	$ 20,000	$ 30,000	$ 15,000
Receivables	75,000	75,000	75,000	75,000
Inventory	350,000	350,000	350,000	350,000
Total current assets	$ 440,000	$ 445,000	$ 455,000	$ 440,000
Fixed assets	180,000	170,000	160,000	150,000
All other	30,000	30,000	30,000	30,000
Total assets	$ 650,000	$ 645,000	$ 645,000	$ 620,000
Due banks	$ 100,000	$ 90,000	$ 75,000	$ 85,000
Due trade	120,000	115,000	100,000	95,000
Total current liabilities	$ 220,000	$ 205,000	$ 175,000	$ 180,000
Long-term liabilities	130,000	125,000	115,000	110,000
Total	$ 350,000	$ 330,000	$ 290,000	$ 290,000
Net worth	300,000	315,000	355,000	330,000
Total liabilities	$ 650,000	$ 645,000	$ 645,000	$ 620,000
Sales	$1,200,000	$1,200,000	$1,200,000	$1,200,000
Working capital	220,000	240,000	280,000	260,000
Net profit	15,000	15,000	40,000	(25,000)

strengthened the XYZ Company's financial position. The marked improvement shown by XYZ during 1971 may be traced to the rise in the profit-to-sales ratio to a 3.33 percent level, substantially above the industry norm, while sales remained steady at $1.2 million. Although sales remained constant, the company's trading ratio (net-sales-to-net-worth) moved closer to normal levels by virtue of the increase in net worth. By once again retaining the year's profits, the XYZ Company bolstered its entire financial structure in impressive fashion. Another year like 1971 would have provided management the opportunity to declare attractive dividends while retaining funds for future growth.

The following year-end closing, unfortunately, found the XYZ Company with a net deficit of $25,000, representing a 2.08 percent loss on unchanged sales volume. Red-ink operations produced the following repercussions.

▪ The current ratio declined; this decline reflected a tightening of working capital.

Table 27

RATIOS	1969	1970	1971	1972	INDUSTRY AVERAGE
Current	2.00 times	2.17 times	2.60 times	2.44 times	2.11 times
Fixed-assets-to-net-worth	60.0 %	54.0 %	45.1 %	45.5 %	46.7 %
Current-liabilities-to-net-worth	73.3	65.1	49.3	54.5	53.8
Total-liabilities-to-net-worth	116.7	104.8	81.7	87.9	96.9
Inventory-to-working-capital	159.1	145.8	125.0	134.6	142.4
Accounts-receivable-to-working-capital	34.1	31.3	26.8	28.8	31.0
Long-term-liabilities-to-working-capital	59.1	52.1	41.1	42.3	37.6
Miscellaneous-assets-to-net-worth	10.0	9.5	8.5	9.1	9.3
Net-profit-to-net-sales	1.25	1.25	3.33	(2.08)	1.84
Net-profit-to-net-worth	5.00	4.76	11.27	(7.58)	6.35
Net-sales-to-fixed-assets	6.67 times	7.06 times	7.50 times	8.00 times	6.80 times
Net-sales-to-net-worth	4.00	3.81	3.38	3.64	3.00
Net-sales-to-inventory	3.43	3.43	3.43	3.43	3.70
Net-sales-to-working-capital	5.45	5.00	4.29	4.62	6.09
Collection period	23 days	23 days	23 days	23 days	22 days

■ The fixed-assets-to-net-worth ratio moved slightly upward despite the reduction of fixed assets through depreciation.

■ Liabilities (current and total) increased relative to net worth; this increase indicated greater short-term creditors' interest in the XYZ Company.

■ The inventory-to-working-capital ratio showed a rise even though inventory turnover remained unchanged; the rise in this ratio reflected the drop in working capital caused by the operating deficit.

■ Receivables-to-working-capital increased for the same reason that the value of the preceding ratio rose.

■ The ratio of long term liabilities to working capital increased, again because of the working-capital reduction.

■ Net-profit-to-net-worth, which—barring substantial income from a source outside the primary operation—obviously goes hand in hand with the profit-to-sales ratio, showed a sharp negative reversal.

- Net-sales-to-fixed-assets continued to climb slowly as a result of depreciation of fixed assets, but it had not yet reached the review point.

- Net-sales-to-net-worth had now turned upward, suggesting the reappearance of overtrading, not because of an increase in sales, but from diminution of the equity capital needed to support the existing volume of sales.

- Miscellaneous-assets-to-net-worth also rose, despite the fact that the dollar amount of this group of assets remained constant.

The other ratios were again held constant for the purposes of this illustration.

We have seen, then, that when profits are earned, even though they may be below industry average, the effect is beneficial. Substandard profits do not, of course, add to the financial health of the business to the extent normally to be expected, but nonetheless a low net profit is helpful. An operating loss, however, exercises a pronounced negative effect upon the company's financial balance, as reflected by other ratios, and hence in this instance the greatest concentration of corrective effort is required on the profit-to-sales ratio. This is not to suggest that either owners or credit grantors should be satisfied with substandard profit. Far from it. Such results must be carefully analyzed in an effort to detect and correct the fault, such correction being a means of reaching or exceeding industry average in the future. But operating losses, which can threaten the life of a business, demand immediate attention and remedial action.

Included in its "Annual Statement Studies," Robert Morris Associates publishes profit-and-loss data, of which commercial printers for the year 1970, shown in Exhibit 4, are representative. In studying this exhibit, note the disparity between the gross-profit and pretax-profit attainment of the smaller companies as opposed to that of the larger units. This, along with 1969 and 1970 medians for gross profit (shown in tabular form in Chapter 6), illustrates the fact that as a general rule the smaller companies achieve higher percentages of gross profit than do their larger competitors. As various expenses are deducted, however, the original edge is usually dissipated, with the larger companies ultimately realizing a higher percentage of net profit on sales. One can logically assume that the smaller companies are, on the average, dealing with customers of small size, those buying in quantities unattractive to the larger producers. As limited competition permits higher unit prices for production runs and deliveries of less quantity, the smaller firms are able to maintain a gross-profit advantage. Why then do the expenses of the smaller companies so greatly exceed those of their larger rivals? In what areas are their expenses higher? The figures point directly at fixed costs, as the smaller companies are evidently unable to achieve or to support a dollar volume of sales adequate to absorb these costs to the same degree as the larger organizations. Where "selling and delivery expense" comparisons can be made between the smaller and the larger manufacturing companies, generally the advantage rests with the firm of smaller size. This edge, however, is not as apparent in the fields of wholesaling and retailing. But in any case, many of these expenses are of a variable rather than a fixed nature, so the reasons that the bigger companies earn larger net profits remain undetermined at this stage.

Let us turn our attention to figures, again drawn from Robert Morris Associates' income supplement, for two areas where fixed costs are predominant: officers' salaries and other general and administrative expenses. Table 28 shows these figures—expressed as a percentage of income—for several industries. The figures indicate that fixed costs present a substantial hurdle for the smaller companies. While they transact a larger volume of sales related to net worth than do the larger concerns, this tendency to overtrade does not generate sufficient dollar volume of sales to afford the coverage of fixed costs attained by the bigger companies through a lower rate of capital turnover. Without exception, the table shows the smaller companies' sales dollars bearing a burden of officers' salaries anywhere from two to four times as great as that of their larger competitors. The $50,000 salary of a vice president of a company transacting annual sales of $50 million has considerably less impact on the sales dollar of his

Exhibit 4. Profit-and-loss data, commercial printers.

	MANUFACTURERS OF COMMERCIAL PRINTING (EXCEPT LITHOGRAPHIC) 42 STATEMENTS ENDED ON OR ABOUT JUNE 30, 1970 45 STATEMENTS ENDED ON OR ABOUT DECEMBER 31, 1970				ADDITIONAL OPERATING DATA
UNDER $250M	$250M AND LESS THAN $1MM	$1MM AND LESS THAN $10MM	$10MM AND LESS THAN $25MM	ALL SIZES	ASSET SIZE
19	45	23		87	NUMBER OF STATEMENTS
100.0%	100.0%	100.0%		100.0%	Net Sales
64.4	70.0	77.6		74.8	Cost of Sales
35.6	30.0	22.4		25.2	Gross Profit
7.1	10.7	8.3		9.0	Selling and Delivery Expense
10.7	4.0	2.7		3.4	Officers' Salaries
16.1	12.3	6.3		8.5	Other General Administrative Expense
.6	.6	2.2		1.7	All Other Expense Net
1.1	2.5	2.8		2.7	Profit Before Taxes
17	45	23		85	NUMBER OF STATEMENTS
3.2%	3.1%	2.6%		2.8%	Depreciation and Amortization (As % of Net Sales)
13	28	16		57	NUMBER OF STATEMENTS
2.4%	2.6%	1.7%		2.0%	Lease and Rental Expense (As % of Net Sales)
15	43	23		81	NUMBER OF STATEMENTS (Corporations only)
.4%	.9%	1.0%		.9%	Income Tax (As % of Net Sales)
	25	19		49	NUMBER OF STATEMENTS (Corporations only)
	3.8	2.1		3.0	Cash Flow/Current Maturity LT Debt

firm than does $20,000 compensation for an executive of a company doing only $1 million of business annually. Unfortunately, far too many officers of small companies feel that the title of president or vice president automatically entitles its holder to a major income, whether the business can afford this luxury or not. And, ironically, many undercapitalized businesses will lend these same officers money for their personal needs. Indeed, many creditors seem to view such questionable loans with complete calm and detachment, evidencing as much surprise as the owners themselves when they meet in the bankruptcy courts.

	MANUFACTURERS OF COMMERCIAL PRINTING (LITHOGRAPHIC)				ADDITIONAL OPERATING DATA
	38 STATEMENTS ENDED ON OR ABOUT JUNE 30, 1970 42 STATEMENTS ENDED ON OR ABOUT DECEMBER 31, 1970				
UNDER $250M	$250M AND LESS THAN $1MM	$1MM AND LESS THAN $10MM	$10MM AND LESS THAN $25MM	ALL SIZES	ASSET SIZE
24	37	19		80	NUMBER OF STATEMENTS
100.0%	100.0%	100.0%		100.0%	Net Sales
68.6	71.7	77.1		75.1	Cost of Sales
31.4	28.3	22.9		24.9	Gross Profit
7.8	11.0	9.6		9.9	Selling and Delivery Expense
8.3	5.2	2.4		3.5	Officers' Salaries
12.2	8.0	5.2		6.4	Other General Administrative Expense
1.4	.9	.8		.9	All Other Expense Net
1.6	3.2	4.8		4.2	Profit Before Taxes
23	35	19		77	NUMBER OF STATEMENTS
2.9%	2.9%	4.4%		3.9%	Depreciation and Amortization (As % of Net Sales)
13	19	10		42	NUMBER OF STATEMENTS
2.9%	2.2%	1.2%		1.6%	Lease and Rental Expense (As % of Net Sales)
23	36	19		78	NUMBER OF STATEMENTS (Corporations only)
.7%	1.3%	2.8%		2.3%	Income Tax (As % of Net Sales)
11	23	14		48	NUMBER OF STATEMENTS (Corporations only)
3.5	3.6	3.8		3.6	Cash Flow / Current Maturity LT Debt

© 1971 Robert Morris Associates.

In most industries "other general and administrative expenses" related to the sales dollar are again higher for the small company than for the large organization. Complete details are unfortunately not available now; but because this catchall group consumes anywhere from five to eighteen cents on each dollar of income, we clearly must supplement our present financial information so that in the future any analyst studying any company within a recognized industry can determine "par for the course" regarding office salaries, legal and accounting fees, rent, cost of heat and light, and travel and entertainment expenses. (The de-

Table 28

	OFFICERS' SALARIES			GENERAL AND ADMINISTRATIVE EXPENSES		
	UNDER $250M	$250M AND LESS THAN $1MM	$1MM AND LESS THAN $10MM	UNDER $250M	$250M AND LESS THAN $1MM	$1MM AND LESS THAN $10MM
WHOLESALE TRADE						
Automotive equipment	5.3%	3.3%	1.6%	10.9%	11.0%	8.9%
Electrical supplies and apparatus	7.7	3.9	1.5	10.3	8.3	6.0
Fruits and vegetables	4.7	2.1	1.2	8.5	5.8	4.7
General groceries	6.4	1.6	.7	13.7	7.0	4.3
Wine, liquor, and beer	3.1	1.7	.9	6.5	4.9	4.3
Furniture	6.2	3.7	3.1	12.4	11.4	8.6
Hardware and paint	6.3	3.8	1.3	8.6	10.0	8.5
Metal products (except scrap)	4.7	4.3	1.7	9.8	9.5	7.0
Plumbing and heating equipment and supplies	4.7	3.5	1.7	9.7	9.3	9.2
Building materials	4.9	2.6	1.6	9.5	8.3	7.1
Lumber and millwork	2.5	2.3	1.6	4.4	6.4	7.0
Heavy commercial and industrial machinery and equipment	5.9	4.3	1.7	9.6	9.6	8.7
Mill supply house	4.4	3.4	1.7	10.2	12.3	8.2
Dry goods	6.1	3.2	2.3	7.1	5.8	6.9
RETAIL TRADE						
Building materials	4.7	3.7	2.5	11.4	.9.7	9.7
Lumber	6.2	3.5	2.1	11.8	10.3	12.2
Dry goods and general merchandise	6.2	3.7	4.3	13.2	14.4	12.9
Farm equipment	3.6	2.3	1.8	9.8	10.7	12.1
Furniture	8.0	4.3	2.8	13.8	16.5	16.9
Autos, new and used	2.4	1.1	.7	8.5	9.8	8.2
MANUFACTURING						
Bread and other bakery products	5.7	2.9	1.7	14.8	10.5	5.1
Wood furniture: upholstered	6.2	3.4	1.9	7.7	7.8	5.4

Table 28 (*continued*)

	OFFICERS' SALARIES			GENERAL AND ADMINISTRATIVE EXPENSES		
	UNDER $250M	$250M AND LESS THAN $1MM	$1MM AND LESS THAN $10MM	UNDER $250M	$250M AND LESS THAN $1MM	$1MM AND LESS THAN $10MM
Electronic components and accessories	8.4	5.4	N.A.	18.4	10.1	N.A.
Machine shops: jobbing and repairing	7.0	5.5	3.4	10.0	7.9	12.0
Special dies and tools, die sets, jigs, and fixtures	7.1	5.4	2.3	10.7	9.2	6.3
Special industrial machinery	10.6	4.8	2.2	12.2	10.6	8.3
Fabricated steel structures	4.9	2.9	2.1	11.4	8.1	5.5
Miscellaneous plastic products	5.9	4.6	2.6	10.1	7.2	6.0
Concrete brick, block, and other products	7.1	4.5	3.2	10.1	12.3	7.9

Table 29

	COMPANY M	COMPANY N	COMPANY O	COMPANY P
Net profit-to-net-sales	6.95%	3.50%	.89%	(2.75%)
Industry average	3.42	3.42	3.42	3.42

velopment and publication of industry figures will be discussed in detail in Chapter 7.)

Very briefly, let us observe the performance of the hypothetical Companies M, N, O, and P with respect to the net-profit-to-net-sales ratio, as presented in Table 29. Company M's profit on sales is most attractive and is undoubtedly strengthening every element of the concern's financial structure—to the extent that this profit is real and is retained in the business. Management must be alert, however, to the possibility of generating a greater profit return on capital through the expansion of sales at a lower margin. If the company's capital position is sufficient to support increased business activity without the incurrence of additional expense, sales of $5 million at 6 percent net profit will obviously produce more total revenue than will $4 million volume at 7 percent. Some critics may say—on the assumption that some new product or new idea has given Company M an immediate edge that will be dissipated as others in the industry introduce competitive products or ideas—that such a high rate is temporary at best. Such an opinion may or may not ultimately prove to be true, but for the present, at least, Company M is benefiting from each dollar of sales to a greater extent than the industry in general and is to be commended. The initiative shown in gaining the company's current position indicates creativity in management, and such creativity may very well lead M to even further future advantages over its less imaginative competitors. The analyst should never be alarmed by profitability—unless, of course, such profit is fraudulently or ignorantly created by unrealistic asset valuation or inadequate provision for bad debts or depreciation.

Company N is near the industry norm. To the extent that it retains an average portion of its profit in the business, its financial ratios will benefit no more and no less than those of its typical competitor.

Company O earned a slight profit on each dollar of sales, and even this minimal amount will aid in attaining overall objectives. By failing to keep pace with the average firm in its line, O is losing some ground within the industry, but its internal financial balance will not be adversely affected. Company O's management, however, should be far from satisfied with its present accomplishments and should study the entire area of costs to determine why the company is unable to match the attainment of the typical concern with which it competes. Management may find that the company's difficulty is a low sales level, an inadequate markup, or weak internal cost control.

Company P has glaring, immediate problems. No company can survive a chronic loss situation. If Company P's present results represent an extension of similar deficits from past years, management urgently needs to study every industry ratio and every industry cost percentage with extreme care to determine the company's area or areas of fundamental weakness. Unless corrective steps are taken soon, Company P is faced with inevitable extinction. If, on the other hand, Company P has been a profitable enterprise until recently, a second standard of measurement is available to it. Not only can management study the company's position in relation to industry averages, but it is able to make item-by-item comparisons with Company P's own past performance to detect just which areas weakened during the past year. Working with financial understanding, management can take direct action to reduce excessive expenses, resume profitable operations, and restore financial balance.

Because the net-profit-to-net-sales ratio affects the entire range of key financial measures, it obviously must be regarded as one of the six primary ratios.

Miscellaneous-Assets-to-Net-Worth

Before considering the significance of the *miscellaneous-assets-to-net-worth ratio,* we must define "miscellaneous assets," a term which includes all assets that are not current assets, not fixed assets, and not intangible assets. Among the assets most frequently classified as miscellaneous are the following:

- Due from officers, directors, or employees (representing loans or advances).
- Investments in or advances to subsidiaries.
- Loans or advances to affiliated companies (usually firms related through mutual ownership).
- Prepaid expenses and deferred charges.[1]
- Investment in other than readily marketable securities.

---

[1] Accountants differ regarding the classification of these items as either current or miscellaneous assets. The most widely circulated source of industry averages excludes "prepaid and deferred" from current assets; and since comparison is meaningless unless ratios are derived from uniformly classified figures, this item is included here as "miscellaneous." An industry preparing its own ratios can categorize figures according to any generally accepted accounting method, provided, of course, that the assignment of these items is made clear to those reviewing the industry averages.

- Any long-term receivables, such as a mortgage receivable.
- Inventory of supplies.[2]
- Cash value of life insurance.

It is true that such miscellaneous assets do not constitute a prominent part of the average balance sheet, and in only perhaps one case out of 15 does the ratio of miscellaneous assets to net worth indicate the basic cause of a company's financial imbalance. But, if we are to have a ratio approach which assures the analyst of reasonable certainty in his final determination of cause and cure, we cannot afford even a 5 percent or 10 percent margin of error.

The ratio of miscellaneous assets to net worth is computed by dividing total miscellaneous assets by tangible net worth. A company possessing miscellaneous assets valued at $20,000 and net worth of $110,000 has, then, a ratio of 18.2 percent.

As we noted in considering the fixed-assets-to-net-worth ratio, every company has a limited amount of invested capital with which to achieve its objectives. Commitment of an inordinate proportion of this capital in miscellaneous assets restricts working capital and productive fixed assets and may concurrently increase the company's debt position. To establish the relative importance of the miscellaneous-assets-to-net-worth ratio, let us examine 1970 figures which show averages for 121 lines of manufacturers, 55 lines of wholesalers, and 44 lines of retailers. These figures are reproduced in Table 30. Of the 121 manufacturing lines included in the study, 13 industries reported a median of 20 percent or more of their net worth in miscellaneous assets, with a high mark of 32.0 percent. In wholesaling, 13 of the 55 industries showed 20 percent or more; the highest industry average was 59.6 percent. Among retailers, more than one-quarter had 20 percent or more of their net worth invested in miscellaneous assets, and one line averaged 74.2 percent.

In the cases which we consider in this book, the miscel-

---

[2] While the segregation of supplies from regular merchandise inventory is desirable, again the industry and the individual analyst must be guided by common practice, to insure uniformity in the compilation of ratios. If most units in the industry do not distinguish between merchandise inventory and supplies inventory, then this item should be included as a part of current assets under the inventory heading.

Table 30

MANUFACTURERS

Upper quartile	16.6%
Median	12.2
Lower quartile	9.0

WHOLESALERS

Upper quartile	19.7
Median	15.7
Lower quartile	10.8

RETAILERS

Upper quartile	20.1
Median	14.5
Lower quartile	11.3

These figures are derived from data copyrighted by Robert Morris Associates, 1971.

laneous-assets-to-net-worth ratio is discussed sparingly because industry averages for this ratio are not at present generally available for direct comparison. The lack of industry average figures makes the application of this ratio difficult for many analysts. Moreover, analysis of miscellaneous assets requires subheadings and individual percentages, similar in many respects to the breakdown and detailing of individual expense items in connection with study of the net-profit-to-net-sales ratio. In order to make specific recommendations, the analyst must know whether excess exposure in this area, for example, is due to borrowings by officers and employees or is a result of investment in business life insurance. While this ratio is considered only briefly here, it is nevertheless recommended for inclusion in any statistical preparation by individual industries.

Although the miscellaneous-assets-to-net-worth ratio indicates the fundamental cause of any difficulty less often than the others, it certainly must be considered among the six causal ratios. Serious distortion in the relationship between miscellaneous assets and net worth has widespread effect. If owners have borrowed heavily from the business, such withdrawals are reflected in a depressed current ratio or in elevated debt ratios. The same result follows from substantial diversion of funds into other assets making up this miscellaneous category. True, in the case of officers' or owners' borrowing, creditors should be most concerned. But owners should scrutinize their own actions, for it is always possible to "kill the goose that laid the golden egg." It has been done too often.

Miscellaneous assets are quite vulnerable to writeoff or markdown from book figures. Money lent to officers is, in many cases, never repaid. Amounts shown as invested in or lent to a subsidiary or affiliate are only as good as the company which received the funds. The owners of the business would be wise to show realistic values on the balance sheet, for otherwise they are simply deceiving themselves. Credit grantors must investigate the companies to which funds have been siphoned to ascertain that book figures reflect true worth. If, for example, the XYZ Company has invested in or lent to its subsidiary a sum of $80,000 and that subsidiary is on the verge of bankruptcy with substantial net-worth deficit, can this asset properly be shown at the full $80,000 figure? To the extent that any miscellaneous asset must be scaled down in value or written off, the recognition of such losses will affect net profit and can easily throw otherwise profitable operations into the loss column. In this event, all ratios relating to profit and net worth will be adversely distorted.

To illustrate, let us examine Companies Q, R, and S with respect to the ratio of miscellaneous assets to net worth, as shown in Table 31. Let us assume that the 14.8 percent industry average can be broken down as indicated in Table 32. Company Q, quite apparently, has been overzealous in diversion of funds into this group of assets. The probable result is a tight current ratio. Profitable expansion of the company's operations may be hampered, for substantial funds which might otherwise be used to support such growth are tied up in miscellaneous assets. Cash discounts are probably being passed, and slowness in trade payment is likely. Suppose that further research into this group of assets indicates the breakdown shown in Table 33 for Company Q. Reasoned conclusions in this case require knowledge of the financial position of the subsidiary and a thorough review of the balances due from employees.

Table 31

	COMPANY Q	COMPANY R	COMPANY S
Miscellaneous-assets-to-net-worth	36.7%	13.6%	4.9%
Industry average	14.8	14.8	14.8

Table 32

Due from related companies	3.6%
Life insurance, cash value	5.4
Prepaid and deferred	3.2
Due from officers, directors, and employees	2.6

Table 33

Due from employees	11.6%
Investment in subsidiary	20.7
Prepaid and deferred	4.4

Specifically, the analyst must discover to which employees loans were granted, how widespread the practice of borrowing from the company has become, the terms or understanding with respect to repayment, and the company's means of collecting its advances. (There have actually been cases—involving substantially higher percentages than in this example—in which money was being carried on the books as due from employees who had terminated their associations with the company a year or two before, whose whereabouts were unknown, and from whom there was no evidence of, or admission of, debt. These reported assets turned out to be 100 percent losses for the benevolent employer who had so freely and generously lent the money.) Whether or not Company Q's book value for these assets is well supported, additional investment in this area must be halted and an effort must be made to recover some of the outstanding funds for more active use in the regular operation of the business.

Company R's performance is, evidently, normal. If its distribution of miscellaneous assets proves to be sound, even though the makeup may vary from standard industry composition, then— other factors being equal—Company R's showing in this area is not subject to question. The liquidity position of Company S is benefiting from its relatively small commitment in miscellaneous assets. The company should, however, study industry percentages to determine, for example, whether the company is passing up investment opportunities or is providing adequately for business continuity through life insurance policies on key officers.

The ratio of miscellaneous assets to net worth must be included among the causal ratios if cause-and-effect analysis is to serve management as a thoroughly effective aid in the making of financial decisions.

4 Application
of the Causal Ratios

Now that we have examined the fifteen ratios which together form the financial picture of a company and we have seen that changes in the six primary ratios necessarily affect the nine secondary ratios, a question arises regarding the order of importance of the six causal measures. How do we ascertain cause or promote cure of a business ill if two of the six primary ratios are at wide variance with industry norms? Or if four are out of line? Or if all six are distorted, what is their rank of importance? The answer to these questions is that no relative weight can arbitrarily be assigned among the six primary ratios. There is considerable interplay between them, and one primary ratio can become distorted through the alteration of one or more of the others. Although no strict rule exists for distinguishing the relative importance of each primary ratio in a situation where more than one differs significantly from industry average, the application of fundamental logic will enable the analyst to assess the role of each.

In many cases, fortunately, only one of the causal ratios is distorted relative to the industry norm, and the analyst's problem is then quite simple. Conceivably, all six may be contributory to a company's plight; but in such an extreme case, the firm under analysis is probably beyond redemption. Generally, however, if three or more basic financial difficulties are discovered—that is, if three or more of the six primary ratios are unfavorably distorted—logical thinking will indicate their order of importance in each instance. By studying each individual case and determining the rank of the causal ratios, the analyst can establish a plan of constructive action to strengthen the company's financial structure. Let us illustrate this point through four hypothetical cases.

Case 1: Manufacturer of Paper Boxes

Established some 14 years ago in a large northern New England town, the XYZ Company is a manufacturer of paper boxes. (The analyst must, of course, be certain to compare the company under consideration with averages for the particular line of activity in which that concern is engaged.) Simplified and condensed balance-sheet figures and summarized sales and profit figures showing the XYZ Company's performance over a four-year period are shown in Table 34. These figures, reduced

Table 34

	1969	1970	1971	1972
Cash	$ 60,000	$ 50,000	$ 20,000	$ 10,000
Receivables	80,000	75,000	75,000	70,000
Inventory	90,000	85,000	85,000	80,000
All other	20,000	20,000	20,000	20,000
Total current	$250,000	$230,000	$200,000	$180,000
Fixed	150,000	145,000	140,000	130,000
All other	50,000	50,000	40,000	30,000
Total assets	$450,000	$425,000	$380,000	$340,000
Due banks	—	—	—	—
Due trade	$ 80,000	$ 90,000	$110,000	$145,000
Taxes	10,000	—	—	—
All other	—	—	—	—
Total current	$ 90,000	$ 90,000	$110,000	$145,000
Long-term liabilities	60,000	55,000	50,000	45,000
Total liabilities	$150,000	$145,000	$160,000	$190,000
Net worth	$300,000	$280,000	$220,000	$150,000
Total	$450,000	$425,000	$380,000	$340,000
Net sales	$900,000	$850,000	$800,000	$750,000
Net profit	30,000	(20,000)	(60,000)	(70,000)
Working capital	160,000	140,000	90,000	35,000

Table 35

	1969	1970	1971	1972	IND. AVG.
Current ratio	2.78 times	2.56 times	1.82 times	1.24 times	2.83 times
Fixed-assets-to-net-worth	50.0 %	51.8 %	63.6 %	86.7 %	50.9 %
Current-liabilities-to-net-worth	30.0	32.1	50.0	96.7	27.6
Total-liabilities-to-net-worth	50.0	51.8	72.7	126.7	59.3
Inventory-to-working-capital	56.3	60.7	94.4	228.6	67.6
Receivables-to-working-capital	50.0	53.6	83.3	200.0	39.4
Long-term-liabilities-to-working-capital	37.5	39.3	55.6	128.6	63.3
Net-profit-to-net-sales	3.33	(2.35)	(7.50)	(9.33)	3.18
Net-profit-to-net-worth	10.00	(7.14)	(27.27)	(46.67)	7.64
Net-sales-to-fixed-assets	6.00 times	5.86 times	5.71 times	5.77 times	5.00 times
Net-sales-to-net-worth	3.00	3.04	3.64	5.00	2.40
Net-sales-to-working-capital	5.63	6.07	8.89	21.43	5.94
Net-sales-to-inventory	10.00	10.00	9.41	9.38	9.20
Collection period	32 days	32 days	34 days	34 days	32 days
Miscellaneous-assets-to-net-worth	16.7 %	17.9 %	18.2 %	20.0 %	10.7 %

to ratios and compared to a five-year industry average, are shown in Table 35. (In a thoroughly professional analysis, the analyst would not rely on just one set of industry figures to cover four years' performance; instead, industry averages for 1969 would be matched to the company's 1969 ratios, 1970 figures for each would be compared, and so on. Our present purpose, however, is best served by more simplified figures.)

The distinction between cause and effect, between primary and secondary ratios, must be kept in mind by the analyst who studies these figures. First, he should take a cursory look at the current state of the XYZ Company's primary or causal ratios, noting the satisfactory, the unsatisfactory, and those which require further study.

1. *Fixed-assets-to-net-worth.* With 86.7 percent against industry average of 50.9 percent, the XYZ Company appears to have excess investment in fixed assets relative to capital. This ratio is "bad" or at best "doubtful."

2. *Net-profit-to-net-sales.* Loss of 9.33 percent on each dollar of sales, in contrast with industry average profit of 3.18 percent,

certainly reflects an alarming situation and immediately places XYZ's performance in the "bad" category.

3. *Net-sales-to-net-worth.* With XYZ showing a trading ratio of 5 times per year, in contrast with the industry average of 2.4, this measure points to an overtrading situation and should prompt the analyst to mark this ratio, too, as "bad."

4. *Net-sales-to-inventory.* The XYZ Company "turns" its inventory 9.4 times annually as opposed to 9.3 times for the average company in its line of activity. Since XYZ is doing a bit better than average job, the analyst accordingly classifies the company "good" in this department.

5. *Collection period.* The XYZ Company's 34 days compares favorably with the 32-day average for the industry. While the company is two days "over par," this is hardly an important adverse deviation, and the XYZ Company is clearly "good" from the point of view of maintaining overall collectibility of receivables.

6. *Miscellaneous-assets-to-net-worth.* The present investment of 20 percent in this area is twice as great as the industry average of 10.7 percent. Any such major variance requires investigation; thus a preliminary assessment of this ratio shows it as "bad."

In identifying the XYZ Company's basic problems, the analyst need no longer be concerned with those areas where performance is satisfactory; he can discard from further study two primary ratios, net-sales-to-inventory and collection period. Four ratios must undergo additional examination:

Fixed-assets-to-net-worth.
Net-profit-to-net-sales.
Net-sales-to-net-worth.
Miscellaneous-assets-to-net-worth.

Looking more closely at the fixed-assets-to-net-worth ratio, the analyst sees that in 1969 the XYZ Company was strictly average and that this ratio has become distorted over the ensuing three years. Was this unfavorable development due to an expansion program which diverted an increasingly large share of the company's capital into fixed assets? Clearly not, for the total investment in fixed assets actually declined $20,000 through depreciation between 1969 and 1972. The net-sales-to-fixed-assets ratio, further, indicates that the XYZ Company is getting greater activity from its plant and machinery than is true of the industry as a whole. It is quite apparent, then, that the primary fixed-assets-to-net-worth ratio has become top-heavy solely through the decline in net worth, rather than as a result of increased expenditures for productive assets. While the analyst should bear in mind the lack of balance in this ratio, he must nevertheless conclude that fixed assets to net worth, in this case, is not the primary cause of the XYZ Company's difficulties.

Turning next to the net-profit-to-net-sales ratio, the analyst must take note that, during the past three years, the company has lost money on sales and that the rate of loss has been increasing dramatically. The effects of these losses are now widespread. Net worth has been cut in half as the cumulative result of three disastrous years, and it has already been seen that the diminution of capital has created an illusion of excessive fixed assets. Losses have added to debt, virtually eliminating working capital. A close scrutiny of the XYZ Company's operating statements should immediately disclose the fundamental reasons for the tremendous reversal from a successful 1969 performance, and clearly, corrective steps must be taken immediately.

As the analyst observes the third unfavorable ratio, net-sales-to-net-worth, his first impression might be that the XYZ Company is overtrading—that is, its sales volume appears to be too great for its capital structure. While this is true, XYZ's overtrading is, in fact, *technical* overtrading; the fault lies with shrinkage of net worth through losses rather than with increased sales. In 1969 the company's sales were greater by $150,000, yet it was not overtrading then. The analyst, therefore, will rightly conclude that declining sales could not contribute to overtrading but that the increase of this ratio results from the continuing heavy losses which have cut net worth in half. As the XYZ Company first begins to push sales back to normal profitable levels (assuming that costs can be greatly modified to permit a profit on sales), it will encounter definite strain because of capital depletion. However, in the present study, the analyst can discard overtrading as one of the XYZ Company's basic faults.

Next, the analyst must turn his attention to the miscellaneous-assets-to-net-worth ratio, which at 20 percent is twice as high as the industry average. Noting that even in 1969 the diversion of funds into this group of assets was high, he must recognize that the company has taken corrective steps in the interim; miscellaneous assets, which amounted to $50,000 in 1969, have been reduced to $30,000 in 1972. Had the XYZ Company's net worth even remained constant, this ratio would be entirely normal for 1972. The exaggeration of this ratio results solely from shrinkage of net worth, which is in turn attributable to the loss on sales. Miscellaneous assets, then, are eliminated as a possible cause of the XYZ Company's present financial predicament.

Although four primary ratios of the XYZ Company are at considerable variance with industry averages, the application of logic has enabled the analyst to determine the fundamental problem, a continuing loss on sales, and a possible secondary difficulty, declining sales volume. Thorough study of the income statement and comparison of operating expenses with those of the industry as a whole should guide the management of this company toward resumption of profitable operations and recovery of financial balance. (The compilation and application of industry expense figures are explored in the following chapters.)

Case 2: Manufacturer of Stoves

In this case, the ABC Company, a manufacturer of stoves, has provided only the current annual statement for analysis. (All too often, prior years' results, which furnish the important element of trend, are unavailable to the analyst.) The ABC Company's 1972 statement shows the figures recorded in Table 36. The concern's ratios for the year under study, compared with industry averages, are shown in Table 37. The analyst should again concentrate on the six primary ratios to ascertain the ABC Company's basic financial position:

1. *Fixed-assets-to-net-worth.* ABC's figure is quite high at 40 percent—nearly 1.5 times industry average—and the analyst is obliged to mark this ratio "bad" or "doubtful," requiring further study.

Table 36

Cash	$ 10,000
Receivables	130,000
Inventory	200,000
All other	10,000
Total current	$350,000
Fixed	80,000
All other	20,000
Total assets	$450,000
Due banks	$ 50,000
Due trade	150,000
Taxes	5,000
All other	15,000
Total current	$220,000
Long-term liabilities	30,000
Total liabilities	$250,000
Net worth	200,000
Total	$450,000
Net sales	$600,000
Net profit	15,000
Working capital	130,000

Table 37

PRIMARY	ABC COMPANY	INDUSTRY AVERAGE
1. Fixed-assets-to-net-worth	40.00%	28.10%
2. Net-profit-to-net-sales	2.50	1.94
3. Net-sales-to-net-worth	3.00 times	2.84 times
4. Net-sales-to-inventory	3.00	6.00
5. Collection period	79 days	47 days
6. Miscellaneous-assets-to-net-worth	10.00	9.7
SECONDARY		
1. Current ratio	1.59 times	3.46 times
2. Current-liabilities-to-net-worth	110.00%	28.70%
3. Total-liabilities-to-net-worth	125.00	62.40
4. Inventory-to-working-capital	153.8	69.30
5. Receivables-to-working-capital	100.00	51.80
6. Long-term-liabilities-to-working-capital	23.10	25.70
7. Net-profit-to-net-worth	7.50	5.62
8. Net-sales-to-fixed-assets	7.50 times	10.10 times
9. Net-sales-to-working-capital	4.62	4.83

2. *Net-profit-to-net-sales.* The ABC Company shapes up favorably in this area, recording profit of 2.5 percent on sales, compared with an industry average of 1.94 percent. Accordingly, this ratio can be labeled "good."

3. *Net-sales-to-net-worth.* The ABC Company's annual turnover of net worth is 3 times, which is comparable to the 2.84 times attained by the median company in the industry. This ratio, too, is satisfactory.

4. *Net-sales-to-inventory.* While ABC is "turning" inventory at an annual rate of only 3 times, its average competitor achieves a rate of 6 times; this indicates the likelihood of serious problems. With regard to inventory, ABC's performance is clearly substandard.

5. *Collection period.* As the industry average is 47 days, ABC is operating at a definite competitive disadvantage with its 79-day collection period. The analyst should mark this ratio "bad."

6. *Miscellaneous-assets-to-net-worth.* The ABC Company's showing is almost identical with the industry norm, so the analyst can quickly dismiss this ratio as contributing to any financial problems the company may have.

Setting aside for the moment those ratios which were found to be roughly average or better, the analyst has narrowed his immediate field of study to just three errant ratios: (1) fixed-assets-to-net-worth, (2) net-sales-to-inventory, and (3) collection-period.

First, the analyst should consider the inventory turnover ratio, or net-sales-to-inventory. In an earlier discussion, we noted that many evils are associated with stagnant, slow-moving inventory. Some of these evils are clearly present in the ABC Company's operations, and all are likely to appear in time. If the ABC Company were able to bring its inventory exposure down to a level no greater than industry average, $100,000 in cash funds now tied up in stock would be released. Applying these funds against current obligations would aid materially in generating an improved working-capital balance that would reinforce the current ratio. Moreover, the lower ABC brings its inventory exposure, consistent with maintaining sales level, the less likely is the company to sustain losses through writeoff of inventory value from obsolescence, physical deterioration, or reduced salability of merchandise. The ABC Company needs a complete review of its buying program, as well as a thorough study of the condition and status of present inventory. A sound inventory control must be established to permit an orderly reduction of stock by utilizing excess supplies and buying only those materials required by production plans. With such positive corrective steps will come greater flexibility and relief from creditor pressure.

Next, the analyst should look at the collection period, another problem area which is exercising an adverse influence on the ABC Company's financial balance. By reviewing its credit-and-collection policy and making its necessary reforms to lower the collection period to the 47-day industry average, management would unfreeze $50,000 additional cash for paying current bills. If the company's principal weakness has been a hit-or-miss collection program of relatively recent origin and if its basic credit risks are of average credit acceptability, the institution of a regular, diplomatic follow-up program would soon indicate to ABC's customers that payment according to terms is expected and would start the checks rolling into the company's bank account. If, however, the company has taken an indifferent collection attitude for several years, its customers have undoubtedly developed their own payment rhythms, and an abrupt attempt to change the pattern might meet resistance and possibly result in loss of goodwill and sales.

Should the 79-day collection period prove to represent credit extension to bad risks, then the company has a much more serious problem. Despite management's best collection efforts, many weak risks must pay very slowly because of their own cash limitations. If the ABC Company cannot afford the luxury of carrying heavy receivables, it must either cut off future credit to these accounts or insist on very short terms, which would oblige the weak accounts to shop elsewhere. And, of course, the obvious risk of bad-debt loss apparent in an inordinately lengthy collection period may turn into a grim reality and bite deeply into ABC's profits. Having let matters get so far out of control, the company can probably look forward to either a loss of sales or an actual loss of money in bad debts as it endeavors to bring its receivables back closer to industry average. In the event that the company is totally successful in its objective, receivables will be reduced from the present $130,000 level to approximately $80,000.

If the ABC Company is able to effect reform in both inventory control and receivables management without suffering financial reverses, these two actions will give the company a 2.86 current ratio, compared with its present 1.59 ratio, and normality will be restored to its working-capital position. To rectify such serious deviations from normal without disrupting the entire sales and merchandising program will take some time, and the sooner management sets to the task the more likely it will be to meet with success.

The third ratio which was marked as deficient is fixed-assets-to-net-worth. By contrast with the serious inventory and receivables problems, the ABC Company's excessive investment in fixed assets pales almost to insignificance, for the company has been able to achieve a better-than-average profit notwithstanding. Further, if correction can be successfully accomplished in the inventory and receivables areas, current and total debt will be within acceptable limits and management will be afforded the freedom of action and flexibility it must have to compensate for the abnormality of this one primary ratio; depreciation charges will soon bring fixed assets into proper perspective, not only with respect to net worth but also relative to sales. Moreover, the difference between industry average (28.1 percent) and the company's present position (40 percent) represents a tie-up of only $24,000, a small amount compared to ABC's excess exposure in receivables and inventory, which aggregates $150,000.

We have again seen that through the application of basic logic the analyst is able to pinpoint the fundamental causes of financial imbalance—in this case, receivables and inventory difficulties—so that action may be taken to restore and enhance the company's competitive position.

Case 3: Wholesale Hardware Firm

This case study concerns the P&Q Company, a wholesale hardware firm, whose financial statement at December 31, 1971

Table 38

Cash	$ 100,000
Receivables	740,000
Inventory	2,000,000
All other	10,000
Total current	$2,850,000
Fixed	150,000
All other	100,000
Total assets	$3,100,000
Due banks	$ 500,000
Due trade	1,900,000
Taxes	50,000
All other	50,000
Total current	$2,500,000
Long-term liabilities	100,000
Total liabilities	$2,600,000
Net worth	500,000
Total	$3,100,000
Net sales	$6,000,000
Net profit	120,000
Working capital	350,000

fiscal closing showed the figures reproduced in Table 38. Reduced to ratios, P&Q's figures are compared with industry averages in Table 39. By any standard of measurement, the P&Q Company has problems, multiple problems of a serious nature. An analyst unfamiliar with cause and effect, or with the distinction between primary and secondary ratios, might instinctively focus his attention on those ratios that are most alarmingly distorted, starting with the current ratio and concentrating heavily on the debt and working-capital ratios, the astronomical size of which immediately catches the eye. But recognizing that these distortions result from other causes, that they do not of themselves cause, the analyst can omit these secondary ratios from his initial analysis and instead concentrate on the six primary ratios.

■ First, P&Q's fixed-assets-to-net-worth ratio is high—30 percent against an industry average of 14.6 percent. This ratio clearly requires further study.

■ Next, the net-profit-to-net-sales ratio appears good at 2

Table 39

	P&Q COMPANY	INDUSTRY AVERAGE
Current ratio	1.14 times	3.69 times
Fixed-assets-to-net-worth	30.0%	14.6%
Current-liabilities-to-net-worth	500.0	31.7
Total-liabilities-to-net-worth	520.0	67.6
Inventory-to-working-capital	571.4	83.7
Receivables-to-working-capital	211.4	35.7
Long-term-liabilities-to- working-capital	28.6	20.6
Net-profit-to-net-sales	2.00	1.44
Net-profit-to-net-worth	24.00	4.43
Net-sales-to-fixed-assets	40.00 times	19.50 times
Net-sales-to-net-worth	12.00	2.85
Net-sales-to-working-capital	17.14	3.56
Net-sales-to-inventory	3.00	4.00
Collection-period	45 days	39 days
Miscellaneous-assets-to-net- worth	20.0%	11.2%

percent, somewhat above the industry norm of 1.44 percent. The analyst can therefore dismiss this ratio from consideration as a possible cause of P&Q's difficulties.

▪ Third, the net-sales-to-inventory ratio shows a sluggish "turnover" rate of 3 times per year, in contrast to 4 times for the industry. Further study of this ratio is suggested.

▪ Fourth, net-sales-to-net-worth is abnormally high, with capital turnover of 12 times per year as opposed to an industry standard of only 2.85 times. This ratio definitely demands review.

▪ Fifth, the P&Q Company's 45-day collection period is significantly higher than the 39-day average for its industry. This ratio, likewise, must be subjected to scrutiny.

▪ Finally, the miscellaneous-assets-to-net-worth ratio, nearly twice as high as the 11.2 percent characteristic of the industry, indicates a condition requiring further investigation.

Five primary ratios have been found to be unfavorably distorted, and all are contributing in some degree to the P&Q Company's present plight. Which of these is the fundamental cause? Or are all five of equal importance? The experienced analyst will recognize this as a classic case of overtrading, replete with all the ills that characterize extreme examples of that financial malady. The P&Q Company has reached the stage where its credit standing and its very existence are threatened. Corrective steps must be taken. The company is already unable to meet trade bills as they come due; and should a strike, a fire, or some other disruptive event occur, management would in all probability be obliged to seek relief in bankruptcy court. In order to solve its fundamental problem of financial imbalance, the P&Q Company must attract additional equity capital or effect a drastic reduction in sales volume, or possibly combine both courses of action. As a temporary means of relief—although not a permanent solution—it might explore the possibility of a major long-term financing program.

Fortunately, the company has achieved an attractive profit on sales, better than that which characterizes its industry. For those impressed by profit return on invested capital, the P&Q Company shows a whopping 24 percent a year—yet the company is in jeopardy because of its strained working-capital position, which is certain to impair its general credit standing. Investment bankers might well look on the P&Q Company with favor and assist it in promoting either common- or preferred-stock issues to add the roughly $1 million in equity capital needed to support present sales volume. Similarly, Small Business Investment Corporation (SBIC) financing might provide the relief needed. But either of these alternatives involves risk of dilution or loss of ownership control. Of course, existing stockholders or associates themselves might be willing to invest added funds to bolster net worth. If equity capital is not available or cannot be secured without extreme disadvantages to P&Q's owners, they can perhaps buy time through long-term borrowing. Such financing is, of course, not a permanent substitute for invested funds, as it merely shifts the burden of debt and imposes a fixed obligation to operate profitably. Principal and interest payments on such long-term debt must be met, and bond holders or note holders cannot be expected to have the same degree of patience or forebearance as stockholders.

Since the P&Q Company has little unpledged equity in "permanent" assets to serve as collateral for secured borrowing, there is no certainty that it could successfully negotiate long-term financing. Despite its present good rate of profit return, the P&Q Company's general credit standing is probably not sufficient to support major unsecured long-term financing, such as a $1 million debenture issue. The company's largest assets, receivables and inventory, are reasonably attractive, but in general these assets serve as collateral for short-term loans or advances, and borrowing against them would contribute very little toward alleviating the company's overall problems.

If no additional capital-stock investment is available to the P&Q Company and if it is unable to arrange relief in the form of long-term financing, management has little choice but to curb the company's burgeoning sales volume. An exaggeration of P&Q's overtrading trend—or even a continuation of its present strained level of operations—would carry with it tremendous peril to the company's very survival. The P&Q Company is already at the mercy of creditors and is unable to meet terms of purchase. To try under these circumstances to maintain current sales levels or to increase them in the hope of adding profit is to court disaster. Instead, P&Q must recognize that there are safe levels beyond which a business cannot expand without additional capital or without some built-in compensating advantages. A car has a maximum safe speed, above which strain can cause mechanical breakdown and tragedy. Roads and highways are built with clear recognition that certain curves can be safely driven at 50 miles per hour, but not at speeds of 90 or 100 miles per hour. Without specially designed cars and parts, the racing driver could not attain the record speeds produced in today's competition.

The P&Q Company could speed more rapidly than its competitors if it were able to build some compensating advantages into its financial makeup. If, for example, it were to negotiate the sale and leaseback of its fixed assets, a good portion of its $150,000 investment would be "in the till" for the purpose of debt payment. If it were able to turn its inventory at a rate better than industry average (perhaps 6 times annually as opposed to its present 3 times a year), it would "unfreeze" $1 million of the $2 million currently tied up in stock. If the company were to collect its receivables more quickly than the average concern in its line, this too would be an advantage that would allow P&Q to indulge in some degree of overtrading. For instance, the realization of a 32-day collection period (as opposed to the industry average of 39 days and P&Q's own 45-day performance) would release $215,000 more cash for payment of current obligations. And if a portion of the company's $100,000 investment in miscellaneous assets were recovered from officers, employees, or affiliated companies, working capital would again benefit. Adding together the more than $100,000 generated from fixed assets, the $1 million from inventory, and the $215,000 from receivables, along with $50,000 from miscellaneous assets, management finds an impressive sum potentially available to bolster working capital. To the extent that any or all of these areas are improved, overtrading will become a less pressing problem. Such is the significance of compensating advantages.

Without additional invested capital or long-term borrowing or the creation of compensating advantages, the P&Q Company has little choice but to retrench—to pull sales back to levels which its capital capacity can support. The industry average suggests that sales in the neighborhood of $1 million can be carried without overtrading strain. Such a drastic curtailment must be carefully planned to avoid complete disruption of established patterns, but P&Q's extreme overtrading must be curbed rapidly.

Through studies of the profitability of individual accounts and the institution of selective selling, the unprofitable or the undesirable accounts can be weeded out. Some customers on the books are, in all likelihood, outside of P&Q's normal trading radius; freight or service costs on these accounts probably leave little or no profit from handling their orders. Other customers undoubtedly require the maintenance of certain specialized slow-moving inventory items, not salable to the majority of P&Q's customers; the culling of these accounts would aid in alleviating two current problems, inventory stagnation and overtrading. Many habitual deductors, low-profit volume accounts, marginal credit risks, and slow-paying customers might also be eliminated to advantage. Other companies better financed than P&Q may profitably cultivate many of these accounts, but if the P&Q Company is to survive, its management must face the realities which require reduction of sales. As it returns toward a state of financial balance, the P&Q Company will find the flexibility to chart imaginative programs which, if based upon financial understanding, will promote sound, sensible sales growth.

As in our previous illustrations, logical application of cause-and-effect ratio analysis has given the analyst insight into the firm's multiple difficulties, and it has suggested means of restoring financial balance and enabling the company to meet the challenges of competition on a solid financial footing.

Case 4: Manufacturer of Plastic Products

For a final illustration of basic analysis of the company's financial position through the application of the cause-and-effect technique, let us observe LMN Corporation, a manufacturer of plastic products. The company's fiscal closing figures for the years 1970 through 1972 are shown in Table 40. In analyzing LMN's recent progress and present condition, we shall follow our standard practice of converting this data to the 15 financial ratios and injecting

Table 40

	1970	1971	1972
Cash	$ 100,000	$ 50,000	$ 50,000
Receivables	210,000	270,000	335,000
Inventory	380,000	560,000	875,000
All other	30,000	60,000	50,000
Total current	$ 720,000	$ 940,000	$1,310,000
Fixed	600,000	900,000	1,200,000
All other	30,000	60,000	100,000
Total assets	$1,350,000	$1,900,000	$2,610,000
Total current liabilities	$ 300,000	$ 480,000	$1,010,000
Long-term liabilities	50,000	220,000	300,000
Total liabilities	$ 350,000	$ 700,000	$1,310,000
Net worth	1,000,000	1,200,000	1,300,000
Total	$1,350,000	$1,900,000	$2,610,000
Net sales	$1,700,000	$2,400,000	$3,500,000
Net profit	85,000	132,000	225,000
Working capital	420,000	460,000	300,000

available industry averages for comparison. These figures are shown in Table 41. (In this instance the average for the industry is derived by melding the median figures from three separate statistical sources as a means of leveling off differences, thus making the industry figure easier to use.) Concentrating on the six causal relationships, the experienced analyst will begin his study with a review of the primary ratios.

1. *Fixed-assets-to-net-worth.* In comparison with industry norm, the LMN Corporation evidences heavy investment in plant and equipment relative to equity capital. Although the degree of deviation is not alarming, this ratio requires further examination.

Table 41

	LMN CORPORATION			INDUSTRY AVERAGE
	1970	1971	1972	
Current ratio	2.40 times	1.96 times	1.30 times	1.70 times
Fixed-assets-to-net-worth	60.0%	75.0%	92.3	70.%
Current-liabilities-to-net worth	30.0	40.0	77.7	59.0
Total-liabilities-to-net-worth	35.0	58.3	100.8	95.5
Inventory-to-working-capital	90.5	121.7	291.7	103.2
Trade-receivables-to-working-capital	50.0	58.7	111.7	105.8
Long-term-liabilities-to-working-capital	11.9	47.8	100.0	93.4
Net-profit-to-net-sales	5.00	5.50	6.43	3.25
Miscellaneous-assets-to-net-worth	3.0	5.0	7.7	20.3
Net-sales-to-fixed-assets	2.8 times	2.7 times	2.9 times	4.4 times
Net-sales-to-net-worth	1.7	2.0	2.7	3.3
Net-sales-to-working-capital	4.0	5.2	11.7	7.3
Net-sales-to-inventory	4.5	4.3	4.0	8.4
Net-profit-to-net-worth	8.50%	11.00%	17.31%	16.40%
Collection-period	45 days	41 days	35 days	56 days

2. *Net-profit-to-net-sales.* During each of the three years under study, the LMN Corporation has surpassed the industry profit average. The analyst can therefore mark the company's accomplishments in this area as excellent.

3. *Net-sales-to-net-worth.* While the company is undertrading to a discernible extent, the two-year trend of its trading ratio is reassuring. This measure, however, must be considered in greater detail.

4. *Net-sales-to-inventory.* Industry performance shows clearly that the LMN Corporation is substantially below average. This ratio must be underscored as definitely deficient.

5. *Collection period.* The LMN Corporation has consistently bettered industry averages in the collection of receivables, and its trend reflects an increasingly rapid flow of cash into the company's bank account. While the analyst can at this point classify the LMN attainment as good, any such extreme divergence from normal requires further examination.

6. *Miscellaneous-assets-to-net-worth.* Although the company's minimal investment in miscellaneous assets—far below the industry norm—may be inadequate to meet future contingencies, this ratio has been exerting a favorable influence on the company's financial structure.

Next, the analyst should subject to more thorough scrutiny the three ratios which he has marked for further study.

1. *Fixed-assets-to-net-worth.* In just two years, the LMN Corporation has increased fixed assets $600,000 over and above depreciation charges. This increase has caused the ratio of fixed assets to net worth to rise from 60.0 percent to 92.3 percent. Despite its phenomenal 105 percent sales expansion during the same period, the company's capital-good outlay appears somewhat excessive. This is because its utilization of physical facilities has remained below the industry standard as determined by the secondary ratio, net-sales-to-fixed-assets. However, since the company has probably reached a plateau where further outlay for fixed assets will not be necessary for some time, this ratio will rise to industry average through depreciation charges as well as through any growth in sales during fiscal 1973. Although its trend must be watched closely, LMN's investment in plant and equip-

ment has not had the effect of depressing its profit-to-sales ratio—which, on the contrary, has continued to climb markedly—so the analyst can, in this case, discount fixed assets as a significant negative influence.

2. *Net-sales-to-net-worth.* A hasty glance at the LMN Corporation's 2.7 ratio, which is noticeably below the industry average, might lead to a conclusion that the company's undertrading on capital is a dangerous practice. The analyst must remember, however, that undertrading is positively harmful only if a company's sales level is inadequate to return a reasonable profit or if it results in operating losses. The LMN Corporation is a demonstrably profitable concern—far above average in this respect—and hence its low trading ratio has not proved to be a major detriment. The trend, moreover, is distinctly favorable; in two years, LMN's ratio has moved upward from 1.7 to 2.7 and its capital has grown appreciably through retention of extraordinarily good profits. Although increased trading would in all probability enhance the profit picture still further, the company's financial balance is certainly not suffering from its present level of sales relative to net worth.

3. *Collection-period.* The analyst must consider whether the LMN Corporation's terms structure is too restrictive, for the difference between its collection period of 35 days and the 56-day average of its industry is quite significant. As we have seen, negativism in credit dealings with customers normally results in diminishing sales. That the LMN Corporation has actually increased business—highly profitable business at that—by more than 100 percent during the past two years indicates that its ability to convert receivables to cash at a relatively rapid rate is a definite plus factor, a compensating advantage.

Thus, by process of elimination, the analyst has determined that only one primary financial relationship is exerting an unfavorable influence on the LMN Corporation. That relationship is net-sales-to-inventory. The company's inventory turnover is seriously deficient, roughly half the rate enjoyed by its average competitor. Management is evidently unaware of the gravity of the situation, for it is diverting funds into stock at an ever increasing pace, an additional $315,000 commitment having been made during the past fiscal year alone. Although in actual dollars and cents the LMN Corporation has recently added more to fixed assets than to inventory, its investment in plant and equipment relative to net worth has remained much closer to industry average. Inventory turnover, however, has been substandard since 1970 or earlier, and the trend is downward (from 4.5 times in 1970 to 4.0 times in 1972).

One of the immediate effects of sluggish inventory movement is apparent in the company's current ratio of 1.30, which compares unfavorably with the industry norm of 1.70. Had the $380,000 inventory figure for 1970 been held constant, and had the $495,000 additional investment during 1971 and 1972 been used instead for current-debt reduction, the current ratio would have climbed to roughly 1.6, or very nearly average for the industry. Inventory-to-working-capital would have declined to 126.7 percent, still above par but substantially below the present alarming figure of 291.7 percent. Current and total debt would have been even further improved over the company's present acceptable positions relative to net worth. Yet LMN's inventory turnover rate would rise to but 9.2 times annually, only slightly above the industry norm of 8.4 times per year.

Were it not for the compensating advantages which LMN has built into its financial structure (most notably its short collection period and its extremely attractive profit return), the company would find its competitive position considerably handicapped by its poor purchasing and merchandising performance. Management of the corporation must devote serious thought to implementing more effective means of inventory control, or all its impressive gains may be jeopardized. A decline in materials prices, a recession or depression, a drop in sales, writeoffs of obsolete or damaged materials—all the potential dangers to the overinventoried company, as emphasized in our study of the net-sales-to-inventory ratio—are now threats to the LMN Corporation's profit and progress. But through understanding of its single major difficulty, management can take direct action to correct this situation and thus enhance the company's sound competitive position. Once again, cause-and-effect ratio analysis has provided the answers sought by management.

The foregoing cases, in which the most basic analysis was applied, demonstrate that the primary causes of financial imbalance can be readily detected by means of the cause-and-effect technique. Complete ratio analysis is illustrated in detail in Chapter 6.

CORRECTIVE MEASURES

A parallel may be drawn between financial imbalance and physical illness, with the analyst—whether he be the owner or an officer of the business, one of its credit grantors, or an independent industry analyst—assuming the role of doctor. While a wise individual consults his physician regularly in order to be assured that his health remains good or to detect possible incipient disease, many persons neglect medical attention until their illnesses are far advanced. Companies, too, often seek guidance only after financial distress has reached serious proportions, but the informed business principal knows the value of a periodic financial review.

Symptoms of financial disease include tightening of working capital, increasing debt pressure, and distortion of any of the nine secondary ratios. The degree of deviation from normal indicates the seriousness of the situation and the speed with which curative measures must be applied. Medical journals report that certain symptoms are common to several different physical illnesses, but they note that various methods of diagnosis plus consultation with experts will disclose the true cause underlying the symptoms. Unless a doctor knows with reasonable certainty the identity of the disease he is treating, he must be cautious in advising medication or surgery because each disease has its own cure and the prescription for one might complicate or increase the severity of another. To treat a symptom without knowing its cause is as dangerous to the business patient as it is to the medical patient. To gain a familiarity with fundamental financial diagnosis through cause-and-effect ratio analysis, we have examined various causes of financial imbalance in the previous pages. But accurate diagnosis will not, by itself, bring about recovery. Once the analyst has determined the cause of a company's financial difficulties, he must be aware of the corrective actions available in order to offer sound, specific recommendations.

The analyst will often encounter a company beset by working-capital deficiency, as determined through examination of these five ratios:

Current ratio.
Inventory-to-working-capital.
Receivables-to-working-capital.
Long-term-liabilities-to-working-capital.
Net-sales-to-working-capital.

How is the current ratio to be strengthened or working capital increased? The answer, of course, depends in large part upon the fundamental cause of the working-capital deficiency. Is there one broad universal cure for working-capital problems, a cure that will be permanent? Some businessmen may say, "Yes, add something to invested capital. Increase net worth and add the cash to the bank account or pay some current bills." But this course of action does not necessarily produce a permanent solution. It is, instead, similar to a blood transfusion, which—unless basic corrective measures are taken—may have to be repeated again and again because it provides only temporary relief. Through his understanding of cause-and-effect relationships, the analyst knows that a depressed current ratio is symptomatic of any one—or a combination—of six deep-seated illnesses:

Excessive fixed assets.
Operating losses.
Overtrading.
Sluggish or questionable inventory.
Slow or uncollectible receivables.
Diversion of funds into miscellaneous assets.

A cure for excessive fixed assets cannot apply with equal effectiveness to a case of slow accounts receivable, for the two problems are fundamentally dissimilar. Nor are operating losses likely to require the same medication as overtrading. Clearly, the analyst-doctor must prescribe his working-capital cure only after he knows why working capital is in its present condition.

To illustrate another common symptom of financial imbalance, suppose that the debt structure of the XYZ Company is top-heavy and that its operating freedom has been severely curtailed. Is there a panacea which will insure the permanent financial health of the XYZ Company? Someone may suggest, "Profits must be earned and retained in the business." But if debt is heavy due to overtrading, even profitable operations may not prevent the XYZ Company from becoming a profitable bankrupt. Or excessive fixed assets—often the fundamental cause of burdensome debt—may bring rising costs and make profit difficult, if not impossible, to realize. Profit is, of course, one of the ingredients of the cure that applies, but it is no universal elixir. The realization of adequate profit is, in itself, dependent upon a certain degree of overall financial soundness. It is obvious, then, that cure depends on diagnosis and treatment of cause and not on a general palliative for the symptom.

We shall now consider a few of the fundamental causes of financial imbalance that are likely to be encountered by an analyst and briefly note specific corrective measures that can be applied.

Excessive Fixed Assets

If after thorough examination of a company the analyst should find that fixed assets are excessive with respect to net worth, several courses of action are open to remedy this situation—some permanent, some simply expedient.

- *Raising additional capital from existing owners or through attracting outside investors*. The latter move may take the form of bringing in additional partners or incorporating and selling stock—perhaps even "going public."
- *Selling idle machinery and parts, unused vehicles, and unnecessary equipment*. Other companies in the same or related industries may profitably use this equipment and may gladly pay cash for it. As production needs change, often excess equipment—with actual cash value—is simply shunted to one side. Many an organization has started with good used equipment bought from a competing firm.
- *Arranging sale and leaseback of plant and equipment*. Such

arrangements may be made with commercial leasing companies or other financial institutions specializing in this type of program.

- *Restricting further investment in fixed assets.* New equipment can be leased from manufacturers or other leasing sources as needed.

- *Developing compensating advantages.* Some such advantages might be improved inventory turnover, faster collection of receivables, and higher profit return that would permit greater-than-average investment in fixed assets.

In order to bolster working capital impaired by excessive fixed assets, these additional steps might be taken.

- *Securing long-term loans from banks, finance companies, or factors.*

- *Resorting to Small Business Administration (SBA) loans or Small Business Investment Company (SBIC) financing.* The 5.5 percent SBA rate has proved quite attractive to borrowing companies, which must have been refused loans by commercial banking institutions in order to qualify for the government program. SBIC financing has generally taken the form of subscription to debentures of the borrowing company, convertible at the option of SBIC to the debtor's common stock at the fair value of that stock at the time the loan was made. The exercise of the option depends primarily on the degree of profitability attained by the borrower. If the conversion to stock privilege is opted, original ownership control becomes weakened, threatened, or even lost.

- *Seeking longer terms from key suppliers.* This might be accomplished by securing a "frozen" line of credit—such as $20,000 or $50,000—with all purchases in excess of that amount to be discounted on regular terms. Or the company might convert its existing open-account balance (say $50,000) to interest-bearing notes payable periodically over a 12- to 24-month period with current purchases to be discounted on regular terms. Or "temporary" 90- or 120-day terms might be secured from suppliers to permit completion of the marketing cycle without the strain of more rapidly maturing trade obligations.

The foregoing is not a complete list of alternatives, but it suggests that there are a great many ways to deal with excessive fixed assets. A single approach is, of course, seldom sufficient; the solution to this problem generally consists of a combination of measures. Any action which accomplishes either a reduction of fixed assets or an increase in invested capital is in the nature of a permanent cure. Others which involve borrowing—and which affect neither fixed assets nor net worth directly—are temporary expedients which simply shift the burden from current debt to longer-term obligations, thus "buying time" for the over-extended company to effect essential corrective measures. Retained earnings will in time build net worth; depreciation charges will decrease fixed assets. Thus, unless the degree of imbalance is insurmountably high, this combination may ultimately restore equilibrium. But the assumption of heavy fixed-term debt brings with it many hazards of which the borrowing company needs to be fully aware.

With respect to leasing, the company contemplating such action must give careful consideration to the cost factor. A relatively new method of financing, leasing is gaining favor and popularity at a very rapid rate. Generally, a security deposit—ranging from one month's payment in advance to 15 percent of the total rental called for under the lease—is required in addition to an annual charge of roughly 10 to 18 percent of original cost. The rather wide variance in the deposit and leasing charges is attributable to differences in customer credit worthiness and to the relative resalability of the leased property.

Lease agreements are of various types, some of which embrace all maintenance costs. Such an agreement will clearly establish in advance the total expense involved and will thus eliminate uncertainty. Proponents of leasing assert that, in the final analysis, costs are quite moderate when consideration is given to offsetting savings such as the five that follow.

1. The elimination of depreciation.
2. The possibility that the 7 percent federal investment-tax credit may be passed on by the leasing company to the customer.
3. The availability of new equipment beyond the customer's immediate ability to purchase; this can lead to profits in excess of leasing charges.

4. Reduction of strain on working capital; this promotes flexibility of action.

5. Enhancement of the lessee's overall competitive position, which is certainly of great value although it cannot be directly measured in dollars and cents.

To qualify for most sale-and-leaseback arrangements, however, a company must be reasonably well established.

Abnormal Collection-Period Ratio

If a collection period is abnormally high or abnormally low, the following points should be considered.

▪ *Selling terms can be either shortened or lengthened.* The analyst must first consider the competitive element, for many accounts are motivated in their purchasing not only by quality of product and price, but by terms of sale and credit arrangements as well. Each company's terms, however, must be determined by individual circumstances and need not exactly parallel those of others in the same industry.

▪ *Cash discount can be injected into selling terms, or existing cash discount can be increased, or cash discount can be eliminated entirely, thus restricting all sales to a net basis.* The choice will depend upon the particular needs of the company under analysis. The effect of any of these discount choices will vary, of course, with the manner in which the matter is approached and activated.

▪ *Greater selectivity in accepting accounts can be imposed or liberalization of credit policy can be instituted.* The choice, again, will depend on the nature of the particular company's problem.

▪ *Either a more systematic collection follow-up can be established or the relaxing of arbitrary payment demands can be inaugurated.* Again, the choice depends upon the individual collection situation.

▪ *A professional credit manager can be hired, or the education and training of the employee now handling the credit function can be initiated.* Both courses of action can pay dividends in the stabilizing of the entire credit-and-collection program.

■ *Slow receivables can be factored or discounted with a finance company or bank.* Again a cost element enters the picture, for factoring and discounting services are not free. If increased sales can be stimulated through such a move or if the immediate release of cash is adequate to permit the earning of purchase discounts to offset the added financing costs, then this approach may be entirely justified. But if, despite the increase in available funds, the company will still be obliged to struggle along, able to pay bills on a net basis at best, then little benefit will have been gained, and the costs will eat heavily into profit. The company contemplating such a move must also consider the suspicion (invalid though it may be) about the concern's solvency sometimes created among trade creditors—a suspicion occasionally shared by customers. Much depends on the type of receivables financing, whether it be old-line factoring or discounting of individual receivables or blanket borrowing against receivables, as well as on the recourse element and notification feature.

■ *Credit insurance can be obtained to protect against abnormal bad-debt loss.* If, however, the company has run a very loose credit program, the premiums for credit protection are likely to be quite high. Moreover, insurance policies will not insure against normal bad-debt loss, and thus a high percentage of accounts may be uninsurable.

■ *Compensating advantages can, perhaps, be developed.* Such advantages, if sufficiently great, could permit the company to carry excess receivables until they can be brought under control.

The foregoing list is not complete, but it does indicate various alternative approaches available to the company in the event that analysis discloses collection period to be one of its basic causal problems.

Sluggish Movement of Stock

If the net-sales-to-inventory ratio shows sluggish movement of stock, the company again has available many corrective actions, a number of which are included in the following list.

■ *Study of inventory records to detect items no longer used in the present manufacturing or marketing program.* Frequently while such forgotten items gather dust in the warehouse, they are carried on the books at original purchase price. Efforts should be made to realize cash from such stagnant but sometimes valuable materials. They can be moved as distressed goods if no other market is available.

▪ *Review of the turnover rate of the various inventory components.* Those components for which demand is exceedingly low relative to supply on hand should be noted. Salesmen can then place emphasis on movement of these items, and at the same time, they can attempt to curtail the reorder of those for which little demand is evident.

▪ *Establishment of perpetual inventory records to insure that articles are not purchased in excessive quantity or in advance of need.* At the same time, care must be taken to maintain an adequate supply of vital parts. Data processing has rendered inventory control considerably more precise than it once was and has contributed greatly toward the shrinking importance of inventory in the working-capital structure of modern businesses.

▪ *Purchase of merchandise on consignment.* The choice of this approach depends, of course, upon satisfactory agreements with major suppliers. Consignment purchasing makes inventory available without the necessity of remitting payment until the merchandise is actually consumed. Such an arrangement can provide the company with a complete line of goods beyond its capacity to secure in advance through its own cash-flow capacity. Using the consigned stock and completing its marketing cycle, the company can use its current sales revenue to meet its obligations. Consignment agreements thus reduce the concern's inventory exposure and provide impetus to sales, while the supplier, who holds title to the consigned goods, is exposed only to the risk of loss on the accounts receivable created as the goods are withdrawn. A greater-than-average amount of paperwork is necessarily involved in this type of arrangement.

▪ *Initiation of field warehousing.* Field warehousing accomplishes essentially the same objectives as consignment, except that the supplier is in a more secure position because of the watchful actions of the warehousing company and the issuance of a warehouse receipt. This receipt can be used for borrowing purposes by the supplier, yet the goods are in the purchaser's warehouse (under the supervision and control of the warehouse company) for immediate access, provided that the terms and conditions of the agreement are met.

■ *Arrangement of loans on inventory.* Sources of such financing include banks, finance companies, and factors. Although such loans are generally of a short-term nature and provide no permanent solution to slow movement of inventory, they may aid the company in revamping inventory procedures, speeding turnover, and averting the need for future loans.

■ *Delegation of the purchasing and inventory control function to a single responsible person.* Such delegation minimizes duplication of orders and promotes inventory balance consistent with production or marketing needs.

■ *Study of the physical layout of the warehouse and storage areas.* If necessary, alteration of design and methods can be made to insure ready access to materials as needed.

■ *Promotion of increased sales while holding inventory levels constant.* This fundamental approach is so obvious that it hardly needs mentioning; but it does require action in two areas, and all too often emphasis is placed on sales alone.

■ *Development of compensating advantages to offset the competitive disadvantage of slow inventory turnover.*

This incomplete list illustrates only a few of the many ways that inventory problems may be attacked.

Overtrading or Undertrading

In the event that the net-sales-to-net-worth ratio is distorted beyond reasonable bounds, what choices of action are open to the company to restore financial balance? The answer, of course, depends in large measure upon whether the company is overtrading or undertrading. Among many alternatives, let us consider just a few.

■ *When undertrading is the problem, the analyst must consider the degree of profitability currently enjoyed.* If sales are adequate to afford a good profit, the company may have excess and idle funds which might be utilized for expansion or might be temporarily invested in the money market. If, on the other hand, operations are unprofitable, then added sales will aid in eliminating red ink—unless, of course, certain cost factors preclude the possibility of profit at competitive prices, in which case the concern must make radical changes or cease operations.

Are substandard sales the result of an incomplete line of merchandise? If so, what other items must be added? Should the company add to its sales force or replace the salesmen now employed? Should it change its approach to reaching the market and perhaps place more emphasis upon advertising or exhibits at industry shows? A study of expense percentages of the sales dollar in contrast with industry averages will often indicate a more effective means of distributing promotional dollars to bolster sales. Or does the company have a noncompetitive product that should be redesigned? Or is its pricing-and-terms position due for revamping? Or have restrictive credit policies held sales back? Or is this concern so miscast in its present role that it should close up shop and retire from the business scene as gracefully and inexpensively as possible? The answers to these questions can be found through detailed analysis.

▪ *If the company is overtrading, then again a vital consideration in effecting remedial measures is the degree and actuality of profit.* In assessing actuality, the analyst must determine whether reported profit is subject to drastic markdown through either inventory overvaluation or the existence of extremely doubtful receivables. In instances where the overtrading is highly profitable, there is an impelling reason to attract additional capital or develop compensating advantages so that the profitable venture will not be threatened with extinction because it has overreached its financial resources. As we have seen earlier, compensating advantages take the form of better-than-average performance in other key areas, such as receivables collection, inventory turnover, fixed-assets investment, and miscellaneous-assets control. That operations are profitable and that the single deficient component is capital should provoke the interest of investors. Management must be alert, however, to the possibility of dilution or loss of ownership control in the process of raising needed funds.

If, on the other hand, overtrading has resulted in losses, then a thorough study must be undertaken to determine the profitability of each customer. Amazingly enough, the company is likely to find several customers who buy at unattractive price levels, who require costly extra services without affording adequate compensation, whose freight costs are excessive, who make arbitrary adjustments or endless deductions from invoices based on alleged unsuitability of goods, who take unearned cash discounts, who require special credit terms, who are extremely slow and expensive to collect from, who represent poor credit risks with high bad-debt loss potential—who, in other words, are undesirable from virtually every point of view. Other accounts will represent varying degrees of profitability and potential. Selective elimination of undesirable customers can prove to be a definite gain, not only because such elimination increases profits but also because it decreases the pressure on capital caused by overtrading. As an alternative to eliminating such accounts, the company can charge them prices sufficient to compensate for the extraordinary services rendered to them. While this type of customer may bluster and threaten to take his business elsewhere, competitors are not likely to bid too aggressively for his unprofitable or disagreeable account.

- *Whether the fault be overtrading or undertrading, borrowing from financial institutions or securing special credit terms can provide temporary relief.* These expedients may permit gradual restoration of the net-sales-to-net-worth ratio into proper balance through more permanent remedial action.

Inordinate Investment in Miscellaneous Assets

If the company's problems should be traced to inordinate investment in miscellaneous assets (which, as we have noted previously, is the responsible factor far less frequently than are distortions of the other five causal ratios), the solutions are perhaps more immediately apparent but are often more difficult to effect. In many instances, excesses in this area involve personalities and perhaps individual self-interest, interest which may easily override that of the business. Loans to officers and employees should be collected and the money put back into the active working funds of the company. Advances to, or investments in, affiliated companies—other interests of the officials—should be called in like manner, unless direct benefit to the parent firm can be demonstrated. If an affiliate has credit standing of its own, it should be encouraged to borrow through normal channels rather than tap the resources of the parent company. If, on the other hand, its credit strength is insufficient to merit loan consideration from financial institutions then the analyst must question whether the parent concern, and its stockholders, should assume such a risk, from which the benefits may be minimal or nonexistent. Because many other factors may enter into the miscellaneous-assets picture, any plan designed to correct an overly high miscellaneous-assets-to-net-worth ratio must be based upon knowledge of the particular areas into which funds have been diverted. Curtailment of excessive outlay for business life insurance obviously requires different action than that applicable to an unusually great capital-stock investment in closely held enterprises. Thorough investigation and specific remedial measures are clearly required in this area.

Operating Losses

If the company's lack of balance derives from operating losses, as indicated by the net-profit-to-net-sales ratio, the analyst must determine whether this situation results from factors connected with any of the other causal ratios or from excessive expenses of an operational nature. In other words, are the losses caused by inadequate sales, inventory writeoffs, or bad debts? Or can they be traced through review of operational expense percentages related to the sales dollar? In the latter case, an item-by-item comparison of expenses will bring to light significant deviations from industry average. Any such variance must be thoroughly scrutinized and related to operating results before nonproductive expenses can be reduced and profitable operations realized. Is the operating loss indicative of a trend? Or is it the result of unusual, nonrecurring expenses? And if, for instance, returns and allowances are excessive, does this situation stem from manufacturing weaknesses or from lack of quality control and inspection? Or is it due to unwarranted claims by certain habitual deductors? If the gross profit percentage is low, then perhaps a review of buying policies or selling prices would prove productive. Standardized, representative, accurate expense percentages compiled by each major industry would obviously be of great aid to the analyst in determining specific deviations from normal performance.

Given understanding of the company's financial condition, management may utilize the services of specialists (in, say, inventory control, sale and leaseback, or business life insurance) as needed. But recognition of the need for improvement must necessarily precede remedial measures, and cause-and-effect ratio analysis heightens management awareness by providing a precise picture of the firm's financial structure. Once the nature of a specific difficulty is determined, management can design and implement the proper corrective actions by drawing upon its business experience and, on occasion, by enlisting the aid of outside consultants.

MAKING POLICY DECISIONS

Because cause-and-effect ratio analysis sets forth, in detail, the financial condition of a company, it can be of significant aid to management in reaching major policy decisions. Alternative projections may be utilized to estimate the effect of contemplated competitive moves upon each element of the company's financial structure and to indicate its resulting position vis-à-vis other businesses in the industry. Obviously, application of cause-and-effect analysis will not produce clairvoyance, but sound estimates of the impact of particular actions can be derived by means of this versatile method.

Let us briefly observe the manner in which management might use ratio analysis as a tool in making specific policy decisions. Table 42 shows summarized figures for three separate packers of meat and provisions, all corporations of similar size

Table 42

	COMPANY A	COMPANY B	COMPANY C
Cash	$ 20,000	$ 40,000	$ 30,000
Receivables	66,000	76,000	70,000
Inventory	64,000	64,000	62,000
All other	10,000	10,000	8,000
Total current	$ 160,000	$ 190,000	$ 170,000
Fixed assets	170,000	120,000	80,000
Miscellaneous	52,000	10,000	12,000
Total assets	$ 382,000	$ 320,000	$ 262,000
Due banks	$ 20,000	$ 30,000	$ —
Accounts payable	110,000	40,000	36,000
Taxes	—	6,000	12,000
All other	10,000	14,000	4,000
Total current liabilities	$ 140,000	$ 90,000	$ 52,000
Long-term liabilities	42,000	30,000	10,000
Total liabilities	$ 182,000	$ 120,000	$ 62,000
Net worth	$ 200,000	$ 200,000	$ 200,000
Total	$ 382,000	$ 320,000	$ 262,000
Working capital	$ 20,000	$ 100,000	$ 118,000
Net sales	1,000,000	2,000,000	2,500,000
Net profit	(5,000)	15,000	25,000

and business age and all operating in the same general vicinity. Obviously, Company A is, at best, marginal; but it is hardly an unusual case. Company B approximates industry average in most respects, while Company C is an organization reflecting excellent financial condition, considerably better than normal. To illustrate how these three companies compare with normal performance for their industry, Table 43 presents all 15 ratios for each concern and injects published figures for packers of meat derived by averaging out median figures from three separate statistical sources. There was wide variation between the three, and the industry norm resulted from amalgamation of these divergent medians.

Company A, through reference to the industry average for comparison, is clearly shown to be fighting for its very existence, and its present performance does not give rise to optimism regarding the ultimate outcome of that struggle. Concentrating on the causal ratios, the analyst sees that Company A's fixed assets

Table 43

	COMPANY A	COMPANY B	COMPANY C	INDUSTRY AVERAGE
Current ratio	1.14 times	2.11 times	3.27 times	2.10 times
Fixed-assets-to-net-worth	85.0%	60.0%	40.0%	61.4%
Current-liabilities-to-net-worth	70.0	45.0	26.0	63.3
Total-liabilities-to-net-worth	91.0	60.0	31.0	95.7
Inventory-to-working-capital	320.0	64.0	52.5	80.1
Trade-receivables-to-working-capital	330.0	76.0	59.3	94.6
Long-term-liabilities-to-working-capital	210.0	30.0	8.5	68.8
Miscellaneous-assets-to-net-worth	26.0	5.0	6.0	12.7
Net-profit-to-net-sales	(.50)	.75	1.00	.93
Net-profit-to-net-worth	(2.50)	7.50	12.50	11.8
Net-sales-to-fixed-assets	5.88 times	16.67 times	31.25 times	15.9 times
Net-sales-to-net-worth	5.00	10.00	12.50	11.7
Net-sales-to-working-capital	50.00	20.00	21.19	22.9
Net-sales-to-inventory	15.63	31.25	40.32	32.2
Collection period	24 days	14 days	10 days	14 days

are excessive with respect to invested capital, its net loss on sales is cause for deep concern, its undertrading (low net-sales-to-net-worth) is apparent, its sluggish inventory is a source of difficulty, as is its excessively high collection period, and its diversion of funds into miscellaneous assets is abnormally high. As direct by-products of these six causal factors, the company's working capital is deficient and highly dependent upon substandard inventory and receivables, and its overall survival is in grave doubt. Strong remedial measures must be applied, and applied quickly, to save Company A from extinction. On the other hand, Company B has achieved stability and has established a strong foundation for further growth and progress. Company C has developed enviable balance, and its freedom of action is exceedingly great.

With this background, let us note several typical management questions that each company might have need to consider. First, let us suppose that an improved property adjoining the company's plant has recently been listed for sale. Should the company purchase this property and integrate it with existing facilities at a total cost of $70,000? The answer in Company A's case must be a resounding "no." Let us study the reasons behind this decision in some detail. Company A's fixed-asset exposure is already too great for its net worth—85 percent. If A should assume a $70,000 expansion program in its present overtaxed condition, the result would be a fixed-assets burden that would place the company's existence in greater jeopardy. Although an exceedingly optimistic observer may ponder possible long-range advantages in purchasing contiguous property, concern for Company A's immediate survival dictates a negative answer to the proposal. Moreover, the need for enlarged facilities is not evident. Sales, for example, are insufficient for proper utilization of the existing plant. The analyst will note the net-sales-to-fixed-assets ratio of 5.88 times, as opposed to an industry standard of 15.9 times. This ratio demonstrates that present facilities (if they are roughly comparable to those of the average firm in the industry) should be ample to support physical production three or four times as great as present levels.

If no additional equity capital is available—and in the face of operating losses, low sales, and extreme lack of balance, capital would not be easy to attract from investors, whether they be principals of Company A or outsiders—what would happen to the working-capital and debt structure should Company A attempt this expansion by means of creditor support? If the company should try to finance this acquisition from present working capital, it would incur a deficit of $50,000. The concern's current ratio would decline to a level below 1-to-1. Through postponement of payment of creditors' bills, the company would invite lawsuits and other forms of collection pressure. The debt structure, already high, would rise well above net worth, threatening total loss of freedom in management action. Finally, Company A possesses no compensating advantages to offset the foregoing deficiencies. If, for instance, its inventory turned better or its receivables were not so slow and doubtful, some liquid funds would be generated to offset overexpansion. But the company is deficient in these areas and others, and no internal support can be found. Even given compensating advantages, Company A would have little basis for considering expansion under present circumstances.

Company B might well devote serious thought to acquiring the neighboring property. Company B's management must review several factors in reaching a decision. Have sales been climbing rapidly in the past two or three years, or have they tended to stabilize? If sales are gaining momentum, then the proposed addition to plant capacity can be viewed with some degree of favor. The analyst can see that Company B's utilization of present facilities has already reached industry average; net-sales-to-fixed-assets is 16.67 times per year as against an industry average of 15.9 times. Further, the company's fixed-assets-to-net-worth ratio is not excessive: 60 percent as opposed to an industry norm of 61.4 percent. True, an additional $70,000 investment in plant would push Company B above average, but not beyond the point of ultimate financial redemption. The company would feel strain, beyond doubt, but, all other factors remaining roughly equal, the strain should not be unbearable. The major determinants are, then, Company B's present rate of sales growth and the sales and profit increases projected on the basis of the proposed expansion.

What effect would Company B find on its working-capital and debt structure from the combination of fixed-asset expansion and future sales growth? The answer must be conditioned upon the type of financing that is available for the contemplated enlargement of the plant. If $30,000 could be secured through long-term mortgage borrowing, debt pressure would be heavy but not oppressive. Available sources indicate the industrywide long-term-liabilities-to-working-capital ratio is characteristically nearly 70 percent. Adding $30,000 to present long-term liabilities, Company B would have $60,000 in this category. The remaining $40,000 would come from working capital, which would be reduced to $60,000. Company B's long-term-liabilities-to-working-capital ratio, then, would move steeply upward to 100 percent, a high but tolerable proportion—tolerable, that is, if two or three other factors remained favorable (or became more so). The current ratio would drop to approximately 1.5, which temporarily would not be too dangerously far from the average pace reported by sources of industry figures.

In part, too, the decision to expand must be based on the relationship between the projected sales increase and the projected profit accruing from the expansion. While Company B's trading ratio is in good balance now—net-sales-to-net-worth being 10 times versus the industry norm of 11.7—a 50 percent sales increase would push Company B close to an overtrading position. Unless inventory turnover, receivables collection, or profit attainment can be markedly accelerated as compensating advantages, substantially greater sales volume will push debt upward and bring pressure on working capital. Thus the calculated rate of profit attainment on sales is quite important, for if sales do not increase enough to cover the additional fixed costs, the expansion will hurt rather than help financial balance. Yet an excessively rapid sales increase would subject B to considerable trading pressure.

Company B, in other words, is at the crossroads, and the timing of management's decision to expand is of paramount importance. Should management defer the addition to plant until the company's financial situation becomes somewhat more solid, or does it stand to gain an immediate competitive edge which might be lost through indecision? And is that advantage of sufficient long-range importance to justify the strain that will almost certainly follow? By understanding its present financial position and by becoming aware of changes that will result from its contemplated expansionary move, the management of Company B can arrive at informed answers to these questions. In the event that it does add to existing facilities, Company B will, temporarily at least, fall from a balanced condition to one of imbalance; but if, through reference to industry norms, management succeeds in restoring equilibrium, the company will then stand at a higher level.

Because of Company C's solid financial foundation, a proposal to purchase the adjoining property necessitates little soul-searching by management in reaching the conclusion that well-considered expansion is both supportable and wise. The need for added facilities is illustrated by the high degree of utilization of present fixed assets (31.25 times per year). The extent of plant expansion, however, must be predicated upon the amount of sales increase that Company C can realistically expect. Company C's investment in plant and equipment would not become particularly high through a $70,000 addition in this area, because the fixed-assets-to-net-worth ratio would rise to no more than 70 percent, not too far above the industry norm. The company has sufficient working capital to support the bulk of such expansion independently if it chooses, and it has ample room for long-term financing if this should prove more appealing. The profit picture is quite good, and Company C can withstand any temporary reduction in return during the period of construction or transition. Both receivables collection and inventory turnover are exceptionally good and will aid in supporting a diversion of funds. For that matter, if Company C's sales expansion should be based in part on the assumption of somewhat more marginal credit risks, it can afford selective acceptance of certain accounts that do not measure up to its present high standards. If profit can be generated through additional sales to more marginal customers, Company C stands to gain, for its past performance in controlling accounts indicates that its bad-debt losses are unlikely to reach even the industry average of 1.1 percent. The management of Company C can, then, undertake any expansion plans that it finds justifiable on the basis of projected sales with the assurance that the company's financial condition will support expansion up to the proposed $70,000.

Companies A, B, and C each have the same question to answer, and each must arrive at its decision on the basis of an understanding of its relative strengths and weaknesses, which are clearly disclosed by cause-and-effect ratio analysis. As we have noted and as we shall explore at length in the final chapter, accurate and complete industry statistics can—let us optimistically say, will—make the analyst's efforts considerably less difficult and his results more exact. Without totally reliable industry data, businessmen are not able at present to utilize ratio analysis with as great precision as would be desirable, and management—particularly management of the smaller firm—often encounters difficulty in attempting to project the net effect any major decision will have on its company's total financial balance and competitive position.

Referring again to the hypothetical Companies A, B, and C, let us consider another situation requiring evaluation and decision by management. In this case, one of the company's officers desires to borrow $15,000 to make a down payment on a farm and residential property. He proposes to repay the advance over a three-year period through salary deductions, to give the company a second mortgage, and to pay 5 percent interest. Overlooking the propriety and the policy aspects of this request, let us see if A, B, and C, respectively, can afford to accommodate this officer.

A preliminary matter to be considered is the location of such a transaction on the balance sheet. It could be shown as an amount "due from officers," or in view of the collateralized nature of the proposed arrangement, it might be termed an "investment" or even a "mortgage receivable." Under any of these headings, it would be classified as a miscellaneous asset.

How, then, does Company A shape up with respect to the industry average for the miscellaneous-assets-to-net-worth ratio? It currently has a $52,000 exposure in this type of asset, roughly 26 percent of its net worth and double the proportion held by the average firm, according to industry figures. To add $15,000 in this area would cause one-third of the company's total equity capital to be tied up in miscellaneous assets, many of which have little or no direct relevance to the corporate purpose, the processing of meat. Suppose that analysis of the makeup of Company A's present $52,000 miscellaneous-assets figure should disclose the breakdown shown in Table 44. From these figures the analyst can see that Company A has been quite generous in its financial support of personal projects of certain individuals associated with the organization. Precedent has been set, but this does not con-

Table 44

Due from officers, directors, employees	$36,000
Investment in affiliated company	10,000
Prepaid and deferred	6,000
	$52,000

firm the wisdom of earlier advances or the financial merit of the present proposal. A review of the miscellaneous-assets-to-net-worth ratio—coupled with previous knowledge of A's limited working capital, heavy debt structure, and operating losses—clearly indicates that the company's answer should be a polite but firm "no" to the overtures of its officer for this $15,000 loan. This transaction would, for one thing, virtually wipe out the company's working capital. With obvious difficulty in attempting to meet suppliers' terms now, Company A can ill afford any further drain, which might well bring total ruin. Those who feel that the loan request in this example is highly unlikely have probably reviewed very few financial statements of marginal concerns. There are innumerable cases of heavy borrowing from company resources on the part of executives, the examples often coming from companies operating with deficit net worth. In such situations, creditors must share the blame with the owners, for their tolerance and continued unquestioning credit extension encourages and perpetuates this practice. The executives often realize that the future of their company is limited, but as long as suppliers permit extension of high salaries and condone "tapping the till" while they await payment, little other than conscience will dissuade them from continuing these practices. At this late stage, creditors stand to lose more than the owners themselves.

Neither Company B nor Company C evidences a disproportionate ratio of miscellaneous assets to net worth, nor is either plagued by the acute financial stress of Company A. The financial positions of both concerns could support the proposed advance (although the effect of this move would be more perceptible to B), and hence for both B and C the decision rests on ethical grounds—or even considerations of company morale—which fall outside the financial area in the realm of basic personnel policy.

Let us examine one more major question requiring top management decision. Each of the three companies has storage space available and is soliciting more contract business as a means of boosting sales. Contract arrangements will call for the maintenance of approximately $40,000 more in inventory to support an additional $500,000 in sales because the contract customer has agreed to take one year's requirements from the company in return for the privilege of ordering out quantities of a special-order product (in this case, particular cuts of meat) as needed over a period of 12 months.

Let us now study the manner in which Company A should approach this proposal, which is based upon three assumptions: (1) Annual sales would increase $500,000, (2) inventory exposure would rise on the average $40,000, and (3) the selling price would be constant.

If Company A should accept this potential business, it must expect to encounter a number of consequences at the outset. Its critically low net-sales-to-inventory ratio, already one of A's prime problems, would suffer further reduction to approximately 14.5 times per year by addition of slow-moving contract inventory. If the analyst assumes that the new contract buyers represent sound credit risks who can and will pay within 10 days, the addition of $500,000 volume of 10-day accounts would exert a beneficial influence on the collection-period ratio, which would decline to 19 days. This lower collection period, however, would still be far too high and, further, would tend to camouflage persisting credit-and-collections weaknesses which definitely require correction. Net-sales-to-fixed-assets would improve; the added volume would obviously mean greater and more efficient utilization of existing plant and machinery. Net-sales-to-net-worth would also improve, as Company A is now undertrading. Since the $40,000 inventory exposure would be matched by a comparable rise of roughly $40,000 in accounts payable, the net effect on the current ratio would be a decline below the present critical level. Working capital would sustain acute stress from exceedingly rapid turnover; the impact of new sales would produce a rate of 75 times per year, a pace that may be beyond Company A's ability to support. (Although a substantial number of companies with deficit working capital are able to discount, these concerns are bolstered by compensating advantages not enjoyed by Company A.) The added $40,000 current debt would place Company A in a highly vulnerable current-liabilities-to-net-worth position—roughly 90 percent—while total-debt-to-net-worth would push substantially beyond 100 percent. Although the actual dollar amount of working capital would be virtually unchanged, the addition of $40,000 in inventory would raise the ratio of inventory to working capital to a staggering 520 percent. Receivables-to-working-capital would also rise, probably at about the same rate as inventory, because the contract sales would be on a credit rather than a cash basis.

If Company A were able to survive these initial developments, it might derive two long-range benefits.

- Net-profit-to-net-sales might improve to breakeven level or above. This gain might be offset to the extent that the working-capital pinch might cause the loss of purchase discounts.
- Net-profit-to-net-worth would, of course, benefit if profits were earned or losses reduced.

While management might be greatly tempted to take on this volume, it would be risking financial suicide in the process. The company needs the sales and it needs the profit, but to enjoy these rewards it must first put its house in order, which means immediate concentration on the three major areas of substandard performance—inventory, accounts receivable, and miscellaneous assets. If, however, Company A can bring about substantial correction of its deficiencies prior to the assumption of the proposed contract business, it may well be able to absorb this additional sales volume (and attendant inventory pressure) without undue strain. Through concentrated remedial effort, Company A can release anywhere from $50,000 to $100,000 of frozen funds to boost working capital and to reduce debt. The release of these funds would give Company A the flexibility it so sorely needs to take advantage of enticing opportunities such as this one. If the company should attempt to expand without taking action to correct its three critical weaknesses, it may have occasion to review this move in the bankruptcy courts.

Because of Company B's considerably more stable financial position, it can entertain the option of accepting this contract business with far less trepidation than Company A experienced. Undertaking this proposal would involve the following developments for B.

■ The net-sales-to-net-worth ratio would increase to 12.5 but would remain within the bounds of normality.

■ The net-sales-to-fixed-assets ratio would rise to 20.82, or only slightly above industry average.

■ The net-sales-to-inventory ratio would decline to 24 times per year, in contrast with today's 31.25 times. Company B's performance in this area would become slightly substandard, for normal industry expectancy is 32.2 times per year.

■ Collection period would decline to 13 days, if the assumption can be made that the new accounts would pay within ten days from date of billing.

■ The net-profit-to-net-sales ratio would probably rise fractionally, but without other data this supposition cannot be confirmed.

■ The miscellaneous-assets-to-net-worth ratio would be unaffected except as net worth might be increased by additional retained profit.

Of the six primary ratios, then, only inventory turnover would be adversely affected, and the positive elements would more than compensate for the single negative aspect of the proposed move. The probable secondary effects of the contemplated contract arrangement for Company B are as follows:

■ Company B's current ratio would drop initially to approximately 1.75—anathema to the unswerving disciple of the 2-to-1 yardstick—but still not dangerously below industry levels.

■ Working-capital turnover (net-sales-to-working-capital) might reflect some strain in rising to 25 times per year, but that level would not be beyond reasonable proportions.

■ Company B's current debt might rise to a maximum of 65 percent and total debt to 80 percent, both well within industry norm.

■ Inventory-to-working-capital would rise above 100 percent but would remain in the normal range.

■ Receivables-to-working-capital would rise to 90 percent (if the analyst assumes that ten-day accounts are added). This is roughly average for the industry.

The positive features clearly predominate in this case, and since neither of the anticipated unfavorable changes foretells major difficulty, Company B can pursue this new business with enthusiasm.

If Company B can operate, and plan for the future, with confidence in continued financial balance, how much more easily can Company C do so! The only factor requiring detailed study by the management of Company C is the probable need for additional plant or equipment if substantial enlargement of present sales volume should be undertaken. While we assumed at the outset that all three companies had ample storage space, C's rate of utilization of plant and equipment is evidently approaching the maximum (with a net-sales-to-fixed-assets ratio of 31.25 times per year), unless a significant proportion of its fixed assets are leased. However, C's enviable position of high liquidity and low debt would make normal fixed-asset expansion easily assimilable.

Other major policy moves—including such matters as reducing or raising prices, shortening or lengthening selling terms, investing in a subsidiary, and attracting equity capital through selling common or preferred stock—and the projected effects of such moves can, likewise, be clearly understood through the application of cause-and-effect ratio analysis.

5   Guidelines for Applying the Cause-and-Effect Technique

Certain common misconceptions regarding ratio analysis must be dispelled before the analyst can use the cause-and-effect method successfully. Ten cardinal points are commended to the individual who wishes to master the technique of cause-and-effect ratio analysis.

- Ignore isolated figures; financial balance is relative.
- Strive for decimal accuracy.
- Compare likes; ratios of a company under study must be related to averages for the line of business in which the particular concern is engaged.
- Relate individual averages to industry norms of the same, or nearest available, year.
- Study any substantial deviation from normal—either high or low.
- Avoid concentration on astronomically high percentages or spectacular variances; the significant ratios may be less sensational in appearance.
- Remember that a ratio measures both components.
- Recognize the seasonal factor and make appropriate allowance for it.
- Watch for trends.
- Be alert to compensating advantages.

Let us examine each of these points in some detail.

The first rule in ratio analysis is that *isolated figures mean nothing*. What would the owner of the XYZ Company—or the credit manager of a supplier to the XYZ Company—benefit from knowing that XYZ's inventory in 1970 was $150,000? Or that in 1971 it rose to $250,000? Or that in 1972 it increased further, approaching $350,000? What conclusions could he reach? And what significance should management attach to the fact that the company's receivables were $175,000 in 1970, $190,000 in 1971, and $260,000 in 1972? Any decisions reached on the basis of such isolated figures are in the realm of sheer speculation—not only groundless but dangerous—for nothing on a financial statement stands alone. To add meaning to these figures, the analyst must relate them in a logical, causal pattern to other significant data. Through ratio analysis, management can measure and interpret changes, thus establishing a foundation for sound decisions.

Dollars invested in inventory is naturally of interest to the analyst of the XYZ Company's statement, but to determine if either the amount or the trend is justified, this commitment must be considered in the light of other factors. Turnover is of primary interest. In other words, is inventory moving? Is there an accumulation of slow-turning items which may be subject to physical deterioration, obsolescence, or change in style or price? Fundamentally, is the XYZ Company an efficient merchandiser? The answers to these questions are indicated by relating inventory to net sales. Suppose that the analyst finds that the XYZ Company's sales, inventory, and net-sales-to-inventory ratio for the period 1970–1972 are those shown in Table 45. The trend of the net-sales-to-inventory ratio indicates, by any standard of measurement, a favorable development in inventory turnover and refutes any negative opinion derived from the study of inventory figures alone. Relating inventory figures to other key data will answer

Table 45

	SALES	INVENTORY	NET-SALES-TO-INVENTORY
1970	$ 750,000	$150,000	5.0 times
1971	1,500,000	250,000	6.0
1972	2,275,000	350,000	6.5

Table 46

CURRENT ASSETS	1970	1971	1972
Cash	$ 40,000	$ 50,000	$ 50,000
Accounts receivable	175,000	190,000	260,000
Inventory	150,000	250,000	350,000
Total current	$365,000	$490,000	$660,000
CURRENT LIABILITIES			
Notes payable—bank	$ 30,000	$ 20,000	$ 20,000
Accounts payable	120,000	140,000	180,000
Accruals	15,000	10,000	10,000
Federal income tax	20,000	30,000	40,000
Total current	$185,000	$200,000	$250,000
Working capital	$180,000	$290,000	$410,000

a second important question: is the XYZ Company's bill-paying
capacity threatened by the rapid rise in this one asset item? Remember that inventory has increased substantially in the period
1970–1972; but the inventory figures, standing alone, do not resolve the question. If, however, the analyst relates these figures
directly to working capital (by means of the inventory-to-working-capital ratio) or traces their effect on working capital
(through the current ratio), then conjecture is eliminated and
real meaning emerges. Assume that XYZ's figures for current assets and current liabilities shaped up for 1970, 1971, and 1972
as shown in Table 46. Reduced to ratio form, these figures indicate the inventory-to-working-capital and current ratio trends
shown in Table 47. The stable picture of inventory-to-working-
capital, made apparent through elementary application of the
ratio technique, again demonstrates that a conclusion hastily
drawn from inventory figures alone is misleading. The current
ratio, for the three years under study, actually shows improvement. Thus the analyst sees that inventory accumulation has had

Table 47

	INVENTORY-TO-WORKING-CAPITAL	CURRENT RATIO
1970	83.3%	1.97 times
1971	86.2	2.45
1972	85.4	2.64

no detrimental effect on the XYZ Company's liquidity or on its ability to meet its obligations. On the contrary, 1972's inventory, as seen in relation to other financial-statement items, is healthier than 1970's or 1971's. This fact is not, however, at all apparent from a study of the balance-sheet dollars-and-cents figures for inventory.

Let us examine for a moment the XYZ Company's accounts receivable to see what changes have actually taken place in this area. Can the analyst logically assume from the rise in receivables that the company's credit department has let down its guard and is accepting questionable credit risks and courting potential bad-debt losses? Before making any such assessment, the analyst must relate receivables to sales, to the XYZ Company's selling terms, and to industry averages in order to place this item in perspective. By computing the collection-period ratio, the analyst establishes the following trend:

1970	85 days
1971	46
1972	42

He sees that the receivables picture has improved substantially during the past two years, collection period having been cut in half during that time. If the XYZ Company's selling terms of 1 percent 10th prox have remained constant during the period, then its receivables are considerably more collectible than they were in 1970 or even in 1971. Total receivables must, finally, be related to working capital to determine whether the rising exposure in this asset has tended to restrict the company's ability to meet trade or other current obligations. This ratio shows:

1970	97.2%
1971	65.5
1972	63.4

Obviously, working capital has become considerably less dependent on receivables in each of the years following the dangerous receivables exposure of 1970. While study of the receivables figures alone suggests definite problems in this area, rudimentary ratio analysis indicates that the XYZ Company is entitled to a vote of confidence for its credit-and-collections performance.

We turn now to the second cardinal point: *decimal accuracy is a must.* An analyst who is unsure of the proper location of the decimal point should either look for a new vocation or hire an assistant who has mastered this field of study. What a difference the location of the decimal makes! If the industry average for fixed-assets-to-net-worth were 73.2 percent and correct calculation of a particular company's ratio showed 66.7 percent, an individual would have no difficulty in correctly appraising the company's performance as being very close to normal in this particular area. If, however, the analyst had come up with an answer of 667 percent, he would undoubtedly be alarmed by the apparently heavy exposure and would likely place the blame for any of the company's problems squarely on capital goods. If, on the other hand, his arithmetic showed only 6.67 percent, he would surely express amazement at the company's capacity to generate sales of such magnitude on such a modest investment in productive assets; or he might well conclude that the company is leasing all of its property and would approach his analysis based largely on that conclusion.

A factor contributing to decimal confusion is the present practice of expressing certain ratios in "times" and the others (with the exception of collection period) in "percent." For example, we refer to a company's current ratio as being 2-to-1, 3-to-1, or 3.2-to-1. This means that current assets are 2 times as great as current liabilities, 3 times as great, or 3.2 times as great. Inventory turnover (net-sales-to-inventory) is likewise recorded as 8.7 times or 11.3 times. Yet, when we refer to profit-to-sales or debt-to-net-worth, we express these ratios as 2.86 percent or 83.1 percent. Lack of uniformity is not a major problem to an experienced analyst, but it does create decimal problems for the beginner. This difficulty might be alleviated in large measure by expressing in percent all ratios except the collection period, which is most conveniently shown in "days." But, since the business community remains—for the most part—dependent upon currently published averages for industry comparison, analysts must for the present continue to work with ratios expressed in the traditional fashion while recognizing the advantages of uniformity in this area.

Turning now to the third important consideration in the application of ratio analysis, the analyst must always remember to *compare likes*. He must avoid reliance on rule-of-thumb values for assessing individual ratios. There is no "typical American business" against which all other businesses can be measured. Neither can a strictly typical or average retail bakery, or a typical hardware manufacturer, or a typical paper wholesaler be found. Certain norms, however, can be determined for each line of business activity (although industry averages are subject to considerable refinement, as we shall see in Chapter 7).

We have previously noted several sources of industry statistics which, in the aggregate, evidence an awareness of the need for

1. Matching the ratios of a particular company to norms for its line of business activity.

2. Comparing the individual concern's figures with those of companies of roughly the same size.

3. Recognizing geographical peculiarities and the corresponding different problems for local, regional, and national concerns.

4. Allowing for varying degrees of diversification, and compiling figures for dual or multiple lines.

5. Developing operating-statement information to pinpoint any deviations from average in operating expenses and profit attainment.

These factors are all valid and exceedingly important in arriving at meaningful conclusions with respect to the present financial position of the individual company and to the direction the concern is taking. Significant progress has been made over the years in supplying such data for analytical purposes, but much more remains to be done. The 2-to-1 current ratio clearly cannot have general applicability for any and every business, regardless of line. And, certainly, no company should blindly accept the 2-to-1 standard as a guide for its own operation. In 1970, for instance, a 1.52 current ratio was typical for manufacturers of dairy products, whereas 3.39 was average for hardware manufac-

Table 48

INDUSTRY	COLLECTION PERIOD
Meat packers	13 days
Vegetable oils	19
Candy and confectioners' supplies	24
Flavoring extracts and syrups	33
Wines, distilled liquors, and liqueurs	38
Household electrical appliances	42
Advertising displays and devices	49
Perfumes and cosmetics	55
Hats	59
Fertilizers	62

© 1971 Robert Morris Associates

turers, according to Dun & Bradstreet. Rules of thumb applied to other ratios should be similarly scrutinized or, better, ignored altogether.

Recognizing that the problems and pressures of each line of business activity are unique, an analyst of an individual concern's financial statement must make every effort to match its particular ratios with those of firms most closely related to it. The importance of measuring the ratios of a particular concern against averages taken from the financial reports of companies in its line of activity cannot be overemphasized. To illustrate the wide disparity between median averages of different industries, let us observe selected manufacturers' collection-period figures (in days) for the year 1970, as shown in Table 48. Consider, also, fixed-assets-to-net-worth for manufacturers (1970), expressed as percentages and shown in Table 49. Median averages for the other financial ratios show a similar disparity between industries, not only in manufacturing, but in the wholesale and retail trades as well. Because such variables as business size, age, and location definitely influence a company's financial balance, they also should be accorded recognition in the compilation of industry averages; figures reflecting these variables can probably be developed best under the auspices of trade associations. In Chapter 7 we shall observe the significance of several key variables; specific means of providing accurate, meaningful industry figures are also presented in later pages.

Next, we must consider the need to *relate individual averages to industry norms of the same, or nearest available, year.* In analyzing a company's financial statement for December 31, 1971, the analyst cannot hope for accuracy if he compares that concern's ratios against those of its industry for 1964. The American economy is hardly static. The dollar amount of the gross national product changes from year to year; the unemployment rate is subject to movement; housing starts do not remain constant. The conditions, the operations, and the attainment within each industry likewise undergo alteration with time; these constant changes render the chronological matching of industry and individual company ratios a necessity. Certain lines of business, moreover, are subject to rather severe fluctuations from one year to the next as a result of weather conditions, government policy, or labor agreements.

Consider Table 50, which shows the six-year trend in five typical industries, chosen at random, for the period 1965–1970. Let us suppose that the XYZ Company is a manufacturer of office and store fixtures and that we are analyzing its 1969 statement. In the event that we found its net profit return on sales to be 1.30 percent, our conclusions would be markedly different if we referred to 1965 industry figures rather than those for 1969. In 1965, according to Dun & Bradstreet, the industry showed a 1.26

Table 49

INDUSTRY	FIXED-ASSETS-TO-NET-WORTH
Fur goods	4.0%
Men's and boys' work clothing	15.7
Mattresses and bedsprings	24.1
Millwork	36.0
Hosiery	47.7
Screw machine products	55.2
Industrial chemicals	63.7
Malt liquors	75.0

Source: Dun & Bradstreet

percent average, and the XYZ Company was operating at a perfectly normal level of income—as compared to 1965 averages. Yet when we relate its 1.30 percent profit-to-sales ratio to the industry average of 3.07 percent for the year 1969, its performance appears woefully deficient by contrast. The XYZ statement reflected 1969 conditions, and to furnish an accurate comparison, the analyst needs to measure the attainments of the company under study against industry results for the same period.

As another example, the current ratio for petroleum refiners was 1.43 in 1965, or 33 percent above the 1.09 attainment in 1970. Clearly, if an analyst attempted to measure a company's 1970 ratio against 1965 industry figures, his conclusions would prove faulty because of significant changes within this particular industry. For one final illustration of change wrought by time, refer

Table 50

YEAR	CURRENT RATIO	NET-PROFIT-TO-NET-SALES	TOTAL-LIABILITIES-TO-NET-WORTH
	OFFICE AND STORE FIXTURES		
1965	1.98 times	1.26%	85.8%
1966	2.24	2.07	105.1
1967	2.23	2.44	103.6
1968	2.46	2.98	160.0
1969	2.08	3.07	123.0
1970	2.51	2.06	100.1
	PETROLEUM REFINING		
1965	1.43 times	5.31%	25.0%
1966	1.37	4.63	46.7
1967	1.20	5.05	30.5
1968	1.35	4.13	38.8
1969	1.14	3.76	23.6
1970	1.09	3.41	35.2
	PAPERBOARD CONTAINERS AND BOXES		
1965	2.22 times	3.33%	96.1%
1966	2.08	4.03	82.6
1967	2.38	3.71	79.4
1968	2.45	2.45	78.3
1969	2.43	3.36	83.4
1970	2.90	2.61	87.0

Source: Dun & Bradstreet

again to figures for petroleum refiners. The total-liabilities-to-net-worth ratio for 1966 was twice that for the 1969 closing.

Because of the significance of the time factor, which brings frequent and rapid change in a dynamic industry, timely industry data is an extremely important element in the development of precise information through ratio analysis. At the present time, published averages appear some eight to twelve months after December 31 closing, and the analyst has reason to question the total applicability of 1970 industry ratios to a concern's June 30, 1972, figures. But we note hopefully that today, through the confidence of their members, trade associations are in a position to provide current, accurate, representative statistics.

Now let us turn to the rule that the analyst must *study any deviation from normal—either high or low.* Many amateur analysts try to simplify their understanding of ratios by establishing in their minds a pattern of uniformity—that a higher-than-average showing in certain ratios is invariably good or that a low ratio has universal merit in other cases. Such oversimplification, however, can lead to serious errors in analysis. Extreme variance from average must always be subjected to scrutiny, although the analyst must exercise care to avoid the assumption that ratios of spectacular magnitude are necessarily causal. In order to test the adequacy of a particular ratio, that ratio must be placed within the financial framework of the company under consideration through reference to other key measures. In some instances (for example, net-sales-to-inventory) a higher-than-average ratio is *generally* good; in other cases (current-liabilities-to-net-worth, for example), lower than average is *usually* a favorable sign; and for some (such as net-sales-to-net-worth), a substantial deviation in either direction indicates a potential or actual problem. The qualifications that must be included in any general prescription of this nature render such an effort impractical, at best. The point to be remembered is that *any* significant deviation from industry average must be studied in detail.

A particularly apropos incident involved one of my students and his approach to a true-and-false examination. This student sat for fully half the time allotted for the test intently studying the questions, but made no visible motions toward indicating any answers. Finally, after much consternation, he came to the instructor's desk to complain that the examination was grossly unfair because there was no "pattern" that he could detect. On being asked to amplify on the comment, he explained, "There is always a pattern. Some professors put three 'trues' in a row, then a 'false,' while others may put two 'falses,' then two 'trues,' or some other such combination. But there is something wrong with your system." I suggested to this student that if he spent as much time considering the merits of each question as he did in trying to detect an underlying pattern, he would probably score well on the examination. Although complete cause-and-effect ratio analysis yields a very definite picture of a company's financial structure (in the same way that an examination indicates much about an individual's motivation, intelligence, and preparation), no simple, predetermined, "higher-or-lower" pattern can be used to advantage by the analyst. Each ratio must be thoroughly scrutinized and related not only to industry averages but to the company's particular financial structure. Ratio analysis is not designed to substitute for judgment but to aid it.

Next, let us focus our attention on the admonition to *avoid being misled by astronomically high figures*. Figures of great magnitude tend to distract the beginning analyst, who occasionally forgets the basic principles of the cause-and-effect technique. As an illustration, let us turn to Table 51 and scan rough financial-statement figures for the mythical XYZ Company for the year ending December 31, 1971. Certain of these figures, converted to five selected ratios, and the industry averages for these ratios

Table 51

Cash	$ 10,000	Notes payable—bank	$ 40,000
Accounts receivable	150,000	Accounts payable	290,000
Inventory	150,000	Taxes	5,000
Other current	40,000	Other current	5,000
Total current	$ 350,000	Total current	$340,000
Fixed assets	$ 140,000	Long-term liabilities	$ 60,000
Other noncurrent	10,000	Net worth	100,000
Total assets	$ 500,000	Total	$500,000
Net sales	$1,200,000	Net profit	$ 15,000

Table 52

	XYZ COMPANY	INDUSTRY AVERAGE
Current-assets-to-current- liabilities	1.03 times	2.54 times
Fixed-assets-to-net-worth	140.0%	39.7%
Net-sales-to-net-worth	12.0 times	3.28 times
Net-sales-to-inventory	8.0	8.2
Inventory-to-working-capital	1,500.0%	70.3%

are shown in Table 52. Immediately upon seeing the staggeringly high percentage for inventory-to-working-capital, the impulsive analyst will sit bolt upright and sagely conclude that inventory is "way out of line" and that this is the XYZ Company's problem beyond a doubt. A 1,500 percent figure naturally astounds many beginning analysts and portrays to them a condition that screams for attention and for remedy. It follows from such faulty analysis that inventory is completely worthless and that the XYZ Company must immediately institute drastic controls to bring this flagrant violator to terms.

But a calmer and more experienced analyst would recognize that this ratio is a secondary or resultant one and not a cause unto itself. Also, the experienced analyst would quickly detect that inventory turnover (net-sales-to-inventory) is the only ratio of the three primary ratios reviewed that is really in balance. He would recognize that inventory is the one item measured here that meets the test of quality; it does represent salable merchandise and is under adequate control. The able analyst concentrates upon cause and would, without hesitation, place the blame squarely where it belongs—on overtrading and on excessive fixed assets. If overtrading were brought under control, either through additional capital investment or through more selective and profit-minded selling—which would reduce sales and perhaps even increase profit—then working capital would benefit greatly. And if fixed-asset investment were reduced through any of a variety of methods (such as sale and leaseback or outright disposal of surplus, nonproductive items) or if long-term borrowing were increased, working capital would gain appreciably. A substantial addition to working capital is needed to bring this ratio within reasonable limits, for working capital, and not inventory, is the XYZ Company's problem. But any figure which stands out as prominently as 1,500 percent tends to throw the beginning analyst off course; it holds his attention so much that he forgets the overreaching importance of cause and effect. In this case, the company's problems stem from excessive net-sales-to-net-worth and from inordinate fixed-assets-to-net-worth; the working-capital squeeze is a product of these two causes. Inventory is a neutral factor and is hardly deserving of the condemnation indicated by a glance at the misleading 1,500 percent ratio.

The seventh cardinal point is that *a ratio measures both sides of the fraction*. Ratios are computed by simple long division. If, for example, the analyst is to determine the fixed-assets-to-net-worth ratio for the XYZ Company, he divides the concern's fixed assets (of, say, $120,000) by its net worth (assumed to be $160,000). The result is expressed as 75 percent. Let us suppose in this case that for the XYZ Company's industry the median average is only 34.2 percent. XYZ's present percentage accordingly appears quite high, and a need for further study is indicated. Many beginning analysts would immediately decide that fixed assets are at fault, whereas this ratio may instead point out a deficiency in net worth. Or, conceivably, the ratio may show that both halves of the fraction contribute to the distorted percentage—that not only are fixed assets high but also net worth is inadequate. One cannot automatically conclude that the top half of the fraction is necessarily the guilty party whenever a ratio reflects a serious deviation from industry average. Because a single ratio demonstrates only the relationship between two elements and does not, in most cases, point to the true adequacy of either component, each key item on the balance sheet and profit-and-loss statement is, whenever practicable, tested not just once, but two or three or more times. Only through multiple measurement can the analyst establish the strength of a particular element within the company's financial framework.

Let us assume that in calculating key ratios relating to fixed assets and to net worth, the analyst has derived the figures shown in Table 53. Obviously, the XYZ Company's net worth is quite deficient relative to its debt structure (current-liabilities-to-net-worth, total-liabilities-to-net-worth) and by comparison with nor-mal for its industry. Moreover, the company is overtrading; it is attempting to transact nearly double the industry's average sales volume on each dollar of invested capital. Since the XYZ Company's net-profit-to-net-sales ratio is exactly industry aver-age, the very high (18 percent) return on net worth again points to a relatively low capital investment. On the other hand, the industry average for net-sales-to-fixed-assets indicates that the XYZ Company's utilization of plant and equipment is reasonably close to par. So, through multiple measurement, the analyst has determined the falsity of any hasty conclusion that fixed assets are excessive. Net worth, instead, is responsible for the XYZ Com-pany's unfavorable showing in this ratio.

Let us explore the idea of multiple measurement a bit further. Suppose that in calculating the ABC Company's inventory-to-working-capital ratio, the analyst finds $300,000 in inventory against working capital of $250,000 (current assets of $700,000 less $450,000 in current liabilities)—a ratio of 120 percent. The industry average is 53.3 percent. The discrepancy indicates that the ABC Company has problems in this area. Other key ratios dealing with these components, inventory and working capital, are shown in Table 54. These figures demonstrate that the placing of blame on the ABC Company's inventory would be premature and in error. All three of the ratios relating to working capital clearly show its deficiency, whereas the primary measurement of inventory portrays a better-than-average turnover and reflects favorably on both inventory and the company's merchandising skill. Working capital, and not inventory, is the cause of distortion in this case.

Thus we have seen that both components are tested by each ratio and that only through total analysis—reference to all 15 ratios—can the strength of each element be known.

Now let us consider the important point that the analyst should *make appropriate allowance for the seasonal factor.* Some industries are subject to very marked seasonal influence. Toy manufacturers, for instance, can expect their major sales to be concentrated in the period preceding the Christmas season. Power mowers and other gardening tools move according to sea-

Table 53

	XYZ COMPANY	INDUSTRY AVERAGE
Fixed-assets-to-net-worth	75.0%	34.2%
Current-liabilities-to-net-worth	81.3	39.6
Total-liabilities-to-net-worth	93.8	48.2
Net-profit-to-net-sales	2.0	2.0
Net-profit-to-net-worth	18.0	10.0
Net-sales-to-net-worth	9.0 times	5.0 times
Net-sales-to-fixed-assets	12.0	14.6

sonal demand. Canners of fruits and vegetables are subject to a different type of seasonal pressure; they are obliged to put up their pack at harvest time but meet a comparatively steady demand throughout the year.

Many companies have successfully countered such seasonal irregularities through diversification, the addition of new lines to their product mixes to fill otherwise slack periods. Power-mower manufacturers, for instance, have popularized the snow blower, which has yielded them more uniform income patterns. Other firms have resorted to varying types of off-season discounts to encourage year-round buying of highly seasonal products. For an item in which consumer interest runs only from spring through late summer, a manufacturer might offer a 4 percent special discount for November purchase and payment, 3 percent for December, 2 percent for January, and 1 percent for February in an effort to move his product and receive prompt payment. Manufacturers of candy boxes must make provision for special

Table 54

	ABC COMPANY	INDUSTRY AVERAGE
Long-term-debt-to-working-capital	60.0%	26.7%
Current-assets-to-current-liabilities	1.56 times	2.67 times
Net-sales-to-working-capital	7.2	2.7
Net-sales-to-inventory	6.0	5.0

seasons—such as Valentine's Day, Easter, Mother's Day, and Christmas—and supplement their regular product lines accordingly. Since these concerns must anticipate the need for heart-shaped boxes long before February 14 and because set-up boxes require extra warehousing and storage space, these manufacturers may try to relieve themselves of this burden and the attendant expense by offering their customers dating arrangements—the privilege of paying for the boxes in January or February if shipment can be made in October. Toy manufacturers also rely heavily on extended datings as a means of moving their products, leveling off their own production loads, and insuring that the shelves and counters of the retail stores are loaded to meet buyers' demands when the Christmas season arrives.

The pattern in many industries shows gradual seasonal variations, which are generally predictable. Barring extremely unusual weather, a brewer can count on a reasonably consistent pattern for his beer sales, month by month, year in and year out, with the heaviest concentration during hot weather. On the other hand, companies in many industries encounter very modest fluctuations, or none at all, throughout the year. Razor-blade sales are relatively stable, as are the sales of detergents.

What does the seasonal influence mean to the analyst? Let us find the answer through a brief examination of the XYZ Com-

Table 55

January	$ 100,000
February	120,000
March	200,000
April	350,000
May	510,000
June	370,000
July	160,000
August	125,000
September	100,000
October	70,000
November	70,000
December	80,000
Total	$2,255,000
Average monthly sales	$ 187,500

pany, whose sales take the pattern shown in Table 55. We shall assume that the XYZ Company closes its books on April 30. Inventory at that time might well be as much as $800,000 or $900,000 in anticipation of peak sales during May and June. Basing the company's net-sales-to-inventory ratio on the figure $850,000, the analyst would conclude that inventory turned only some 2.5 times per year, whereas industry average might be 8.7 times annually. The analyst who failed to take the seasonal influence into consideration would then label the XYZ Company a poor merchandiser with an extremely dangerous inventory exposure. Or at May 31, receivables for the XYZ Company could very well be $700,000 or more on net 30-day terms. On annual sales of $2,255,000 (assumed to be entirely on credit), credit-sales-per-day would be $6,178. Applying this figure to $700,000 receivables, the analyst would arrive at a collection-period ratio of more than 113 days. Finding the industry average to be 36 days, the analyst who overlooked the seasonal factor could, logically enough, say, "The XYZ Company's receivables are in terrible shape, and the books must be loaded with bad debts." Had the XYZ Company, instead, brought its auditors in for a November 30 closing, the analyst might very well have found:

Accounts receivable	$ 98,000
Inventory	150,000

These figures related to sales would show:

Inventory turnover	15 times
Collection period	16 days

Conclusions based upon study of April or May statements would be diametrically opposed to those derived from the review of November figures.

To facilitate compilation and comparison of financial data, among other reasons, the accounting profession has advocated the adoption of natural or fiscal year closings that coincide with the end of a company's peak season in place of the arbitrary calendar year closing at December 31. By so doing, seasonal businesses would show their most liquid condition, and the profit or loss at that date would be more indicative of their true attainments for the year than are figures taken in the midst of their most active periods. Moreover, with stock and production demands at a minimum, physical count is expedited. Receivables and payables are, likewise, more easily verified when they are at or near the low point for the year.

Failure to allow for the effects of year-end closing date in the analysis of seasonal industries is one of the major weaknesses of presently published ratios. Both of the major reporting services compile their figures from statements of companies who close their books at or near December 31 of each year. But through the application of modern data processing methods, trade associations can now publish figures for their respective industries four times annually to reflect the different closing dates of companies within the industries. Among seasonal industries in particular, the need for more complete, precise data is indeed great.

The ninth rule for the analyst to bear in mind is that *trend is exceedingly important.* The analyst must direct particular attention to the financial trend of the business, as reflected in the 15 ratios. If a year-by-year study of the company showed a continuing or increasing deviation of one or more of the primary ratios, the analyst would have reason to conclude that at least one of the following conditions existed:

1. Management was unaware of the nature of its problem.
2. Management did not know how to cope with its difficulty; either it had taken no steps to restore financial balance, or measures which it had taken had proved ineffectual.
3. Management lacked either the power or the resources to check and reverse the trend.
4. Management did not have sufficient staff to carry out its good intentions.
5. External conditions, beyond the control of management, precluded the effectiveness of corrective measures.

If, on the other hand, a trend reflects steady improvement in key ratios which were once seriously deficient, any present distortion must be viewed in that light. And should long-term

Table 56

YEAR	XYZ COMPANY	INDUSTRY AVERAGE
	FIXED-ASSETS-TO-NET-WORTH	
1968	52.1%	34.9%
1969	66.5	33.5
1970	83.7	31.8
1971	104.8	32.3
1972	121.6	30.4
	COLLECTION PERIOD	
1968	48 days	20 days
1969	53	20
1970	39	27
1971	36	32
1972	33	34
	TOTAL-DEBT-TO-NET-WORTH	
1968	148.6%	86.0%
1969	171.3	73.0
1970	159.8	92.6
1971	156.4	86.3
1972	160.3	91.2

developments point to the addition of competitive advantages, management is due for commendation, and the analyst may view temporary deviations in other areas with relative equanimity.

Let us observe the five-year trends of a few ratios of the hypothetical XYZ Company and compare them with industry averages, as shown in Table 56. With regard to the fixed-assets-to-net-worth ratio, the XYZ Company's position warranted the attention of management as early as 1968, for at that time the deviation from normal was roughly 50 percent. By 1969 reduction or limitation of fixed-asset investment definitely should have found a priority position in management's plans for the coming year. The analyst can see from only two years' figures that the XYZ Company's trend went in opposition to that of the industry and that this ratio's distortion had increased to double that of the company's average competitor. Yet the ratio for each succeeding year confirms that—in this area at least—the company has gone from bad to worse. According to its latest statement (1972), the company's fixed-assets-to-net-worth ratio has become four times as high as is characteristic of the industry—a truly alarming situation. Without reviewing all other ratios, the analyst cannot pinpoint the cause of the present difficulty, but management is, from all indications, blissfully unaware of the company's plight, or it is unwilling or unable to take corrective action.

Collection period, on the other hand, evidences a change that reflects credit on the company's management. The dramatic reversal of an unfavorable trend is not a matter of chance. The inference to be drawn from the figures at hand is that in 1970 decisive corrective steps were taken by management to overcome a problem that had caught its attention. If the XYZ Company's terms of sales have not changed between 1970 and 1972 and if its terms are typical of those extended within the industry, then in 1970 management evidently initiated substantial improvements in the company's credit-and-collections program. From the figures alone, the analyst cannot ascertain exactly what steps were taken, but he can be reasonably certain that the XYZ Company either became more selective in its acceptance of risks or began to enforce its selling terms more vigorously. In revising its procedures, the company may have assigned credit management and control to a different member of its staff, one whose approach was more effective than that of his predecessor. But the important fact is that the 53-day collection period in evidence in 1969 was recognized and corrected. At that time, the XYZ Company was incurring potential, if not actual, bad-debt losses and was suffering a needless tie-up of working capital. Figures for the next three years clearly show improvement to the point that today the company's collection performance is equal to the standard in its line.

If the XYZ Company's age trend continues downward, management may find sales suffering from undue credit selectivity or overly aggressive action in making collections, for the industry pattern shows an 85 percent increase in days' sales outstanding within the past four years. Such a marked change might suggest growing emphasis throughout the industry on special terms rather than product differences—a trend requiring management attention, even if the company might not wish to meet competition with the tactics of other companies in its line.

The XYZ Company's total-debt-to-net-worth ratio shows a still different pattern. While the company started from a higher debt level than did the average firm in its industry, this ratio has been subject to fluctuations quite similar to the industry pattern. The company's net variation in the four-year span was approximately an 8 percent upward change; for the industry the increase between 1968 and 1972 was 6 percent. Although the XYZ Company should be concerned over its showing in this ratio, its trend indicates no basis for sudden alarm; the degree of distortion was really no greater in 1972 than in 1968. It is, however, no better, and the need for remedial action continues.

Clearly, then, trend adds much meaning to figures taken from a single point in time and must, whenever possible, be included in total analysis.

The final point to be considered in this chapter is that the analyst must *learn to recognize compensating advantages*. The analyst must guard against becoming alarmed by variant key ratios without first noting compensating or offsetting advantages which may permit the company to prosper while maintaining a somewhat unorthodox financial structure. He must be fully aware that deficiencies in one area can be offset by strength in other areas and that, as a corollary, no company can or should be average in all aspects of financial balance.

For illustration, let us assume that on its fiscal closing of December 31, 1971, the XYZ Company's audited statement showed the condition outlined in Table 57. In Table 58, these figures are reduced to the 15 key ratios, which are compared with industry averages. Preliminary observations indicate excessive fixed

Table 57

Cash	$ 5,000	Notes payable	$ 20,000
Accounts receivable	70,000	Accounts payable	85,000
Inventory	75,000	Taxes and accruals	20,000
Total current	$150,000	Total current	$125,000
Fixed assets	95,000	Common stock	80,000
Miscellaneous assets	5,000	Earned surplus	45,000
Total	$250,000	Total	$250,000
Sales	$900,000	Net profit	$ 36,000

Table 58

	XYZ COMPANY	INDUSTRY AVERAGE
Current-assets-to-current-liabilities	1.20 times	2.45 times
Net-profit-to-net-sales	4.00%	2.78%
Net-profit-to-net-worth	28.80	8.11
Trade-receivables-to-working-capital	280.00	42.5
Inventory-to-working-capital	300.0	66.1
Net-sales-to-net-worth	7.20 times	2.50 times
Net-sales-to-working-capital	36.00	5.02
Collection period	28 days	36 days
Net-sales-to-inventory	12.0 times	8.0 times
Fixed-assets-to-net-worth	76.0%	42.9%
Current-debt-to-net-worth	100.0	33.9
Total-debt-to-net-worth	100.0	80.9
Net-sales-to-fixed-assets	9.5 times	5.8 times
Long-term-liabilities-to-working-capital	—0—	54.8%
Miscellaneous-assets-to-net-worth	4.0%	7.8%

assets, an overtrading situation, limited working capital, and heavy debt with respect to net worth. These are severe indictments, and many credit managers might find the negative list too imposing and thus either decline to extend the XYZ Company credit or place some rather severe limitations on its exposure. Many owners, too, might become alarmed by these obvious signs of difficulty and make ill-considered decisions, motivated by concern over deviation from normal in so many important areas.

Of the 15 key ratios under consideration, the analyst will note that nine reflect unfavorably on the XYZ Company.

1. *Current-assets-to-current-liabilities.* At 1.20 the current ratio is well below industry average; this is evidence of severe working-capital limitations.

2. *Net-profit-to-net-worth.* At first glance, the company's showing in this area may appear quite impressive, but this ratio actually reflects inadequate net worth rather than abnormally great profit.

3. *Trade-receivables-to-working-capital.* The extreme distortion of this ratio again indicates the XYZ Company's tight working-capital position.

4. *Net-sales-to-net-worth.* A definite overtrading situation is depicted by this ratio; the XYZ Company is attempting to transact nearly three times as great a volume of sales per dollar of invested capital as is the average unit within its industry.

5. *Net-sales-to-working-capital.* This ratio further indicates the strain on working capital, which is turning at a rate four times normal.

6. *Fixed-assets-to-net-worth.* The XYZ Company's investment in plant and equipment related to net worth is nearly twice the industry norm.

7. *Current-liabilities-to-net-worth.* The XYZ Company is carrying roughly three times the current debt on capital that is characteristic of the industry.

8. *Total-debt-to-net-worth.* Although not as distorted as the current-debt indicator, this ratio also portrays above-average debt exposure.

9. *Inventory-to-working-capital.* Severe deviation from normal is indicated by this ratio, which is five times as great as the industry average.

The ratio of miscellaneous assets to net worth is somewhat below the industry average, but in this case the dollar amount involved is nominal. Only 5 of 15 key ratios give the analyst—or the XYZ Company—cause for cheer. In ratio analysis, however, the analyst must not be guided by the number of deviant ratios, but he must instead consider the nature of the favorable ratios to determine to what extent they offset the effects of those which are negative. The ratios showing strength in this case are

Net-profit-to-net-sales.
Collection period.
Net-sales-to-inventory.
Net-sales-to-fixed-assets.
Long-term-debt-to-working-capital.

Can sufficient advantages be generated in these areas to compensate for the deficiencies shown by the nine errant ratios? Cause-and-effect ratio analysis may very well indicate an affirmative answer. When the current ratio or any other ratio which relates to working capital is considered, the analyst must determine the quality underlying the quantities measured by the ratio. In this case, he finds that the XYZ Company has sound, collectible receivables as evidenced by its 28-day collection period, which compares favorably with the 36 days reported by the typical firm in the industry. The XYZ Company also makes a strong showing in the merchandising area, turning its inventory 50 percent more rapidly than average. Between receivables and inventory, the company is generating cash much more quickly than many others in its line. Despite overtrading—or perhaps as a result of it—the XYZ Company's profit return on sales is substantially better than the industry norm. Handling a greater sales volume at a higher rate of profit, the company can quickly reinforce its present shortage in both working capital and net worth. Finally, notwithstanding its heavy exposure in fixed assets relative to net worth, the XYZ Company's investment in modern plant and equipment has enabled it to support greater sales volume per dollar of fixed assets than does its average competitor. Moreover, XYZ has effected production economies to the extent that its profit return, even after depreciation allowance, is above average. And, barring further immediate expansion in this area, the company's fixed-assets-to-net-worth ratio will soon be brought into balance. Fixed assets will decline annually through depreciation charges, while net worth will increase through high earnings, if the analyst can assume that earnings will continue at the current rate and that they will be retained in the business.

A favorable condition which has not been explored is the absence of long-term debt. Should working-capital pressure become too great at any time, long-term or intermediate financing would likely be available to the XYZ Company because its fixed assets are free of encumbrance and should represent satisfactory collateral.

Ratio analysis involves study of the *total* financial picture. The analyst must seek out positive factors that may offset known deficiencies in the financial structure of the company under examination. But he must be equally vigilant in detecting signs of incipient danger that may soon weaken a well-balanced company. By basing his conclusions upon a thorough understanding of the importance of each ratio, the analyst can recommend and undertake positive action with confidence.

6 Liquidity Crisis
or Profit Squeeze?

In 1970 the nation's attention was focused on the spectacular and foreboding financial problems faced by such corporate giants as Penn Central, Lockheed, and, to a lesser extent, Chrysler. Was Penn Central truly representative of industry at large? Was Lockheed? Did their difficulties typify the situation prevailing within the average American company? Was there actually a liquidity crisis for *all* commercial enterprise, as was implied by the concentration of public attention on these individual situations?

This chapter is directed primarily to the impact of 1970 operational results on small and moderate-size firms. It is derived from Robert Morris Associates' "Annual Statement Studies," which place emphasis on companies with asset size of $25 million or less. The vast majority of business concerns included in the Robert Morris Associates survey have total assets of less than $10 million. Translated into dollars of annual sales, this would mean that we are concentrating on organizations that may have as little as a few hundred thousand dollars in revenue yearly up to—on average—less than $50 million.

Rather than centering attention on extremes, it is more important and representative to determine what happened in 1970 to the *average* company, taken from the total spectrum of industries on which RMA compiles its composites and ratios. Hence, the median average was used in each industry for 1969 and again for 1970. The result will constitute one measurement of what took place during that controversial year for the typical American firm.

The liquidity of any company is its ability to meet its daily monetary requirements—its payroll, its trade bills, its debt servicing, and the like—from its normal cash availability. In an earlier chapter, it was pointed out that one means of determining the liquidity of a company is to look at its current ratio; that is, its current assets related to its current liabilities.

Contrasting the median averages for all industry in 1969 and 1970, classified by asset size, we find the following pattern.*

CURRENT RATIO—MANUFACTURERS
(Expressed in times)

	1969	1970
A. UNDER $250M		
Upper quartile	1.9	1.9
Median	1.6	1.6
Lower quartile	1.4	1.3
B. $250M–$1MM		
Upper quartile	1.9	1.9
Median	1.7	1.7
Lower quartile	1.6	1.5
C. $1MM–$10MM		
Upper quartile	2.2	2.2
Median	2.0	2.0
Lower quartile	1.8	1.7
D. $10MM–$25MM		
Upper quartile	2.8	2.9
Median	2.5	2.5
Lower quartile	2.2	2.1
E. ALL SIZES		
Upper quartile	2.1	2.1
Median	1.9	1.9
Lower quartile	1.7	1.7

CURRENT RATIO—WHOLESALERS

	1969	1970
A. UNDER $250M		
Upper quartile	2.1	2.1
Median	2.0	1.9
Lower quartile	1.7	1.6

* All the ratios from pages 177 to 187 are derived from data copyrighted by Robert Morris Associates, 1970 and 1971. (Data for wholesalers in the $10MM–$25MM range was unavailable.)

B. $250M–$1MM	1969	1970
Upper quartile	1.9	1.9
Median	1.8	1.8
Lower quartile	1.6	1.6
C. $1MM–$10MM		
Upper quartile	1.9	1.8
Median	1.6	1.6
Lower quartile	1.4	1.3
D. ALL SIZES		
Upper quartile	2.0	1.9
Median	1.8	1.8
Lower quartile	1.5	1.5

These figures reflect a condition of surprising stability and tend to refute the thesis that illiquidity characterized the general status of American business for fiscal 1970.

An analyst might logically question whether the generally static current ratio reflected by these figures was maintained by increased long-term borrowing to reinforce otherwise narrow working-capital positions. This would mean a transference of high current debt to deferred status, which would be reflected in a high ratio of total debt to net worth. The 1969–1970 picture for that ratio shows the following.

DEBT-TO-WORTH—MANUFACTURERS
(Expressed in times)

A. UNDER $250M	1969	1970
Upper quartile	1.3	1.4
Median	1.1	1.1
Lower quartile	.8	.9
B. $250M–$1MM		
Upper quartile	1.2	1.2
Median	1.0	1.0
Lower quartile	.8	.9
C. $1MM–$10MM		
Upper quartile	1.1	1.1
Median	.9	.9
Lower quartile	.7	.7
D. $10MM–$25MM		
Upper quartile	1.0	1.0
Median	.8	.6
Lower quartile	.6	.5

E. ALL SIZES	1969	1970
Upper quartile	1.1	1.1
Median	.9	.9
Lower quartile	.7	.8

DEBT-TO-WORTH—WHOLESALERS

A. UNDER $250M	1969	1970
Upper quartile	1.1	1.3
Median	1.0	1.1
Lower quartile	.8	.9

B. $250M–$1MM		
Upper quartile	1.8	1.8
Median	1.3	1.3
Lower quartile	1.1	1.0

C. $1MM–$10MM		
Upper quartile	1.6	1.7
Median	1.3	1.4
Lower quartile	1.1	1.1

D. ALL SIZES		
Upper quartile	1.4	1.5
Median	1.2	1.2
Lower quartile	1.1	1.0

Note that these ratios are shown in "times." To translate them to percentages they should be multiplied by 100. For example, 1.3 is the equivalent of 130%.

Again one would reasonably conclude that the typical firm was able to maintain its position of normal liquidity (assuming 1969 to be the norm) by internally generated funds, without adding to its relative debt load.

If the current ratio and the debt-to-worth ratio both held relatively constant, it follows that—on balance—the six causal ratios must have been subject to a similar degree of consistency. They show the following.

COLLECTION PERIOD—MANUFACTURERS
(Expressed as days' sales outstanding)

A. UNDER $250M	1969	1970
Upper quartile	48	46
Median	41	40
Lower quartile	34	35

B. **$250M–$1MM**

	1969	1970
Upper quartile	47	48
Median	43	42
Lower quartile	37	38

C. **$1MM–$10MM**

Upper quartile	53	54
Median	45	45
Lower quartile	39	40

D. **$10MM–$25MM**

Upper quartile	59	66
Median	51	58
Lower quartile	47	49

E. **ALL SIZES**

Upper quartile	50	50
Median	46	44
Lower quartile	39	39

COLLECTION PERIOD—WHOLESALERS

A. **UNDER $250M**

	1969	1970
Upper quartile	41	42
Median	36	36
Lower quartile	28	25

B. **$250M–$1MM**

Upper quartile	46	46
Median	40	41
Lower quartile	29	28

C. **$1MM–$10MM**

Upper quartile	46	46
Median	43	42
Lower quartile	30	27

D. **ALL SIZES**

Upper quartile	45	46
Median	41	42
Lower quartile	28	27

COST-OF-SALES-TO-INVENTORY—MANUFACTURERS
(Expressed in times)

A. **UNDER $250M**

	1969	1970
Upper quartile	9.1	10.4
Median	7.6	6.6
Lower quartile	5.5	5.3

B. $250M–$1MM

	1969	1970
Upper quartile	7.9	8.0
Median	5.9	6.1
Lower quartile	4.8	4.9

C. $1MM–$10MM

Upper quartile	6.2	6.4
Median	4.8	4.6
Lower quartile	3.6	3.6

D. ALL SIZES

Upper quartile	7.0	7.0
Median	5.2	5.1
Lower quartile	4.1	4.2

COST-OF-SALES-TO-INVENTORY—WHOLESALERS

A. UNDER $250M

	1969	1970
Upper quartile	9.5	10.3
Median	6.2	6.2
Lower quartile	4.3	4.9

B. $250M–$1MM

Upper quartile	8.5	8.8
Median	6.0	5.4
Lower quartile	4.8	4.2

C. $1MM–$10MM

Upper quartile	8.2	8.2
Median	5.9	5.7
Lower quartile	4.8	4.3

D. ALL SIZES

Upper quartile	8.5	8.6
Median	5.9	5.5
Lower quartile	4.5	4.2

SALES-TO-WORTH—MANUFACTURERS
(Expressed in times)

A. UNDER $250M

	1969	1970
Upper quartile	6.1	6.2
Median	5.3	4.9
Lower quartile	4.4	4.0

B. $250M–$1MM

Upper quartile	5.5	5.3
Median	4.5	4.3
Lower quartile	3.9	3.7

C. $1MM–$10MM

Upper quartile	4.1	4.2
Median	3.4	3.3
Lower quartile	3.0	2.9

D. $10MM–$25MM	1969	1970
Upper quartile	3.0	3.1
Median	2.6	2.4
Lower quartile	2.4	2.2

E. ALL SIZES		
Upper quartile	4.6	4.5
Median	3.8	3.7
Lower quartile	3.3	3.2

SALES-TO-WORTH—WHOLESALERS

A. UNDER $250M	1969	1970
Upper quartile	7.9	8.4
Median	6.4	7.0
Lower quartile	5.3	5.4

B. $250M–$1MM		
Upper quartile	8.0	7.7
Median	6.6	6.4
Lower quartile	5.7	5.6

C. $1MM–$10MM		
Upper quartile	7.9	7.7
Median	6.9	6.2
Lower quartile	5.2	5.1

D. ALL SIZES		
Upper quartile	7.7	7.4
Median	6.4	6.3
Lower quartile	5.5	5.4

FIXED-ASSETS-TO-NET-WORTH—MANUFACTURERS
(Expressed in times)

A. UNDER $250M	1969	1970
Upper quartile	.8	.7
Median	.5	.7
Lower quartile	.3	.3

B. $250M–$1MM		
Upper quartile	6–.7	.7
Median	.5	.5
Lower quartile	.3	.3

C. $1MM–$10MM		
Upper quartile	.6	.7
Median	.5	.5
Lower quartile	.4	.4

D. $10MM-$25MM	1969	1970
Upper quartile	.6	.7
Median	.5	.5-.6
Lower quartile	.4	.4

E. ALL SIZES		
Upper quartile	.6	.6
Median	.5	.5
Lower quartile	.3	.4

Expressed as percentages, .8 is the same as 80%.

FIXED-ASSETS-TO-NET-WORTH—WHOLESALERS

A. UNDER $250M	1969	1970
Upper quartile	.3	.3
Median	.2	.2
Lower quartile	.1	.1

B. $250M-$1MM		
Upper quartile	.3	.3
Median	.2	.2
Lower quartile	.1	.1

C. $1MM-$10MM		
Upper quartile	.4	.4
Median	.2	.2
Lower quartile	.1	.2

D. ALL SIZES		
Upper quartile	.3	.3
Median	.2	.2
Lower quartile	.1	.1

MISCELLANEOUS-ASSETS-TO-NET-WORTH—MANUFACTURERS
(Expressed in percent)

A. UNDER $250M	1969	1970
Upper quartile	17.8	24.3
Median	12.6	16.7
Lower quartile	9.1	11.5

B. $250M-$1MM		
Upper quartile	16.8	17.4
Median	13.5	14.2
Lower quartile	10.6	11.4

C. $1MM-$10MM		
Upper quartile	16.1	17.1
Median	12.2	13.3
Lower quartile	9.4	10.0

D. $10MM–$25MM	1969	1970
Upper quartile	12.9	14.5
Median	10.1	10.2
Lower quartile	8.6	6.8

E. ALL SIZES		
Upper quartile	14.3	16.6
Median	11.5	12.2
Lower quartile	9.3	9.0

MISCELLANEOUS-ASSETS-TO-NET-WORTH—WHOLESALERS

A. UNDER $250M	1969	1970
Upper quartile	14.1	15.1
Median	10.4	11.6
Lower quartile	7.3	9.7

B. $250M–$1MM		
Upper quartile	17.3	17.2
Median	13.0	13.2
Lower quartile	9.9	9.0

C. $1MM–$10MM		
Upper quartile	18.0	18.3
Median	15.0	15.1
Lower quartile	11.0	11.7

D. ALL SIZES		
Upper quartile	18.5	19.7
Median	13.6	15.7
Lower quartile	9.7	10.8

PRETAX-PROFIT-TO-SALES—MANUFACTURERS
(Expressed in percent)

A. UNDER $250M	1969	1970
Upper quartile	4.1	3.3
Median	2.9	2.1
Lower quartile	1.8	.7

B. $250M–$1MM		
Upper quartile	4.5	3.5
Median	3.9	2.7
Lower quartile	2.6	1.6

C. $1MM–$10MM		
Upper quartile	7.0	5.6
Median	5.6	4.4
Lower quartile	4.7	3.1

D. $10MM–$25MM	1969	1970
Upper quartile	8.5	7.1
Median	7.2	5.4
Lower quartile	5.8	4.1

E. ALL SIZES		
Upper quartile	7.2	5.5
Median	6.0	4.3
Lower quartile	4.7	3.2

PRETAX-PROFIT-TO-SALES—WHOLESALERS

A. UNDER $250M	1969	1970
Upper quartile	3.0	2.6
Median	2.3	1.9
Lower quartile	1.4	1.4

B. $250M–$1MM		
Upper quartile	2.9	2.6
Median	2.5	2.1
Lower quartile	1.9	1.5

C. $1MM–$10MM		
Upper quartile	3.9	3.4
Median	3.3	2.5
Lower quartile	2.2	1.8

D. ALL SIZES		
Upper quartile	3.8	3.1
Median	3.0	2.5
Lower quartile	2.2	1.7

While the foregoing figures reflect a condition of overall constancy with respect to general industrial solvency and freedom from debt, there are other facets to study, other questions to be answered, in order to understand the noteworthy year 1970.

Could it have been possible for the entire business community to maintain its 1969 position in the aggregate, but for certain segments to suffer reverses while other lines of industry flourished? Were there instances where one line of commercial activity was beset by problems at the same time that a member of the field prospered, and vice versa? If liquidity did indeed become eroded for an individual industry or company in 1970, was this generally caused by external forces—that is, an unfavorable economic climate—or could it instead be attributable in any degree to internal mismanagement? We must explore and try to explain any such inconsistencies.

The only causal ratio which suffers in 1970 as contrasted with 1969 is that of profit to sales. As explained earlier, *any* profit in excess of dividends—any *retained* profit—exerts a positive influence on liquidity and debt control, provided that the surplus income is not extravagantly diverted into other channels such as fixed assets, slower-paying receivables, sluggish inventory, or miscellaneous assets. It is only when an individual company fails to keep the profit pace of its competition that any disadvantage becomes apparent.

On the average, the other five causal ratios reflected little if any change, and hence the lowered profit percentages did not prevent the continued maintenance of 1969 current ratio and debt-to-worth ratio levels. Had losses been sustained or had dividend rates exceeded profit return, there would indeed have been pressure exerted upon liquidity.

An interesting feature of the widespread decline in business net profit is the fact that gross-profit percentages actually increased in most instances. Thus it becomes apparent that the year 1970 saw a sharp rise in expenses: selling, delivery, and general and administrative, in particular.

GROSS PROFIT—MANUFACTURERS
(Expressed in percent)

	1969	1970
A. UNDER $250M		
Upper quartile	31.9	32.7
Median	27.1	29.1
Lower quartile	24.0	24.8
B. $250M–$1MM		
Upper quartile	28.2	28.3
Median	23.8	23.2
Lower quartile	20.4	20.0
C. $1MM–$10MM		
Upper quartile	27.2	26.1
Median	22.6	22.1
Lower quartile	18.6	19.2
D. $10MM–$25MM		
Upper quartile	28.0	27.3
Median	24.0	25.4
Lower quartile	19.0	17.8

E. ALL SIZES	1969	1970
Upper quartile	27.9	26.6
Median	23.8	23.5
Lower quartile	19.2	19.7

GROSS PROFIT—WHOLESALERS

A. UNDER $250M	1969	1970
Upper quartile	26.3	27.3
Median	23.6	24.1
Lower quartile	18.7	18.5

B. $250M–$1MM		
Upper quartile	24.3	23.9
Median	20.4	20.5
Lower quartile	15.4	16.4

C. $1MM–$10MM		
Upper quartile	21.2	21.8
Median	17.8	18.1
Lower quartile	13.6	15.6

D. ALL SIZES		
Upper quartile	23.5	22.8
Median	18.7	19.6
Lower quartile	14.1	16.2

The only commercial segment which sustained any decline in current-ratio (liquidity) levels and an increase in debt, relative to net worth, was the smaller wholesalers, those with less than $250,000 in assets. By referring to the preceding tables we can readily see that this is attributable to influences brought to bear by heavier trading on equity (net worth). Their turnover of net worth increased roughly 10 percent, and since all other causal ratios remained unchanged or deviated very little from 1969 levels, this accelerated trading activity alone was sufficient to cause the modest downward movement of the current ratio and the similarly slight increase in the debt-to-worth relationship.

In summary, it appears that 1970 did not create widespread liquidity hardship, and the headlines called attention to the exceptional case rather than to the more widespread industrial stability. It would have been more accurate to refer to a profit decline or to an expense expansion than to spread alarm over the liquidity of the entire economy.

Table 59

INDUSTRY	CURRENT RATIO		DEBT-TO-WORTH	
	1969	1970	1969	1970
Hats	2.4	1.9	70.0%	100.0%
Flavoring extracts and syrups	2.8	1.6	40.0	60.0
Vegetable oils	2.4	2.1	40.0	60.0
Broad woven fabrics, woolens and worsteds	2.8	2.4	40.0	50.0
Electric measuring instruments and testing equipment	2.2	1.8	70.0	111.0

1969 and 1970: A Five-Industry Comparison

Characteristically, not all segments of industry achieved the same results for the year under review. Some did discover their working capital dropping and their relative debt increasing during 1970, while other industries enjoyed the benefits of greater liquidity and a lessening of debt pressure. The five lines of activity shown in Table 59, chosen at random, suffered adverse results in both areas. While the industry average is admittedly not compiled from identical firms for each of these two years, the results are sufficiently representative to serve as a base for drawing general conclusions. Let us examine each of these five industries in the light of possible changes within the six causal ratios over the same span of time, to see whether this will help in delineating the reasons for the adverse trend in each case. All ratios except miscellaneous assets to net worth are copyrighted by Robert Morris Associates, 1970 and 1971.

1. MANUFACTURERS OF HATS

	1969	1970
Fixed-assets-to-net-worth (%)	10	10
Collection period (days)	48	59
Cost-of-sales-to-inventory (days)	78	78
Net-sales-to-net-worth (times)	4.1	4.6
Miscellaneous-assets-to-net-worth (%)	10.5	9.1
Pretax-profit-to-net-sales (%)	2.4	4.7

In diagnosing the reasons for regression, we can immediately discard fixed-assets-to-net-worth, inventory turnover, and miscellaneous-asset investment, since these ratios are unchanged or have varied so slightly as to exert no significant influence. While the profit increase would—if retained in the business—tend to bolster working capital and net worth, its beneficial influence is more than offset by the tie-up of funds in slower receivables and by the more rapid trading activity (net-sales-to-net-worth).

2. MANUFACTURERS OF FLAVORING EXTRACTS AND SYRUPS

	1969	1970
Fixed-assets-to-net-worth (%)	40	60
Collection period (days)	29	33
Cost-of-sales-to-inventory (days)	47	62
Net-sales-to-net-worth (times)	3.3	3.3
Miscellaneous-assets-to-net-worth (%)	10.0	19.4
Pretax-profit-to-net-sales (%)	12.2	2.8

That this industry sustained the most alarming reversal of the five chosen for review is not surprising. Only one ratio remained constant (net-sales-to-net-worth), and all others reflected negative change in varying degrees. The two largest asset items on the industry balance sheet increased sharply, with (1) fixed assets advancing 50 percent in 1970 when related to net worth and (2) inventory investment rising roughly one-third more rapidly than sales. Profit margins fell to levels inadequate to support the concentration of funds in these two areas. The situation was made more critical by a four-day increase in the age of receivables and by doubling the diversion of funds into miscellaneous assets.

3. MANUFACTURERS OF VEGETABLE OILS

	1969	1970
Fixed-assets-to-net-worth (%)	40	50
Collection period (days)	28	19
Cost-of-sales-to-inventory (days)	23	31
Net-sales-to-net-worth (times)	3.8	4.7
Miscellaneous-assets-to-net-worth (%)	30.5	27.2
Pretax-profit-to-net-sales (%)	1.2	4.6

On the positive side we find two factors: the favorable increase in profit and the improved collection of receivables. However, these beneficial influences were more than canceled out by a 25 percent relative increased investment in fixed assets and a 35 percent rise in inventory (respectively related to net worth and to net sales). A 25 percent upward rate of trading activity (net-sales-to-net-worth) was another significant pressure factor. The change in miscellaneous-assets-to-net-worth was too small to figure prominently in the final outcome.

Incidentally, this industry provides a good illustration of the inadequacy of cash-flow analysis as the total determinant in measuring a company's or an industry's ability to bolster its working capital or reduce its debt. With profit nearly four times as high in 1970, and with obviously greater depreciation because of increased fixed-asset investment, the flow of cash would reflect remarkable improvement in 1970. Yet the current ratio dropped and the debt pressure was greater.

4. Manufacturers of Broad Woven Fabrics, Woolens and Worsteds

	1969	1970
Fixed-assets-to-net-worth (%)	30	40
Collection period (days)	45	43
Cost-of-sales-to-inventory (days)	64	84
Net-sales-to-net-worth (times)	2.5	2.5
Miscellaneous-assets-to-net-worth (%)	9.3	9.9
Pretax-profit-to-net-sales (%)	4.6	3.6

As causes for this industry's adverse trend, we must concentrate primarily on two ratios: fixed-assets-to-net-worth and inventory turnover. The major changes which took place in these areas far overshadowed those for the remaining causal ratios. Net-sales-to-net-worth remained constant, while relatively modest variances were recorded in the collection of receivables and in the trading ratio. A declining profit margin also compounded the industry's problems but was minor in influence in contrast with the two ratios already cited as the principal contributors to the worsened liquidity and debt situation.

5. Manufacturers of Electric Measuring Instruments and Test Equipment

	1969	1970
Fixed-assets-to-net-worth (%)	20	40
Collection period (days)	75	61
Cost-of-sales-to-inventory (days)	129	129
Net-sales-to-net-worth (times)	3.0	3.2
Miscellaneous-assets-to-net-worth (%)	9.0	17.2
Pretax-profit-to-net-sales (%)	8.6	4.2

Analysis of this industry shows one ratio substantially improved: the collection period, which dropped 14 days. Inventory turnover remained constant. However, all other ratios regressed and contributed more to the decline in working capital and the heavier debt structure relative to net worth than could be offset by the more favorable receivables picture. In order of contributory importance, regressive factors were (1) a doubled fixed-asset-to-net-worth rate, (2) a nearly 100 percent increased diversion rate of net worth into miscellaneous assets, (3) a slightly accelerated trading ratio, and (4) a profit-to-sales ratio reduced by 50 percent.

In contrast to these five industries used to illustrate 1970 operations which resulted in a narrowed working-capital position and a higher debt-to-worth picture, numerous lines of activity were able to improve their status in both these areas. Let us look at just two fields which can be considered typical of the group that recorded progress.

1. Manufacturers of Furs

	1969	1970
Current-assets-to-current-liabilities (times)	1.8	2.6
Total-liabilities-to-net-worth (times)	1.3	.6
Fixed-assets-to-net-worth (%)	10	0
Collection period (days)	49	53
Cost-of-sales-to-inventory (days)	78	71
Net-sales-to-net-worth (times)	4.7	3.1
Miscellaneous-assets-to-net-worth (%)	14.3	5.7
Pretax-profit-to-net-sales (%)	3.4	3.7

The only causal ratio change from 1969 to 1970 that would adversely affect the liquidity and debt ratios was the collection period, which showed receivables payments lagging by four days. This was more than overcome by improved inventory turnover (seven days), by the virtual elimination of fixed-asset investment, by curtailed diversion of funds into miscellaneous assets, by the lowered trading on equity rate, and by the increased profit attainment on sales.

Some might argue that reduced sales-to-net-worth is not necessarily in the best interests of a company. This is not a point at issue here; we are merely attempting to identify the causes for increased liquidity and lowered debt. A diminished trading ratio tends to reduce pressure in both these areas.

It might also be contested—with some degree of validity—that aggregate profit was less in 1970 than 1969, for the increased return per dollar of sales would be more than balanced out by the diminished revenue volume. This could be true, but it is not a vital point in the present study of liquidity for this industry.

2. MANUFACTURERS OF CANNED AND DRIED FRUITS AND VEGETABLES

	1969	1970
Current-assets-to-current liabilities (times)	1.6	1.8
Total-liabilities-to-net-worth (times)	1.2	1.0
Fixed-assets-to-net-worth (%)	70	60
Collection period (days)	20	22
Cost-of-sales-to-inventory (days)	71	74
Net-sales-to-net-worth (times)	4.2	3.6
Miscellaneous-assets-to-net-worth (%)	13.1	7.3
Pretax-profit-to-net-sales (%)	3.8	4.0

This industry's results represent a mixture of favorable and unfavorable elements. Those which contributed both to a shrinkage of working capital and to increased accumulation of debt were (1) collection period and (2) cost-of-sales-to-inventory. Their degree of change was so modest, however, that the positive influences predominated, resulting in industry-wide improvement. On the plus side, we note (1) fixed-assets-to-net-worth, (2) net-sales-to-net-worth, (3) miscellaneous-assets-to-networth, and (4) pretax-profit-to-net-sales.

Thus it will be seen that on average, the sum total of U.S. manufacturers and wholesalers retained their liquidity positions during 1970 and did so without increasing the previously existing balance between debt and worth. Further, although some industries found their results to be negative, these industries were counterbalanced by others whose financial ratios improved.

Were those whose achievements proved unsatisfactory the victims of external economic influences or of failure to exert proper internal controls, directed primarily to maintaining the existing balance within the area of the six causal ratios?

An answer can perhaps best be derived by studying three major corporations, all engaged in the same general line of business activity. While no two companies transacting annual sales volume in the billion-dollar range will be totally comparable owing to the influence of diversification, Companies A, B, and C are sufficiently compatible that external economic factors would affect each to virtually the same degree.

At 1969 fiscal closing, the 15 ratios for these three organizations showed the conditions seen in Table 60. When final figures

Table 60

	COMPANY A	COMPANY B	COMPANY C
Current-assets-to-current-liabilities (times)	1.67	2.88	2.62
Current-liabilities-to-net-worth (%)	45.7	26.7	22.9
Total-liabilities-to-net-worth (%)	148.0	166.6	103.3
Inventory-to-working-capital (%)	118.5	82.1	77.6
Receivables-to-working-capital (%)	109.1	55.1	64.0
Long-term-liabilities-to-working-capital (%)	266.2	235.1	175.2
Net-profit-to-net-worth (%)	11.66	8.37	10.24
Net-sales-to-fixed-assets (times)	1.3	1.1	1.2
Net-sales-to-working-capital (times)	5.1	3.1	3.5
Fixed-assets-to-net-worth (%)	123.9	146.8	108.5
Net-profit-to-net-sales (%)	7.40	5.44	7.92
Net-sales-to-net-worth (times)	1.58	1.54	1.29
Net-sales-to-inventory (times)	4.3	3.7	4.5
Net-sales-to-inventory (days)	85	98	81
Collection period (days)	78	66	67
Miscellaneous-assets-to-net-worth (%)	47.6	42.8	35.9

Table 61

	COMPANY A	COMPANY B	COMPANY C
Current-assets-to-current-liabilities (times)	1.39	3.06	2.65
Current-liabilities-to-net-worth (%)	58.0	25.8	21.8
Total-liabilities-to-net-worth (%)	158.5	166.9	110.4
Inventory-to-working-capital (%)	174.1	92.1	81.6
Receivables-to-working-capital (%)	142.8	45.3	58.1
Long-term-liabilities-to-working-capital (%)	349.9	220.6	197.2
Net-profit-to-net-worth (%)	8.18	6.69	7.64
Net-sales-to-fixed-assets (times)	1.1	1.1	1.0
Net-sales-to-working-capital (times)	6.1	2.8	3.4
Fixed-assets-to-net-worth (%)	124.3	142.4	116.9
Net-profit-to-net-sales (%)	5.76	4.46	6.27
Net-sales-to-net-worth (times)	1.40	1.50	1.22
Net-sales-to-inventory (times)	3.5	3.1	4.2
Net-sales-to-inventory (days)	104	119	88
Collection period (days)	85	59	63
Miscellaneous-assets-to-net-worth (%)	54.9	45.3	35.8

for 1970 were published, their respective ratios had changed to show the picture in Table 61.

It will be seen that Company A's current ratio declined to a stringently low level, whereas both Companies B and C improved their performance in this same area. A's current-debt position relative to net worth rose sharply, but declines in this ratio were registered by both B and C. A's turnover of working capital (net-sales-to-working-capital) reflected increasing pressure, but B and C showed an easing trend. Since each one is primarily engaged in the same industry, it seems logical that the impact exerted by the economy would be felt equally by all three. This suggests that management policies and internal functional performance may have been of greater importance in the respective attainments of each of these organizations.

No attempt will be made here to pass judgment on the merits of any of their divergent approaches to the same profit and solvency objectives. Our aim is solely to study the causes for changes that took place during 1970.

Before analyzing these results, it should be mentioned that the 1969 debt composition of our subjects was as shown in Table 62. In 1970, the maturities of their liabilities had shifted to the relative positions shown in Table 63.

Since Company A had far greater current-debt pressure and far less liquidity in 1969 than the others, we shall concentrate on the causes for the original condition and on the changes that occurred in the ensuing year. Less intensive analysis will be made of B and C, using them more for purposes of contrast.

It should be noted that for the 1969 fiscal closing, Company A did not surpass its two competitors in any of the six causal ratios. Company C had the best performance in five categories (as they relate to improved liquidity): fixed-assets-to-net-worth, net-profit-to-net-sales, net-sales-to-net-worth, net-sales-to-inventory, and miscellaneous-assets-to-net-worth. Company B led in the collection-period ratio.

It is relatively easy to show why—all other factors being equal—A's current ratio would be lower than that of C in 1969.

■ A had a substantially higher percentage of equity capital invested in fixed assets than C.

■ C's profit per dollar of sales was higher, as were its retained earnings.

■ A's turnover of net worth (its trading ratio) was more rapid. While the figure 1.58 as opposed to 1.29 may seem insignificant, we must remember that we are considering very large corporations in this instance, and what may appear to be a minor deviation actually represents a rate for A that is 44 percent higher

Table 62

	COMPANY A	COMPANY B	COMPANY C
Current debt	35.8%	18.5%	27.1%
Long-term debt	64.2	81.5	72.9

Table 63

	COMPANY A	COMPANY B	COMPANY C
Current debt	42.0%	18.1%	23.5%
Long-term debt	58.0	81.9	76.5

than C's pace. The same degree of difference applies as would be true for smaller companies XYZ and ABC if XYZ's net-sales-to-worth ratio were 8 times per year as opposed to ABC's 11.5 times.

■ C's inventory turnover was slightly better. Spelled out in days, C had a four-day edge over A.

■ C's collection rate of receivables was far better than that attained by A: 11 days, to be exact.

■ A had nearly one-third more of its net worth diverted into miscellaneous assets than did C.

Thus, for every one of the causal ratios, C's position was such that its liquidity and its debt structure received more positive benefit than was true for A.

In comparing A with B for 1969, it is far more difficult to account for B's improved liquidity position. In fact, based upon review of the causal ratios an analyst would assume—all other factors being equal—that A's current ratio would exceed that of B. Each was superior to the other in three ratios, but A had a more decided edge in its areas of advantage.

Company A led Company B in three ratios.

■ *Fixed-assets-to-net-worth.* A had nearly 20 percent more of its equity capital invested in fixed assets than B. Since this is by far the largest single asset item for each, such a degree of variance bears considerable weight.

■ *Net-profit-to-net-sales.* A's attainment was 36 percent better than B. Assuming a corresponding degree of profit retention for each company, A's working capital would enjoy far greater beneficial effect.

■ *Net-sales-to-inventory.* A's turnover rate was 15 to 16 percent more rapid than that of B.

B recorded better attainment than A in the remaining three ratios.

■ *Net-sales-to-net-worth.* A had between 2 and 3 percent greater activity than B. While such deviation would be insignificant in a small business entity, it assumes more importance in major industrial organizations by virtue of their extremely large capital accumulation. Even so, this relatively slight variance has far less impact than the sharper deviations in the three ratios already mentioned, where A's performance was better.

■ *Collection period.* B was 18 percent more effective than A in being paid on its receivables. This balanced out the advantage enjoyed by A in inventory turnover.

■ *Miscellaneous-assets-to-net-worth.* B had 11 percent less of its net worth tied up in such items as investments. Since miscellaneous items loom quite large on each company's books (being greater than receivables in each case and—on average—exceeding inventory) this represented a prominent advantage for B. However, its influence was not sufficient to offset A's showing in both profit attainment and relative fixed-asset investment.

In commenting on the A and B comparison, we indicated that A's working capital should have been superior to that of B *if all other factors had been equal.* They were not equal, however, for we see that B relied far more heavily on term debt than did A. If A had resorted to long-maturity borrowing to the same percentage as B—and used the added proceeds solely for the purpose of current-debt retirement—its current ratio would immediately have soared to 3.24. Its *total*-debt-to-net-worth percentage would have been unchanged, but its current-liabilities-to-net-worth would have dropped to 23.6 percent from 45.7 percent.

A's capacity to convert its debt maturity from long to short term may seem open to question if it is viewed solely in light of the ratio of long-term liabilities to working capital, because A's percentage is already clearly higher than that of B or C. However, as brought out in an earlier chapter, in using the ratio analytical approach it must be remembered that every computation measures *both* halves of each fraction. Thus A's 266.2 percent for 1969 may reflect (1) an excessively high long-term debt structure or (2) an inadequate amount of working capital or (3) a combination of both these possibilities. It has already been established from review of the current ratio and the net-sales-to-working-capital ratio that A's working funds were relatively deficient, and its long-term borrowing percentage was correspondingly low. So it should be clear that longer-maturity debt—if used solely for working-capital purposes—would not have further distorted this ratio, but would instead have improved it. In fact, its percentage would have declined to 196.8 percent, which would have placed it in a position superior to B and not too far from C's 1969 figure.

There is, however, one factor that might have caused A to hesitate about bolstering its liquidity position by means of long-term borrowing to the same degree as B. Interest rates were high in 1970, and each percentage point involved in floating a bond issue would have meant millions of dollars in added cost. It probably seemed preferable to await a decline in rates, and, in the light of more current developments in 1971 and 1972, such a decision would have been proved historically correct.

At the close of 1970, the three companies were bearing the following interest burden when related to sales:

Company A	3.9 percent
Company B	4.4 percent
Company C	3.2 percent

If in early 1971 A had patterned its debt structure along the lines of B, its interest cost on each sales dollar would have risen to 5.3 percent, assuming that an issue could have been sold bearing a 6 percent coupon. At 7 percent the cost would have risen to 5.5 percent of sales, which would have placed A at a considerable competitive disadvantage for many years to come. It is less expensive to rely more heavily upon the support of trade suppliers.

Now that we understand the causes for the relative liquidity standings of our three companies for 1969, we can next focus our attention on the reasons for any changes that took place in this direction for 1970. But before doing so, Table 64 is inserted as a reminder of the way in which upward or downward movement in the six causal ratios influences liquidity and debt.

Now let us see how these key ratios changed during 1970 for Companies A, B, and C:

Fixed-assets-to-net-worth
A. Unchanged
B. Decreased 3 percent
C. Increased 13 percent

Net-profit-to-net-sales
A. Decreased 22 percent
B. Decreased 18 percent
C. Decreased 21 percent
Net-sales-to-inventory
A. Decreased 22 percent
B. Decreased 21 percent
C. Decreased 9 percent
Collection period (rate of turnover)
A. Decreased 9 percent
B. Increased 11 percent
C. Increased 6 percent
Net-sales-to-net-worth
A. Decreased 11 percent
B. Decreased 3 percent
C. Decreased 5 percent
Miscellaneous-assets-to-net-worth
A. Increased 15 percent
B. Increased 6 percent
C. Remained unchanged

Table 64

	EFFECT ON WORKING CAPITAL		EFFECT ON CURRENT AND/OR TOTAL LIABILITIES	
	INCREASED % OR TURNOVER RATE	DECREASED % OR TURNOVER RATE	INCREASED % OR TURNOVER RATE	DECREASED % OR TURNOVER RATE
Fixed-assets-to-net-worth	Negative	Positive	Negative	Positive
Net-profit-to-net-sales	Positive	Negative*	Positive	Negative*
Net-sales-to-net-worth	Negative	Positive	Negative	Positive
Net-sales-to-inventory	Positive	Negative	Positive	Negative
Collection period	Positive†	Negative	Positive†	Negative
Miscellaneous-assets-to-net-worth	Negative	Positive	Negative	Positive

* But still positive or beneficial, unless losses have been sustained. It is only *less* positive when at reduced levels compared with those of competitors or the industry at large.

† By turnover rate we mean a faster collection tempo as expressed in lower days' sales outstanding.

For Company A, there was only one positive element that would favorably affect its working capital and debt picture among the six ratios—the decline in its trading activity as reflected by net sales to net worth. Another positive—but qualified—factor was its profit on sales, even though this was at a considerably reduced rate. While admittedly neither of these developments is desirable for meeting company growth objectives, nevertheless both tend to bolster working capital and reduce debt.

The most significant adverse trends for A were threefold.

1. Inventory turnover slowed down more dramatically for A than for either B or C.
2. A's receivables were collected more slowly in 1970, whereas both B and C reflected improvement.
3. A diverted more funds into miscellaneous assets than did either B or C.

Being more adversely affected in the causal areas than either competitor, it naturally follows that—all other factors being equal—A's current ratio could not keep pace with the others, and it would be subjected to heavier debt pressure.

Comparing B's and C's performance in 1970, C's most significant advantage lay in its superior inventory control. This, however, was more than offset by the considerable change in its respective fixed-asset investments relative to net worth (owing to the magnitude in importance of this asset item on the balance sheets of this particular industry), combined with B's better collection rate for receivables.

As we know from our study of 1969 performance, the major operational handicaps of A, and the lesser disadvantages of C in comparison with B—with respect to liquidity—could have been modified or offset by increased reliance on long-term over short-term debt. We find their relative reliance on long-term debt to reflect the following changes in 1970:

Company A	Declined 10 percent
Company B	Remained unchanged
Company C	Increased 3 percent

Thus we see that while both B and C were able to improve their current ratio and slightly reduce their turnover of working capital, A's current ratio dropped sharply and its working-capital turnover rate increased by roughly 20 percent.

This is not intended as criticism of any of the three companies policy decisions. Each apparently had a different approach to the same goal; A chose to place much of its burden on its current creditors, with increased emphasis on its trade suppliers. This study simply shows how, among three competitors during 1970, one accelerated a liquidity problem, while the other two were able to improve their positions in the same area.

One question posed earlier was whether any major adverse liquidity or debt situation for 1970 was due to external causes or to weakened internal control of the six key areas of financial balance. In the case of Companies A, B, and C, the almost uniform decline in profit return would most certainly indicate that external factors were the primary force. The same would be true for the leveling out of their sales volume as reflected in their net-sales-to-net-worth ratios.

To a considerably lesser extent, the general economic climate could be pointed to as contributing to slower inventory turnover, but this conclusion tends to be negated by C's performance, which was superior to that of A or B. Since they were all subject to the same outside pressures, does this not reflect a sounder approach to maintaining realistic inventory levels on the part of C's management?

Certainly the collection-period ratio points to internal controls as being preeminent. For if adverse general liquidity conditions existed among their respective—and often common—customers, it would have been felt equally by all three companies in their collection efforts. B and C both improved their results in this area; only A sustained reverses.

Again, both in fixed-assets-to-net-worth and in miscellaneous-assets-to-net-worth, the changes which occurred in 1970 appear to have resulted from management decisions rather than from economic forces, which would weigh equally on all three. Only C embarked on a major capital-goods expansion; only A diverted any major amount of working funds into miscellaneous assets.

1969 and 1970: A Medium-size Company

As further illustration of the differing impact of general economic conditions on companies engaged in the same line of activity, let us review the case of ABC Company, a publicly traded concern with annual sales volume of roughly $13 million.

Shown in Table 65 are ABC's 15 ratios for 1969 and 1970 placed beside the same figures for the industry of which it is a member, in order to provide direct trend comparison. In 1969,

Table 65

	ABC COMPANY		INDUSTRY AVERAGE*	
	1969	1970	1969	1970
Current-assets-to-current-liabilities (times)	1.69	2.18	1.73	1.64
Current-liabilities-to-net-worth (%)	119.7	72.5	114.9	125.2
Total-liabilities-to-net-worth (%)	119.7	72.5	125.7	144.5
Inventory-to-working-capital (%)	93.7	65.5	92.0	114.1
Receivables-to-working-capital (%)	148.7	110.6	116.6	108.0
Long-term-liabilities-to-working-capital (%)	—0—	—0—	12.8	18.1
Pretax-profit-to-net-worth (%)	21.95	21.12	26.54	23.36
Net-sales-to-fixed-assets (times)	60.2	104.3	34.5	23.7
Net-sales-to-working-capital (times)	6.2	6.7	6.8	7.9
Fixed-assets-to-net-worth (%)	8.5	5.5	16.7	26.7
Pretax-profit-to-net-sales (%)	4.27	3.69	4.65	3.71
Net-sales-to-net-worth (times)	5.1	5.7	5.8	6.3
Net-sales-to-inventory (times)	6.6	10.2	7.4	6.9
Collection period (days)	87	60	62	50
Miscellaneous-assets-to-net-worth (%)	9.0	8.8	9.7	12.5

* Based on a composite of various statistical sources.

ABC was very close to industry average in the nine effect ratios, with but two notable exceptions: (1) receivables-to-working-capital and (2) net-sales-to-fixed-assets.

The cause-and-effect analytical approach makes it quite simple to determine why these two ratios would depart so widely from industry norm. It can clearly be shown that ABC's working-capital position was not at fault, as evidenced by its very nearly average current ratio and by its lower turnover rate of working capital (net-sales-to-working-capital). Its performance in both these areas indicates that it had less strain than its typical competitor.

Thus, if one-half of the fraction (working capital) is clearly established as having been noncontributory to the distortion in this ratio, it stands to reason that the fault must have rested with receivables as measured by the collection-period ratio. Examination of this ratio shows ABC carrying 87 days' sales on its books as opposed to an industry average of but 62 days.

The other effect ratio where ABC was noticeably variant from industry standard is in net sales to fixed assets. Here the company was making twice as effective use of its fixed assets as was characteristic for its average rival. This is attributable to its lower investment in capital goods as reflected by the causal ratio—fixed assets to net worth—where it had only half as much of its funds tied up as was normal for the industry.

Rather than dwell on ABC's position relative to the industry in 1969, let us instead concentrate on the changes that took place for both during 1970. First we shall consider the shift in the nine effect ratios shown in Table 66, and then try to determine the

Table 66

	ABC COMPANY	INDUSTRY AVERAGE
Current-assets-to-current-liabilities	Improved 29%	Regressed 5%
Current-liabilities-to-net-worth	Improved 39%	Regressed 9%
Total-liabilities-to-net-worth	Improved 39%	Regressed 15%
Inventory-to-working-capital	Improved 30%	Regressed 25%
Receivables-to-working-capital	Improved 26%	Improved 7%
Long-term-liabilities-to-working-capital	No change	Regressed 41%
Pretax-profit-to-net-worth	Regressed 4%	Regressed 12%
Net-sales-to-fixed-assets	Improved 73%	Regressed 31%
Net-sales-to-working-capital	Regressed 8%	Regressed 16%

cause for deviation. From this table it will be seen that ABC was able to move forward on a broad front in the face of a general, although moderate, decline in industry attainment. External economic factors can logically be presumed to have weighed with equal force on all companies within the same line of endeavor, and hence ABC's escape from the general regression must have rested in large part on its more progressive internal control of the six key causal areas that collectively represent financial balance. Following is a summary of its relative performance in these primary ratios.

- *Fixed-assets-to-net-worth.* While the industry embarked on a major capital-goods expansion during 1970, ABC was able to reduce its investment from 1969 levels. As a result, it had only one-fifth the tie-up of funds that was typical for its average competitor. This freed more cash to bolster liquidity and to reduce debt.
- *Pretax-profit-to-net-sales.* While ABC's return declined in 1970, its attrition rate was less than the decline which was characteristic for the industry. ABC's latest position was exactly average.
- *Net-sales-to-net-worth.* While its trading ratio increased at a slightly more rapid pace than industry norm, ABC at 5.7 times per year was lower in 1970 than the 6.3 level for its average competitor. The lower the rate, the less the pressure on working-capital and debt growth, so ABC enjoyed a modest advantage in this area.
- *Net-sales-to-inventory.* ABC recorded a remarkable improvement during 1970. While slightly substandard in turnover during 1969, it lowered its inventory investment in the ensuing year, concurrent with a good increase in sales volume. Since the industry suffered sluggishness in turnover, the year 1970 found ABC's movement of merchandise at a speed considerably faster than normal. This was a major factor in its excellent overall financial attainment for the year.
- *Collection period.* In 1969, ABC faced a critical receivables problem with 87 days' sales outstanding—or 25 days more than the recorded norm of 62 days. While it was still 10 days above

industry average in 1970, it had cut its exposure by 27 days in just one year. Even a modified continuation of this trend would find the company closing this 10-day gap. This is the only ratio where ABC appeared at any disadvantage in relation to standard industry performance.

- *Miscellaneous-assets-to-net-worth.* This ratio is not particularly significant to our study, since neither the industry in general nor ABC in particular had a substantial proportion of net worth diverted to this phase of investment. Even so, ABC's performance was better than par for the course.

Since ABC was now clearly superior to the industry in four causal ratios, equal in one other, and inferior in only one area (while rapidly closing the span in this deficiency), there is little question why its picture of financial balance so far surpassed that of its typical competitor.

In review, we find an industry subject to modest but readily detectable deterioration in liquidity and upward debt pressure in 1970. Yet ABC—a member of that industry—reversed the trend and improved its position in every aspect. Under the circumstances, it is hard to reason that the liquidity decline in the industry was due to external economic influences alone, for ABC was subject to the identical forces and yet flourished in the face of what the others considered to be a generally adverse climate.

Analysts who place their entire faith and trust in cash flow would also be hard-pressed to explain this difference in relative results, for ABC's total cash flow was less than that of its average industry counterparts, and yet ABC improved while the others collectively regressed. One would be wise not to ignore the causal ratios in properly interpreting changes which occur in financial balance.

1969 and 1970: The Effects of a Management Decision

For our concluding study we shall look at a line of commercial activity whose financial ratios reflected improvement in all 15 areas for fiscal 1970. (See Table 67.) For purposes of contrast

Table 67

	DEF COMPANY		INDUSTRY AVERAGE*	
	1969	1970	1969	1970
Current-assets-to-current-liabilities (times)	2.51	1.37	1.84	1.98
Current-liabilities-to-net-worth (%)	63.3	228.0	95.3	85.5
Total-liabilities-to-net-worth (%)	80.0	247.7	113.7	102.6
Inventory-to-working-capital (%)	92.9	192.2	94.4	84.7
Receivables-to-working-capital (%)	73.7	181.1	101.9	96.3
Long-term-liabilities-to-working-capital (%)	17.4	23.5	22.9	20.4
Pretax-profit-to-net-worth (%)	14.5	(4.6)	14.3	15.2
Net-sales-to-fixed-assets (times)	54.2	42.8	32.1	36.8
Net-sales-to-working-capital (times)	7.6	13.6	10.2	9.6
Fixed-assets-to-net-worth (%)	13.5	26.7	25.4	21.7
Pretax-profit-to-net-sales (%)	2.0	(.4)	1.9	2.2
Net-sales-to-net-worth (times)	7.3	11.5	8.3	8.0
Net-sales-to-inventory (times)	8.2	7.1	10.8	11.3
Collection period (days)	35	49	37	37
Miscellaneous-assets-to-net-worth (%)	7.6	8.9	12.6	11.8

* Based on a composite of various statistical sources.

we shall inject a member firm whose performance was the exact reverse. The intent, again, is to show that individual companies are as a rule more directly affected by their own management value judgments than by the general trend of external pressures, whether it be plus or minus.

Even a cursory review of DEF's affairs in 1970 would support the conclusion that it had indeed reached a liquidity crisis and that its future survival depended upon its ability to reverse the trend without further loss of time. It is ironic that it should have been beset with troubles of such magnitude at the very time when its industry was enjoying a better-than-average year. While

DEF's management was prone to blame this plight on forces beyond its control—tight money, the recession, and so forth—an intimate knowledge of its affairs would clearly show that it alone brought on the crisis by just one major management policy miscalculation.

DEF is a smaller business than the others which have been reviewed in this chapter. It is a family-owned venture with a 50-year history of slow but solid and successful growth. By 1969 year-end, annual sales volume had reached levels in excess of $900,000, and DEF was clearly superior to industry average by every standard of financial measurement.

In 1970 an opportunity presented itself to DEF which was considered to be a stroke of great good fortune. The entire sales force of a rival organization located perhaps 100 miles distant informed DEF's management that they would consider switching allegiance and joining with DEF if certain conditions could be agreed upon. Management felt that this offered the opportunity to more than double the company's sales volume, expanding into a lucrative market with assured distribution. The top managers reasoned that some duplicated expenses could be eliminated, thus increasing profit, and they believed their liquidity position was such that they could support a sharply increased sales level with minimum strain. Agreement accordingly was reached and DEF looked forward to 1970 with great anticipation.

In actual fact, however, when the fiscal year ended the situation was as follows.

- Whereas the members of the original sales force had each averaged $180,000 per year, the new group contributed less than $50,000 in revenue per man. Increased sales-related expenses—salaries and commissions, automobile costs, group insurance, sales meetings expenses, and the like—eroded gross profit to the point that an operating loss was sustained. This deficiency naturally reduced net worth and working capital, adversely affecting all ratios of which they are a part.
- Inventory rose not only in total dollars, but in relation to sales. While volume increased, inventory accumulation moved up even more rapidly. This was due to pressures exerted by the

new sales representatives, who urged DEF to add to stock those product lines which the sales people were most accustomed to selling. Hence, all ratios related to inventory—and to working capital—were distorted because of the excess dollars tied up in more sluggishly turning merchandise.

- An increased investment in receivables proved necessary. Either the new sales people were able to hold only the weaker and slower-paying of their former accounts, or they were obliged to grant special terms to their old customers to convert them to DEF buyers. The collection period rose 14 days, again striking a blow at working capital as well—and further aggravating all ratios involving either of these elements.

- Fixed assets rose rapidly relative to net worth and also to sales (as measured by net-sales-to-fixed-assets). New delivery equipment and cars were required to service the expanded territory and the enlarged sales force. Further downward pressure thus was exerted on working capital.

- While sales rose at a disappointing rate as far as original management expectations were concerned, they nevertheless proved oppressive, for net worth actually declined through the attrition caused by operating losses. Thus DEF's trading ratio increased by roughly 60 percent and its turnover rate of working capital virtually doubled.

- There was even a modest degree of adversity caused by a higher percentage of investment in miscellaneous assets relative to net worth. This resulted mainly from the decline in DEF's capital account through losses, but even so there was a small added diversion of cash to the miscellaneous group, which further compounded the multiple problems.

Not only was the net result of all these six reverses in the causal ratios felt in diminished liquidity, but each key ratio also has direct influence on the debt structure of the company. Overtrading, sluggish inventory, slow-paying receivables, operating losses, and the funneling of funds into fixed or miscellaneous assets—all drain away money that would normally be available for debt repayment. As a result, the current debt of DEF—related to net worth—increased almost fourfold in just one year. From a light debt pressure position of 63 percent, it rose to an alarmingly high 228 percent.

This case is illustrative both of an individual company going in a direction opposite from the general industry trend, and of the tremendous impact on the fate of a concern caused by one major policy decision.

In summary, this chapter advances the thesis that there was no general liquidity crisis for industry as a whole for 1970, at least among the smaller and moderate-size manufacturers and wholesalers. Instead, there was a prevailing squeeze on profit. Further, where declines were registered, either for an industry or for individual entities, they were influenced more by internal policy moves than by widespread economic adversity.

7 The Uses of Industrywide Statistics

A number of the cases presented in the previous chapters demonstrate that the industry averages currently available for comparison with the ratios of individual companies are at considerable variance. And even if accurate aggregate figures were available for all lines of business activity, the analyst would have reason to question the applicability of median averages—derived from *all* firms in the industry—to the specific company in which he is interested. Certainly, industry figures are vastly superior to vague notions of financial structure or to rules of thumb covering the entire range of commercial activity; but size, location, fiscal closing, and many other factors obviously influence the individual concern's financial statement and give rise to a need for more detailed industry data. (The term "industry," of course, refers to any line of business activity and includes retailing and wholesaling as well as manufacturing operations.)

Sources of Statistics

In recognizing the influence of size on the composition of the assets and liabilities as well as the operating results of individual concerns, Robert Morris Associates has rendered great service to the analyst by segregating its data into four separate groupings according to asset size for each industry, in addition to supplying aggregate all-inclusive industry averages. A typical page from the 1971 edition of the RMA "Annual Statement Studies" (Exhibit 5) clearly shows that the characteristics of each size grouping within an industry are quite dissimilar. If, for example, one were to compare the figures of a footwear manufacturer with assets of $9 million against those which typify the smallest category in terms of size ($250,000 to $1 million in this case), totally erroneous conclusions would be reached.

On average, the median industry ratios published by Dun & Bradstreet reflect substantially better financial attainment in all areas than those portrayed in the Robert Morris study for any given line of activity. That is, as a general rule the current ratio is higher, the debt-to-worth structure lower, the trading ratio lower, and so forth.

This is very likely due to a greater emphasis on the larger or more solvent companies in the compilation of Dun & Bradstreet statistics. This would naturally follow where averages are derived from statements published by publicly traded corporations or from figures submitted by companies to the reporting agency for purposes of establishing a credit rating. Those concerns that are required by the Securities and Exchange Commission to make their financial facts public would generally be considerably larger than the typical member of their industry. Those privately owned companies that voluntarily supply statements to establish their credit standing are probably above average in overall financial stability. While there are obvious exceptions to this generalization, a large proportion of the businesses that are beset with financial problems are reluctant to make their figures available for publication. It must be recognized that the smaller and the unbalanced organizations represent a very substantial segment of our industrial population. To the extent that their representation is absent or minimized in the compilation of averages, those averages will be subject to some degree of bias or distortion, reflecting greater financial stability than is truly characteristic of an industry.

Thus, where size is the main variable to consider, Robert Morris Associates' figures are more representative of the smaller or moderate-size business, whereas Dun & Bradstreet's averages are more representative of the larger organizations.

Exhibit 5. Typical annual statements.

MANUFACTURERS OF JEWELRY, PRECIOUS METALS

37 STATEMENTS ENDED ON OR ABOUT JUNE 30, 1970
46 STATEMENTS ENDED ON OR ABOUT DECEMBER 31, 1970

ASSET SIZE	UNDER $250M	$250M AND LESS THAN $1MM	$1MM AND LESS THAN $10MM	$10MM AND LESS THAN $25MM	ALL SIZES
NUMBER OF STATEMENTS	15	39	26		83
ASSETS	%	%	%	%	%
Cash	7.1	4.9	4.2		4.2
Marketable Securities	.0	1.3	1.2		.7
Receivables Net	27.1	34.9	34.7		30.3
Inventory Net	54.2	39.5	36.5		37.4
All Other Current	1.2	4.5	4.2		2.6
Total Current	89.6	85.1	80.7		75.3
Fixed Assets Net	8.3	9.6	11.2		14.5
All Other Noncurrent	2.1	5.3	8.1		10.2
Total	100.0	100.0	100.0		100.0
LIABILITIES					
Due to Banks – Short Term	9.1	15.1	15.9		13.1
Due to Trade	21.8	20.2	13.4		11.3
Income Taxes	.3	1.1	3.1		3.3
Current Maturities LT Debt	.8	1.1	1.2		1.4
All Other Current	9.6	11.8	8.6		13.2
Total Current Debt	41.6	49.3	42.2		42.3
Noncurrent Debt, Unsubordinated	7.8	4.5	4.8		8.1
Total Unsubordinated Debt	49.4	53.8	47.0		50.3
Subordinated Debt	3.7	1.0	1.1		1.3
Tangible Net Worth	46.9	45.2	51.9		48.4
Total	100.0	100.0	100.0		100.0
INCOME DATA					
Net Sales	100.0	100.0	100.0		100.0
Cost of Sales	71.1	69.4	70.6		67.8
Gross Profit	28.9	30.6	29.4		32.2
All Other Expense Net	27.9	28.1	26.6		29.0
Profit Before Taxes	1.0	2.4	2.9		3.2

MANUFACTURERS OF FOOTWEAR

19 STATEMENTS ENDED ON OR ABOUT JUNE 30, 1970
62 STATEMENTS ENDED ON OR ABOUT DECEMBER 31, 1970

ASSET SIZE	UNDER $250M	$250M AND LESS THAN $1MM	$1MM AND LESS THAN $10MM	$10MM AND LESS THAN $25MM	ALL SIZES
NUMBER OF STATEMENTS		22	43	12	81
ASSETS	%	%	%	%	%
Cash		10.4	5.4	9.5	8.0
Marketable Securities		.8	.3	1.8	1.2
Receivables Net		29.2	33.3	24.5	28.0
Inventory Net		37.1	36.6	35.4	35.9
All Other Current		2.3	2.5	5.8	4.5
Total Current		79.9	78.2	77.0	77.5
Fixed Assets Net		14.8	12.5	16.7	15.0
All Other Noncurrent		5.3	9.3	6.4	7.4
Total		100.0	100.0	100.0	100.0
LIABILITIES					
Due to Banks – Short Term		13.9	11.0	22.0	17.6
Due to Trade		19.6	12.7	7.1	9.7
Income Taxes		3.5	2.6	1.6	2.1
Current Maturities LT Debt		.6	1.2	1.3	1.2
All Other Current		8.9	11.1	7.8	9.1
Total Current Debt		46.5	38.5	39.9	39.6
Noncurrent Debt, Unsubordinated		2.5	6.3	14.9	11.2
Total Unsubordinated Debt		49.1	44.8	54.8	50.8
Subordinated Debt		1.4	.8	1.6	1.3
Tangible Net Worth		49.6	54.4	43.6	47.9
Total		100.0	100.0	100.0	100.0
INCOME DATA					
Net Sales		100.0	100.0	100.0	100.0
Cost of Sales		82.3	80.3	79.9	80.2
Gross Profit		17.7	19.7	20.1	19.8
All Other Expense Net		17.8	16.7	15.9	16.4
Profit Before Taxes		-.1	3.0	4.2	3.5

RATIOS								
Quick	1.5	1.2	1.7	1.6	1.4	1.4	1.3	1.4
	1.1	1.0	1.1	1.1	.8	.8	.8	.9
	.7	.8	.6	.6	.6	.6	.7	.5
Current	2.9	2.7	3.0	2.5	2.7	2.5	2.5	3.2
	2.0	1.8	2.1	2.1	1.8	1.8	1.7	2.0
	1.7	1.6	1.7	1.6	1.4	1.5	1.2	1.5
Fixed/Worth	.1	.3	.1	.1	.0	.0	.0	.0
	.3	.4	.2	.2	.2	.2	.1	.1
	.4	.4	.3	.4	.4	.3	.4	.4
Debt/Worth	.5	.8	.5	.6	.5	.5	.6	.5
	.9	1.8	.9	.8	1.2	1.3	1.4	1.0
	1.6	2.3	1.5	1.3	2.1	1.8	2.2	1.7
Unsubordinated Debt/Capital Funds	.5	.5	.5	.5	.5	.5	.6	.5
	.8	1.8	.9	.8	1.2	1.2	1.3	.8
	1.5	2.3	1.5	1.3	2.0	1.7	2.2	1.7
Sales/Receivables	38 9.4	51 7.0	39 9.2	34 10.7	41 8.7	37 9.8	51 7.0	35 10.2
	55 6.5	74 4.9	57 6.3	47 7.7	60 6.0	56 6.4	68 5.3	55 6.5
	71 5.1	77 4.7	66 5.5	66 5.5	92 3.9	100 3.6	97 3.7	90 4.0
Cost Sales/Inventory	50 7.2	84 4.3	51 7.0	44 8.1	72 5.0	75 4.8	68 5.3	78 4.6
	82 4.4	109 3.3	82 4.4	62 5.8	129 2.8	113 3.2	133 2.7	171 2.1
	106 3.4	109 3.3	106 3.4	95 3.8	190 1.9	171 2.1	190 1.9	277 1.3
Sales/Working Capital	7.4	4.2	8.9	7.2	8.4	7.1	8.8	6.9
	5.2	3.9	5.3	5.6	4.7	4.8	4.2	4.4
	3.7	3.7	3.6	3.5	2.6	2.3	2.7	2.2
Sales/Worth	6.2	4.6	6.3	6.7	5.9	5.9	6.4	5.9
	4.4	4.2	4.2	4.4	3.4	3.2	4.2	3.2
	3.3	3.1	3.3	3.6	2.6	2.6	2.6	2.1
% Profit Before Taxes/Worth	21.9	17.6	23.7	24.6	20.2	17.6	18.9	20.6
	11.4	10.0	14.0	13.5	9.0	8.2	11.1	.0
	3.8	9.6	2.9	2.0	1.1	2.1	2.4	-9.6
% Profit Before Taxes/Total Assets	12.6	10.8	12.7	10.4	8.7	11.8	8.6	5.8
	5.9	5.6	6.2	6.3	3.8	3.5	5.0	.0
	1.8	3.0	1.4	1.3	.4	1.3	.8	-5.6
Net Sales	$695369M	$340786M	$318356M	$34936M	$237844M	$108849M	$35214MM	$3733M
Total Assets	376377M	221102M	141177M	13455M	141303M	66645M	19493M	1910M

© 1971 Robert Morris Associates

Shortcomings in Current Statistics

These two sources of statistical data have done the very best they can to provide business with guidance tools, subject to the limitations of the information available to them. It remains now for industry itself, acting in concert through trade associations or through individual effort, to provide the missing facts and to refine them so as to form the framework within which any management decision can be reached with full advance knowledge of the impact of its implementation.

If one is to compare his company's performance with that of its exact industry counterpart, there are many possible variables—other than size—which might influence the profile of what he should consider as average.

- *Age of the business.* A business which is one year old seldom has the same characteristics as one which has been operating for 25 years.
- *Geographical factors.* There are often differences of consequence between a company in Alabama and its industry counterpart in Minnesota.
- *Community influence.* The circumstances facing a retailer in a large metropolitan area (such as New York or Chicago) are markedly different from those of a store owner in a rural hamlet.
- *Product or sales emphasis.* A restaurant with complete bar service has little direct correlation with one that has no liquor license. A paper wholesaler, selling entirely to institutions (hospitals and schools, for instance), cannot expect his financial picture to parallel that of a rival whose promotional efforts are directed totally to industrial customers.

The list of possible significant variant factors could be greatly expanded. Several that are important to one industry may not be important to another. Only a thorough and intimate working knowledge of a given line of commercial activity can provide the answers.

Another extremely important ingredient of analysis that is inadequately covered today for most of American business is a detailed percentage breakdown of individual cost elements. How much of its sales dollar does the average company within an industry spend for rent? for legal and accounting fees? for light and heat? for salesmen's commissions? for repairs and maintenance?

If a manager is dissatisfied with his net-profit-to-net-sales attainment, can he use current publicly available statistical data to determine the cause for his relatively unsatisfactory performance? Even if a company's profit is superior to industry norms, is it not possible to gain even greater advantage from the knowledge of what others are allocating to clearly identifiable expense categories? It is not enough to know that total selling and delivery expense is 13 percent or that general and administrative expense is 6.4 percent, for what one company considers in expense category A, another may treat as category B. Further, aggregate totals do not identify the individual expenses which together make up the sum. Every component expense part must be studied on its own if the analyst is to detect the specific areas where his subject's accomplishments are deviant from normal.

The source material from which to derive the most meaningful and personalized averages has always been present, but has seldom been tapped and properly used. It resides within each American business establishment's books and records—its balance sheet and profit-and-loss statement—and should be shared with others for the common good. The principal deterrents to making these vital figures readily available for inclusion in statistical guides which would benefit all participants have been the following.

- Many company owners have felt that their confidentiality would be violated, that the anonymity of their highly personal financial condition would not be respected. This kind of entrepreneur is fearful that rivals will gain access to his figures and use them to his competitive disadvantage.
- Lack of standardized accounting procedures has made it difficult to classify all expense items or even all balance sheet entries uniformly.
- All too seldom has there been a vehicle through which data on companies within the same industry could be accumulated,

digested, analyzed, and fed back to the member firms in an understandable and useful form.

▪ In those cases where statements have been gathered and used in the compilation of standards, the resulting averages have lacked direct correlation to any individual participant. They have been too broad-based to be applicable and have failed to recognize the variables that would permit the recipient of the study to turn to a given page and say with certainty, "These figures pertain directly to me."

▪ Until the advent of electronic data processing, any statistical staff was hard-pressed to handle all the figures manually and still publish the final averages before they were almost too stale to be of value.

▪ Very rarely has there been any comprehensible explanatory text accompanying the tables, pointing out trends and pertinent developments within the industry. While the figures could be interpreted by professional statisticians, the thrust of the analysts' comments was not clear to the person for whom the survey was intended—the businessman himself.

The day is now at hand when all these handicaps can be overcome. As companies engage more actively in sharing information, each individually will be the beneficiary. Business firms then will have readily available to them the precise tools they need for making each policy decision in the light of its effect on their financial structure and on their relative posture with respect to the norm for the industry. This is not to suggest that any concern should strive to be average—that is scarcely a desirable objective—but knowledge of what is characteristic of one's industry puts decisions into perspective and casts the light of reason on moves that would otherwise be made on the basis of hunches or intuition.

Industry Surveys

In my view, the most outstanding contribution that has been made in industry statistical guidance has been provided by a private firm. Eli Lilly and Company of Indianapolis has for nearly

40 years published "The Lilly Digest," which serves as an operating guide for more than 70,000 annual users. This publication is based on the financial information provided by more than two thousand community pharmacies throughout the United States. The 74-page documented and illustrated analysis of pharmacies permits each individual druggist to recognize the cogent variables that identify him, so that the financial profile he selects has direct relevance to his own operation.

Few companies have attempted to emulate the service that Eli Lilly and Company provides for the community pharmacy. Aside from the public-spiritedness and the sales promotional aspects which are involved, most companies have neither the staff nor the concentration of interest in one specific segment of industry to warrant dedication to such projects for the benefit of their customers or for business at large.

It is more to be expected that such guidance will to an increasing extent be furnished by the trade associations which are functioning in virtually every line of commercial, industrial, professional, and service activity. They should serve as the most appropriate means to overcome earlier objections that have hampered the development and dissemination of data for financial guidance to fulfill the needs of today's business executive.

Many associations are not yet providing the financial facts and figures their members need for management guidance. In recent years, however, a number of progressive associations have made great strides in gaining the interest and support of their members for the development of industry data, and many of these organizations are now entirely capable of instituting truly meaningful financial programs. Such an opportunity is open also to trade groups which have never actually undertaken a service of this kind but which recognize the value of association surveys covering the financial features of their respective industries.

The value of industrywide figures lies in their broad applicability as standards by which the businessman can evaluate his company's position and measure its progress. The company manager who can draw upon an association survey to learn more about the conditions prevailing in his line will be that much better equipped to determine the strengths and weaknesses of his business and get the most from the resources of his organization. Yet today much of the financial data made available by associations falls short of the mark—usefulness to the members—because the following cardinal principles have not been fully recognized and consistently incorporated in industry surveys.

- Information presented to the members must provide insight into all major financial relationships that affect a company's profits, growth, and stability.
- Data must be drawn from a sufficiently large sample of companies to insure that the resulting statistics are truly representative of the entire industry.
- Figures must be subdivided according to such important variables as company size, age, location, and statement date.
- Statistical tables must be accompanied by a written analysis of trends and other key findings.
- Published reports must contain a thorough explanation of how the information can be used by the businessman to measure the financial condition and operating results of his company.

Each of the foregoing points deserves to be explored in some detail. First of all, how complete must financial data be to have real usefulness for the businessman? There is no definitive answer to this question, since a company in any one industry faces a particular set of operating conditions which require a financial structure different from that of a company in another industry. Nevertheless, a good working guide is this: The data should be sufficiently complete to enable a businessman to evaluate every major item on his financial statement in relation to the characteristic performance of his industry. Businesses of small and medium size, which cannot afford staffs of financial analysts and statisticians, can gain particular benefit from the information provided through association surveys.

The number of companies included in an industry survey will affect the extent to which the resulting figures are an accurate reflection of industry conditions. One approach in compiling industry data is to contact every company (the census approach). Alternatively, the study can be limited to a selected group which is believed to be representative of the industry (the sampling method). At first glance the sampling method appears to be the most economical means of gathering information, and in some cases it is. However, unless a thorough study of variable influences (for example, geographic location or asset size) is undertaken in advance, and unless the sample is accurately chosen and carefully controlled—all of which may be costly efforts—the information obtained may be far from representative of the industry.

Moreover, a small sample may conceal other significant influences (urban versus rural location, for instance) which would become apparent through analysis of more broadly based statistics. For maximum effectiveness, the data should be subdivided according to those variables which prove to be important factors in the industry, thus enabling the businessman to compare his concern's performance with the composite results of companies having similar characteristics. In addition to information about general industry conditions, facts and figures highlighting the advantages and problems associated with specific business features (such as size and age) should be provided to the members.

Analysis of this kind obviously requires responses from a large segment of the industry and is best accomplished through the census method. Because of advances in data processing which permit the rapid and economical organization of large quantities of statistics, the census approach can now be employed to provide far more complete and accurate information than the sampling method for approximately the same cost.

The National Wholesale Druggists' Association (NWDA) uses the census approach, asking all members to submit their confidential financial data to the University of Pennsylvania's Wharton School of Finance, where the statistics are tabulated and an analysis of operations is compiled. NWDA's annual "Operating Survey" has proved to be such a valuable source of industry trends, practices, and profiles that in the 1970 survey, 94 percent of the active membership of the association participated. Thus Francis L. Capers, president of NWDA, could state with assurance that "with such a high degree of input, the Survey certainly reflects an accurate picture of full-service drug wholesaling in the U.S. and provides highly useful benchmarks against which each wholesaler can measure his own individual performance in sales, administration, and operations."

A standardized questionnaire should be used to facilitate data processing and to insure the anonymity of the respondents, who could submit their figures—in confidence—to their association secretary or to an independent research group acting for the industry. Although each association should of course design its own form to gather the particular information most useful to its members, every industry questionnaire should certainly include a section covering significant items of the balance sheet and income statement, as well as data regarding each company's location, age, fiscal closing date, and similar important characteristics. Questions concerning relevant accounting procedures (for instance, each company's method of evaluating inventory and calculating the depreciation of fixed assets) might also be profitably included.

As examples of questionnaires directed toward the variables deemed to be most influential to their individual industries, see Exhibits 6 and 7, taken respectively from the survey forms of Eli Lilly and Company and the National Business Forms Association. While the two have some variables in common—the age of the business, its location, and the degree of active participation by the owners—other factors are distinctly unique for each line of activity. Both of these organizations also provide standardized accounting classifications to insure uniformity in reporting and to permit fast processing of data.

The Eli Lilly and Company survey has been mentioned earlier. The National Business Forms Association, Washington, D.C., is a more recent entrant in the field of statistical guidance for its members. Its survey has been conducted under the guidance of Meredith R. Smith, executive director, and Barry E. Miller, who has acted as the industry's analyst and consultant.

While industry figures for any one year are certainly important to the businessman, the trends revealed in annual figures are particularly significant. The publication of statistical information extending back several years is not always practical, but a written analysis of major trends would provide considerable insight into current figures. Key national and regional developments

Exhibit 6. Survey questionnaire, Eli Lilly and Company.

---

2 prescription summary

> **✓ Don't forget this important section!**

(For the same period of time covered by the Income and Expense Statement)

Number of prescriptions dispensed

New......................... _____   Total ℞ receipts................. $ _____

Renewals .... _____   Prescription inventory .... $ _____

Total........................ _____

3 supplemental information

(Important for the analysis and the Lilly Digest tabulations)

Total fountain sales.. $ _____

Total annual charge sales.. $ _____

Location of pharmacy:	Competition in your market area:	Type of ownership:
☐ Downtown business district	☐ Intense	☐ Sole proprietorship
☐ Neighborhood (suburban or rural)	☐ Average	☐ Partnership
☐ Shopping center	☐ Mild	☐ Corporation
☐ Medical office building		

Hours worked per week by owner(s) and annual salary of each:

_____ , $_____ ; ___ , $_____ ; ___ , $_____

How many of the owners active in the business are pharmacists? _____

Hours worked per week by staff pharmacists other than the owner(s) and annual salary of each:

_____ , $_____ ; ___ , $_____ ; ___ , $_____

Total sales made at cost or reduced margin (physician sales, employee sales, liquor and tobacco sales):

at cost $ _____

at _____ % margin $ _____

Number of hours pharmacy is open per week _____

Size of pharmacy (excluding storage areas) _____ sq. ft.   Size of prescription department _____ sq. ft.

Building in which pharmacy is located is:	Number of years this pharmacy has been in operation under the same ownership:		Did you submit your figures for analysis last year?
☐ Owned	☐ Less than 2 years	☐ 5 to 10 years	☐ Yes
☐ Rented	☐ 2 to 5 years	☐ Over 10 years	☐ No

Lilly Analysis Service, Dept. M-610, Eli Lilly and Company, Indianapolis, Indiana 46206
Please send the analysis report to the personal attention of:

NAME OR P.O. BOX _____

(Please print or type)

STREET _____

CITY _____ STATE _____ ZIP CODE _____

---

in sales, profits, expansion of plant and equipment, inventory control, credit and collections, debt structure, industry growth patterns, and other important areas should be discussed in a detailed analysis included in the annual association report.

But even complete, broadly based financial ratios and operating figures, analyzed in detail and all wrapped up in a beautiful brochure, will not be entirely useful to the businessman unless the application of this information is explained. The practical

Exhibit 7. Survey questionnaire, National Business Forms Association.

1969 Company Operations Survey

_____ Member Company Profile _____

1. Total sales volume $ _____
2. NBFA region _____
3. Age of business _____ Years
4. Market area (Check one or more):
   A. Metropolitan area (500,000 or more), Urban market _____
   B. Metropolitan area (500,000 or more), Suburban market _____
   C. Metropolitan area (100,000 to 500,000), Urban market _____
   D. Metropolitan area (100,000 to 500,000), Suburban market _____
   E. City (25,000 to 100,000) _____
   F. City (small or rural) _____
5. Total sales volume from distribution of forms.................. $ _____
   (Note: If dollar figures are not known, please estimate
            percentage for each item)

Total volume in continuous forms	$ _____
Total volume in unit sets	$ _____
Total volume in machine accounting	$ _____
Total volume in pegboard/pegstrip	$ _____
Total volume in other (Please describe):	
....	$ _____
....	$ _____

   Total sales volume from other business activities.................. $ _____
   Total volume from printing (other than forms) $ _____
   Total volume from other (Please describe):
   .... $ _____
   .... $ _____

6. If you own printing equipment, what percentage of your company's total
   forms volume was printed by your company? _____ %
7. % of sales generated by principals   _____ %
   % of sales generated by salesmen   _____ %
8. Number of orders processed per month (average) _____
9. Total number of active accounts with which you deal over a one-year
   period _____
   (a) Number of active accounts with which you are dealing through an
        average month _____
10. Total number of employees (including your salesmen) _____
11. Total number of salesmen: Full time _____ Part time _____
12. Number of employees other than salesmen:

Customer service/order department	_____
Bookkeeping	_____
Secretarial/Administrative	_____
Warehousing	_____

13. Please explain briefly your company's bookkeeping/accounting system. (For example, are invoices produced and recorded by hand or by use of a machine system?) _____

_____

14. Credit terms extended to customers: _____

15. How many suppliers account for 70% of your total purchases? _____
    (a) What percentage of your total forms purchases go to your "top ten" suppliers? _____ %

16. Please give the credit terms extended by the suppliers which account for 70% of your total forms purchases. _____
    (a) What are the credit terms extended by your top ten suppliers? _____

17. Does the presence or amount of cash discounts in any way influence the amount of your business going to the suppliers? If yes, briefly explain.
    _____
    (a) Does the answer to the foregoing apply equally to principal-generated as well as salesmen-generated business? _____

18. Does your company specialize in serving certain industries (for example, hospitals, schools, trucking companies, food wholesalers)? If so, please specify. _____

    _____

19. If your business is a corporation, what percentage of the outstanding stock is held by the officers and their families? _____ %

20. Percentage of total business given to NBFA manufacturing members _____%

21. Percentage of new business directed to NBFA manufacturers since becoming a dealer member _____%

evaluation of company performance through industrywide financial data must be described in a straightforward manner so that the businessman can judge for himself the value of the association survey as an aid to profitable decisions. An accompanying explanation of the cause-and-effect ratio method and other financial management aids would promote understanding and effective use of industry data.

The association might also provide individual financial counseling for the businessman who desires an independent verification of his own findings or who wishes to gain a more complete, particularized analysis of his company's performance. By drawing upon the wealth of detailed data previously gathered for the association report, an industry analyst could furnish any member company with an extensive evaluation of its specific strengths and weaknesses as compared with other business concerns in its marketing territory. Means of achieving particular company goals, methods of improving performance in possible problem areas, and ways of maximizing superior competitive features could be thoroughly explored in discussions between company management and the industry analyst.

Recognizing that not all recipients of statistical data have the capacity to fully relate the facts as presented to their companies, or may wish an independent verification of any conclusions they have reached on their own, the Lilly Survey (see Exhibit 8) offers to provide an analysis for anyone who wishes it.

The financial counselor or analyst might be a full-time member of the association staff responsible for directing the industry survey and preparing the written reports, or he might be an independent consultant providing counseling for the association on a contract basis. An individual financial counseling service could be furnished to interested members of the association at a cost far less than the fee many companies pay annually to accountants for the preparation of their financial statements. Seminars featuring the application of the association survey to practical business problems, as well as a session in the convention program devoted to analytical comment, could be conducted by the industry counselor to further aid association members in developing financial skills. Special studies of such timely topics as the relative advantages of leasing versus purchase of plant and equipment, current trends in marketing, and changes in credit-and-collection techniques could also be developed from the data contained in the industry survey.

The characteristics and needs of each association will, of course, determine the nature of the financial program to be developed. Statistical techniques and analyses appropriate to a national association having a membership of 2,200 business concerns might well prove unsatisfactory for a regional group with 55 member companies. Therefore, an individual approach to the particular requirements of each association is absolutely necessary.

The personal needs and the total costs of a program for providing meaningful financial information would depend upon both the number of companies participating and the services included. Large national or regional associations might choose to place the industry survey in the hands of a qualified staff member or to seek additional full-time personnel from the outside. In order to

Exhibit 8. Data analysis work sheet, Eli Lilly and Company

if you wish to perform your own analysis, this work sheet will be useful...
if you wish an analysis prepared for you, disregard this work sheet, complete the remaining three pages of this form, and send to the Lilly Analysis Service...

fill in and compare

INCOME AND EXPENSE STATEMENT	Current Data (Dollars)	Current Data (% of Sales)	Last Year's Data (% of Sales)	Lilly Digest Data (Comparable Category) (see page ___)	Notes (♠ or ♥)
Net sales	$	%	%	%	
Cost of goods sold	$	%	%	%	
Gross margin (net sales less cost of goods sold)	$	%	%	%	
Expenses Proprietor's or manager's salary	$	%	%	%	
Employees' wages	$	%	%	%	
Rent	$	%	%	%	
Heat, light, and power	$	%	%	%	
Accounting, legal, and other professional fees	$	%	%	%	
Taxes (except on buildings, income, and profit) and licenses	$	%	%	%	
Insurance (except on buildings)	$	%	%	%	
Interest paid	$	%	%	%	
Repairs	$	%	%	%	
Delivery	$	%	%	%	
Advertising	$	%	%	%	
Depreciation (except on buildings)	$	%	%	%	
Bad debts charged off	$	%	%	%	
Telephone	$	%	%	%	
Miscellaneous	$	%	%	%	
Total expenses	$	%	%	%	
Net operating profit (gross margin less total expenses)	$	%	%	%	

BALANCE SHEET	Current Data (Dollars)	Current Data (% of Sales)	Last Year's Data (% of Sales)	Lilly Digest Data (Comparable Category) (see page ___)	Notes (♠ or ♥)
Current assets	$	%	%	%	
Fixed assets	$	%	%	%	
Total assets	$	%	%	%	
Current liabilities	$	%	%	%	
Long-term liabilities	$	%	%	%	
Total liabilities	$	%	%	%	
Net worth	$	%	%	%	

OTHER CALCULATIONS	Current Data	Last Year's Data	Lilly Digest Data (Comparable Category) (see page ___)	Notes (♠ or ♥)
Inventory turnover	times	times	times	
Prescription sales: prescription inventory	$	$	$	
Average prescription charge	$	$	$	
Number of prescriptions				
Current assets: current liabilities	times	times	times	
Net sales: net working capital	times	times	times	
Long-term liabilities: net working capital	%	%	%	
Accounts payable outstanding	days	days	days	
Net profit: net worth (R.O.I.)	%	%	%	

organize an effective survey and to present the results in a manner meaningful to the association members, the financial program director should be familiar with accounting and the analysis of financial statements, as well as with statistics and data processing. If a financial program is to be useful, it must be well directed.

A special consultant (perhaps "financial adviser" is a better description) may be employed to aid in the development of an industry survey or to administer the entire program. By engaging a consultant on a contract basis, an association can gain the necessary services for an appropriate period without having to retain a specialist for the entire year. Normally, a consultant's services would be needed only during the annual preparation of the financial report. If, for instance, 75 percent of the member companies close their books on December 31, a consultant might be utilized during the month of March, when the annual survey would be published, and perhaps for a brief period during each quarter of the year, when the composite results of companies with fiscal closing in later months would be reviewed.

Although the consultant would not need to be thoroughly familiar with the particular industry under study at the outset (assuming that he possesses the other necessary skills), complete cooperation between the consultant and the association director would be required for the development of an efficient, meaningful program. Valuable counsel can be obtained through certain professional consultants, accountants, bankers, or other individuals experienced in financial analysis and surveys. Careful selection is imperative.

Every trade association has much to gain from conducting a truly useful financial survey. Successful cooperation among members in this important area would encourage more active participation in other group programs, and a financial service of proven value would be a real inducement to the businessman who has not yet joined.

Some individuals may feel that the preparation and dissemination of reliable ratios and cost data will work solely to the advantage of the weaker, more marginal units. True, the struggling company will benefit immensely from acquiring precise, relevant figures through which it may determine its present position and develop plans for advancement; but it is equally true that even the most progressive company in an industry has room for betterment and can profit from confirming its existing advantages and from recognizing potential improvements through more complete knowledge of conditions relating to its line of endeavor. The principals of dynamic, forward-looking companies are often more eager to obtain and benefit from counsel than are those of the weaker units in the field—and that is one reason for their greater success. But the less efficient operator, given an adequate education in the essentials of financial balance, can move forward and add to his industry's stability and progress. Most industries are, after all, in competition with other manufacturers and services, and the industry that provides its members with timely, useful information will advance more rapidly than the one whose constituent companies are less well informed.

The vast majority of companies of small and moderate size hope to grow in time; they aspire to ever greater financial freedom and stability. To achieve this goal they must be able to evaluate their daily progress and problems and to plan future moves with increasing certainty as to their outcome. Evaluation and planning clearly require knowledge; given knowledge, and the confidence that follows, persevering management can succeed.

Cause-and-effect ratio analysis—providing knowledge of the elements of financial balance, of dangers thereto, and of the means to restore and maintain balance—serves as a foundation for sound financial management.

Index

accounts payable, 6
accounts receivable: changes in, 155–156; in current ratio, 20; meaning of, 11
acid-test ratio, 20–21
administrative expenses, officers' salaries and, 96–99
age trend, sales and credit selectivity and, 171
Annual Statement Studies, 16–17, 94, 176, 211–213
assets: items in, 28–29; miscellaneous, 101–102; "permanent," 119; types of, 11–12
associations, in industrywide surveys, 220–227
audited statement, 9

bad-debt loss, 35
balance sheet, 6–7, 13; *see also* financial statement
bankruptcy, 5, 35
Blue Book (*MacRae's Blue Book*), 32
bookkeeping, mechanics of, 6
business population, turnover of, 3

canned fruits and vegetables manufacturers, 1969–70; liquidity status of, 192
capital: changes in, 57–58; equity, 78; invested, 81, 137–138; new, 78–79; sales and, 78
capital-goods investment: as asset item, 29; fixed assets and, 50
capital-stock investment, 120
causal ratios, 55–106; application of, 107–151; concept of, 55–56, 109; corrective measures in, 127–139; distortion of, 107
cause-and-effect ratio analysis, 1–2; compensating advantages in, 172–173; decimal accuracy in, 156; financial items in, 10; guidelines for

applying, 152–175; high figures in, 162–163; isolated figures in, 153; key relationships in, 15; policy decisions and, 139–151; time and seasonal factors in, 161, 164–169; trend in, 169–170
Chrysler Corporation, 176
collection-period ratio, 32, 56, 63–69, 150, 174; abnormal, 132–133; all-industry figures for, 179–180; computation of, 63–64; five-industry comparison of, 188–194, 197; for medium-size company, 1969–70, 204–205; overtrading and, 83; for paper box manufacturer, 110; for plastics manufacturer, 124–125; for stove manufacturer, 114–116; trend in, 171; for wholesale hardware company, 118, 120–121
Commerce Department, U.S., 3
competition, overtrading and, 84
consignment purchasing, 134
cost-of-sales-to-inventory ratio, 70; all-industry figures for, 180–181; five-industry comparison for, 188–194
credit-and-collection programs, 63
credit decisions, basis for, 33–34
credit insurance, 133
credit-interchange services, 33
credit manager, professional, 132
credit needs, in overtrading, 86
credit policy, sales volume and, 66
current assets, 11; changes in, 59
current-assets-to-current-liabilities ratio, 83, 173; for medium-size company, 1969–70, 202–203
current debt: five-industry comparison of, 195; rise in, 150
current liabilities: changes in, 60; current assets and, 22–23; five-industry comparison of, 199
current-liabilities-to-net-worth ratio, 17, 23–27, 83, 174; computation of,

24–25; for medium-size company, 1969–70, 203

current ratio, 17–23, 31, 154; acid-test ratio and, 20; all-industry averages for, 177; computation of, 18; defined, 18; fall in, 150, 187; five-industry comparison of, 1969–70, 188–201; improvement of, 20, 157; limitations of, 21–22; miscellaneous assets and, 103; for medium-size company, 1969–70, 202–205; quantity vs. quality in, 20; working capital and, 59, 92, 128; *see also* liquidity

debt, long-term, 39, 41, 59, 195
debt pressure: increase of, 127; overtrading and, 81
debt ratios: level of, 23–26; miscellaneous assets and, 103
debt-to-net-worth ratio, all-industry averages for, 178–179
decimal accuracy, need for, 156
decisions, financial data in, 8–9
depreciation, elimination of, 131
Donnelly's Red Book, 32
Dun & Bradstreet, Inc., 3, 17, 26, 28, 32, 36–37, 158–160, 211

electric test equipment manufacturers, 1969–70; liquidity status of, 191
employee loans, miscellaneous assets and, 105
equipment costs, 11
equity capital: attracting of, 78; shortage of, 142

failure: inventory loss and, 28; overtrading or undertrading as cause of, 85–87
field warehousing, 134–135
financial counselor, association and, 224–226
financial data, in management decisions, 8–9
financial disease: in corporate giants, 176; corrective measures in, 127–139; operating losses and, 138–139; symptoms of, 127
financial management, 2–5
financial skill, acquisition of, 5–8
financial statement: audited, 9; "estimated," 10; industry method in, 14; interim, 9; items in, 10–14; meaning of, 6; ratio analysis and, 7; understanding of, 8–10; *see also* profit-and-loss statement
financial survey, industrywide, 216–227

five-year trends, in cause-and-effect ratio analysis, 170–171
fixed assets, 11; average capital-goods investment and, 50; capital, 57–58; cause-and-effect relationships and, 60; excessive, 48, 128–132; planning and, 58; outlay for, 49; restrictions on investment in, 130; sales progress and, 46–47, 62; working capital and, 143
fixed-assets-to-net-worth ratio, 46, 56–63, 68, 75, 83, 93, 164, 174; all-industry averages for, 182–183; computing of, 57; five-industry comparison for, 188–194, 196; for medium-size company, 1969–70, 204; for paper box manufacturer, 109–111; for plastics manufacturer, 123–124; for stove manufacturer, 112–113, 116; for wholesale hardware firm, 117
fixed costs, absorption of, 95
flavoring extracts and syrups manufacturers, 1969–70, liquidity status of, 189
funds, diversion of, 128; *see also* capital
fur manufacturers, 1969–70, liquidity status for, 191

general and administrative expenses, 97–99
gross profit, all-industry averages for, 186–187

hat manufacturers, 1969–70, liquidity status of, 188

idle machinery, sale of, 129
income statement, 13; *see also* financial statement
indebtedness, dangers of, 27; *see also* debt ratios
industry norms, individual averages and, 159
industry surveys, 218–219, 222–223
industrywide statistics, use of, 210–227
intangible assets, 11–12
interim statement, 9
Internal Revenue Service, 58
inventory: book figures for, 30; business losses or failure through, 28; cost of sales and, 70; current ratio and, 20, 31; funds frozen in, 74–75; increase in, 29; liquidity and, 154–155; loans on, 135; markdown, 72–73; overtrading and, 86; problems, types of, 71, 86; sluggish movement of,

126, 128, 133–135, 148
inventory control function, 135
inventory-to-working-capital ratio, 17, 27–32, 59, 68, 82–83, 93, 128, 154, 174; changes in, 150; computation of, 27–28; for plastics manufacturer, 126
inventory-turnover ratio, 71–73, 81, 114
invested capital: long-term financing and, 40; in miscellaneous assets, 137–138; in net-sales-to-net-worth ratio, 81

lending, vs. investing, 85
liabilities, 12–13, 20
Lilly, Eli, & Company, 216–217, 220
liquidity: defined, 177; erosion of, 185–186; five-industry comparison in, 199–201; management decision in, 205–209; vs. profit squeeze, 176–209
loans, long-term, 120, 130
Lockheed Aircraft Corporation, 36, 176
long-term-liabilities-to-working-capital ratio, 18, 68, 75, 82–83, 93, 128, 174; computation of, 39
losses, chronic, 100–101
Lyon Furniture Mercantile Agency, 32–33

management: deficiencies in, 3–4; financial understanding of, 1–14; liquidity crisis and, 185–186, 205–209
merchandise, consignment purchases of, 134
miscellaneous assets, 12; inordinate investment in, 137–138; writeoff or markdown of, 104
miscellaneous-assets-to-net-worth ratio, 56, 68, 75, 83, 94, 101–106, 150; all-industry averages for, 183–184; assets included in, 101–102; computation of, 102; five-industry comparison of, 188–194; industry average for, 146–147; for medium-size company, 169–170, 205; for paper box manufacturer, 110, 112; for plastics manufacturer, 124; for stove manufacturer, 114; for wholesale hardware firm, 118
mortgages payable, 11
multiple measurement, concept of, 165

National Association of Credit Management, 33
National Business Forms Association, 220–223

National Wholesale Druggists' Association, 219
net-profit-to-net-sales ratio, 56, 61, 68, 75, 90–101, 103, 149–150, 165, 174; computation of, 90; five-industry averages for, 196; for paper box manufacturer, 109–111; for plastics manufacturer, 124; for stove manufacturer, 114; for wholesale hardware firm, 117–118
net-profit-to-net-worth ratio, 18, 42–46, 61, 68, 75, 82–83, 93–94, 149, 173; computation of, 43
net-sales-to-fixed-assets ratio, 46–51, 83, 94, 150, 174; application of, 47; computation of, 46, 69
net-sales-to-inventory ratio, 56, 69–70, 150, 153, 174; computation of, 69; five-industry comparison for, 196; low, 148; for medium-size company, 1969–70, 204
net-sales-to-net-worth ratio, 68, 75–79, 83, 94, 150, 164, 174; all-industry averages for, 181–182; computation of, 77; five-industry comparison for, 188–194, 196–197; invested capital and, 81; median averages in, 85–89
net-sales-to-working-capital ratio, 18, 51–54, 59, 68, 75, 82–83, 128, 174
net worth: defined, 13, 57; vs. net profit, 82; total debt and, 61
New York Stock Exchange, 7

obsolescence, 11, 73
officers' salaries, sales and expense factors in, 95–96, 98
operating losses, as financial illness, 44, 128
outside investors, attracting of, 129
overtrading: bill payment in, 85; capital and, 79–80; collection period and, 83; competition and, 84; credit needed in, 86; debt pressure and, 81; failure attributable to, 85–86; financial illness and, 128, 135–137; increase in, 86; indebtedness and, 27; indicators of, 88–90; investment and, 85; net-sales-to-net-worth ratio and, 83; price concessions and, 84; profit and, 175; remedial measures in, 136; risk in, 84; trading ratio and, 76
overvaluation, inventory turnover and, 73

paper box manufacturer, causal ratios
  applied to, 108–112
Penn Central Railroad, 176
plant and equipment, sale and leaseback of, 129–130
plant costs, 11
plastics manufacturer, causal ratios for,
  122–127
policy decisions, cause-and-effect ratios
  and, 139–151
pretax-profit-to-sales-ratio, 184–185,
  188–194, 204
price, inventory turnover and, 72
price concessions, overtrading and, 84
profit: all-industry averages for,
  186–187; business health and, 91, 94;
  fixed costs and, 48; net-sales-to-net-
  worth ratio and, 77; overtrading and,
  136, 175
profitability, undertrading and, 135–136
profit-and-loss statement, 6, 13
profit squeeze, vs. liquidity crisis,
  176–209
profits retained in the business, 91

ratio, concept of, 8, 15–54, 164
ratio analysis, 7–8, 175; isolated figures
  in, 153; misconceptions regarding,
  152; total financial picture and, 175;
  see also cause-and-effect ratio analysis
receivables: collectibility of, 66, 128;
  collection-period ratio and, 66; current obligations and, 155; net profit
  and, 91; slow or sluggish, 128, 133;
  vs. working capital, 35, 82; *see also*
  accounts receivable
receivables-to-working-capital ratio, 82,
  93, 128, 149–150, 173
risk: fear of, effects on management
  decisions, 26; in overtrading, 84
Robert Morris Associates, 16–17, 29,
  36, 49, 51, 70, 88, 90, 94–95, 98,
  158, 176–177, 210–211

sales: capital and, 78; excessive concentration on, 4–5; net, *see* net sales
sales volume: credit policy and, 65–66,
  145; vs. general and administrative
  expenses, 97; net worth and, 45;
  officers' salaries and, 95; price concessions and, 80; profit and, 79; ratio
  and, 8
seasonal factor, allowance for, 165–169
Securities and Exchange Commission,
  211
selective selling, 121

slow pay, undertrading and, 87
Small Business Administration, 2–3, 130
Small Business Investment Company,
  130
small company, financial management
  of, 2–5
statistics: industry surveys and,
  210–227; shortcomings of, 214–216;
  sources of, 210–213
stove manufacturer, causal ratios for,
  112–116
suppliers, longer terms for, 130

tax advantages, in lending vs. investing,
  85
time factor, significance of, 12, 160–161
total-liabilities-to-net-worth ratio, 17,
  23–27, 61, 83, 172, 174
trade association, industry surveys and,
  220–227
trade-receivables-to-working-capital
  ratio, 17, 32–38, 59, 75, 83, 173–174;
  see also receivables
trading ratio, 76–77
trend, importance of, 169–170
turnover rate, inventory problems and, 71

undercapitalized businesses, salaries in,
  96
undertrading: capital and, 79; dangers
  of, 86–87, 135–137; failure and, 87;
  slow pay in, 87;
United Beverage Bureau, 32

vegetable oils manufacturers, 1969–70,
  liquidity status of, 189–190

Wharton School of Finance, 219
wholesale hardware firm, causal ratios
  for, 116–122
wholesaling, miscellaneous-assets-to-net-
  worth ratio in, 102
working capital, 30–31, 57–59; current
  ratio and, 59, 92, 128; defined, 12,
  27; five-industry comparison in, 199;
  fixed-asset expenses and, 143; net
  sales and, 51–54, 59; ratios of, 8,
  59; receivables and, 10; tightening
  of, 127; for wholesale meat industry,
  36–37; *see also* net-sales-to-working-
  capital ratio
woven and woolen goods, 1969–70,
  liquidity status in, 190

year-end closing date, allowance for,
  168–169
year-end statement, unaudited, 9–10

AMACOM Paperbacks

John Fenton	The A To Z Of Sales Management	$ 7.95	07580
Hank Seiden	Advertising Pure And Simple	$ 7.95	07510
Alice G. Sargent	The Androgynous Manager	$ 8.95	07601
John D. Arnold	The Art Of Decision Making	$ 6.95	07537
Oxenfeldt & Miller & Dickinson	A Basic Approach To Executive Decision Making	$ 7.95	07551
Curtis W. Symonds	Basic Financial Management	$ 7.95	07563
William R. Osgood	Basics Of Successful Business Planning	$ 7.95	07579
Dickens & Dickens	The Black Manager	$10.95	07564
Ken Cooper	Bodybusiness	$ 5.95	07545
Jones & Trentin	Budgeting	$12.95	07528
Laura Brill	Business Writing Quick And Easy	$ 5.95	07598
Rinella & Robbins	Career Power	$ 7.95	07586
Andrew H. Souerwine	Career Strategies	$ 7.95	07535
Beverly A. Potter	Changing Performance On The Job	$ 9.95	07613
Donna N. Douglass	Choice And Compromise	$ 8.95	07604
Philip R. Lund	Compelling Selling	$ 8.95	07506
Joseph M. Vles	Computer Basics	$ 6.95	07599
Hart & Schleicher	A Conference And Workshop Planner's Manual	$15.95	07003
Leon Wortman	A Deskbook Of Business Management	$14.95	07571
John D. Drake	Effective Interviewing	$ 8.95	07600
James J. Cribbin	Effective Managerial Leadership	$ 6.95	07504
Eugene J. Benge	Elements Of Modern Management	$ 5.95	07519
James E. Kristy & Susan Z. Diamond	Finance Without Fear	$10.95	07587
Edward N. Rausch	Financial Management For Small Business	$ 7.95	07585
Loren B. Belker	The First-Time Manager	$ 6.95	07588
Whitsett & Yorks	From Management Theory to Business Sense	$17.95	07610
Ronald D. Brown	From Selling To Managing	$ 7.95	07500
Murray L. Weidenbaum	The Future Of Business Regulation	$ 5.95	07533
Craig S. Rice	Getting Good People And Keeping Them	$ 8.95	07614
Charles Hughes	Goal Setting	$ 4.95	07520
Richard E. Byrd	A Guide To Personal Risk Taking	$ 7.95	07505
Charles Margerison	How To Assess Your Managerial Style	$ 6.95	07584
S.H. Simmons	How To Be The Life Of The Podium	$ 8.95	07565
D. German & J. German	How To Find A Job When Jobs Are Hard To Find	$ 7.95	07592

Author	Title	Price	Code
W.H. Krause	How To Get Started As A Manufacturer's Representative	$ 8.95	07574
Sal T. Massimino	The Complete Book of Closing Sales	$ 5.95	07593
William A. Delaney	How To Run A Growing Company	$ 6.95	07590
Dean B. Peskin	A Job Loss Survival Manual	$ 5.95	07543
H. Lee Rust	Jobsearch	$ 7.95	07557
Marc J. Lane	Legal Handbook For Small Business	$ 7.95	07612
George T. Vardaman	Making Successful Presentations	$10.95	07616
Norman L. Enger	Management Standards For Developing Information Systems	$ 5.95	07527
Ray A. Killian	Managing Human Resources	$ 6.95	07556
Elam & Paley	Marketing For The Non-Marketing Executive	$ 5.95	07562
Edward S. McKay	The Marketing Mystique	$ 6.95	07522
Donald E. Miller	The Meaningful Interpretation Of Financial Statements	$ 8.95	07513
Robert L. Montgomery	Memory Made Easy	$ 5.95	07548
Donald P. Kenney	Minicomputers	$ 7.95	07560
Frederick D. Buggie	New Product Development Strategies	$ 8.95	07602
Dale D. McConkey	No-Nonsense Delegation	$ 4.95	07517
Hilton & Knoblauch	On Television	$ 6.95	07581
Ellis & Pekar	Planning Basics For Managers	$ 6.95	07591
Alfred R. Oxenfeldt	Pricing Strategies	$10.95	07572
Blake & Mouton	Productivity: The Human Side	$ 5.95	07583
Daniels & Barron	The Professional Secretary	$ 7.95	07576
Herman R. Holtz	Profit From Your Money-Making Ideas	$ 8.95	07553
William E. Rothschild	Putting It All Together	$ 7.95	07555
J.F. Engelberger	Robotics In Practice	$24.95	07587
Don Sheehan	Shut Up And Sell!	$ 7.95	07615
Roger W. Seng	The Skills Of Selling	$ 7.95	07547
Hannan & Berrian & Cribbin & Donis	Success Strategies For The New Sales Manager	$ 8.95	07566
Paula I. Robbins	Successful Midlife Career Change	$ 7.95	07536
Leon Wortman	Successful Small Business Management	$ 8.95	07503
D. Bennett	TA And The Manager	$ 4.95	07511
George A. Brakeley, Jr.	Tested Ways To Successful Fund-Raising	$ 8.95	07568
William A. Delaney	Tricks Of The Manager's Trade	$ 6.95	07603
Alec Benn	The 27 Most Common Mistakes In Advertising	$ 8.95	07554
James Gray, Jr.	The Winning Image	$ 6.95	07611
John Applegath	Working Free	$ 6.95	07582
Allen Weiss	Write What You Mean	$ 5.95	07544
Richard J. Dunsing	You And I Have Simply Got To Stop Meeting This Way	$ 5.95	07558